MW00788465

WHO LE_ _____
MEXICANS
PLAY
IN THE
ROSE BOWL?

Navigating the
Racial Landscape
of America

Hank Olguin

Praise for

WHO LET THE MEXICANS PLAY IN THE ROSE BOWL?

"Hank Olguin's life story is a must read for Americans who want to understand the American Latino experience. Olguin's life, and his descriptions of other Latinos he meets along his journey, depicts a family that has been in America for decades, and in the face of discrimination, figured out how to succeed. He describes that through hard work, belief in oneself, and family support, Latinos like Olguin accomplished and contributed immensely to our nation. Most Americans would be shocked to learn that back in 1959, two "Mexicans" played in the Rose Bowl. Olguin includes his poems throughout the book, and he shares funny and deeply personal feelings about his experiences that will resonate with many of us."

—Federico Peña
Former Mayor of Denver, Former U.S. Secretary
of both Transportation and Energy

"*Who Let the Mexicans Play in the Rose Bowl* is an insightful, often humorous look at the twists and turns of being of Mexican ancestry in the modern United States. In a spell-binding account, we see the incredible journey of Hank Olguin from high school athlete to Bowles Hall and the fraternities at UC Berkeley to the 1959 Rose Bowl (with fellow Chicano Joe Kapp at the helm in Cal's most recent appearance in that iconic bowl), and on to a successful career in the advertising world. Along the way, Olguin offers insights into life as a Chicano in a world adapting to the growing Latina/o presence. *Who Let the Mexicans Play in the Rose Bowl* is required reading for anyone interested in an analysis of Latino identity."

—Kevin R. Johnson
Dean, UC Davis School of Law, Author of *How Did You Get to Be Mexican?— A White/Brown Man's Search for Racial Identity*

"From the Mexican Revolution to the smell of fresh-cut alfalfa in New Mexico to Zoot Suits in Los Angeles, California, to the Blue Suede Shoe Boys of Dallas, Texas, Hank Olguin's beautifully written memoir of growing up Brown in America is full of insight, poetry and soul. The reader is taken through time, under the skin and from behind the eyes of a boy finding his way to a young man finding his place to an elder artist looking back at a life worth living, written with tenderness, humor and great affection. This is a story of family, community and country. This is an American story."

—KJ Sanchez
Founder and CEO of American Records, a theater company,
and Associate Professor and head of Playwriting
and Directing, University of Texas at Austin

"Hank Olguin offers us his engaging and truly inspiring life story, a 99-yard winning touchdown for anyone who has felt sidelined in the American game of life. Entertaining, heartfelt, and courageous, he tells his story with wit and honesty, sharing with us his poignant poetry and love of life and family."

—Emilio Delgado
Actor, Sesame Street's Luis

"Given the current political climate and resurgence of anti-immigrant sentiment, Hank Olguin's memoir, *Who Let the Mexicans Play in the Rose Bowl*? is timely, relevant and important. He is a masterful writer, weaving exquisitely detailed childhood memories through vignettes and poetry together with historical perspective, highlighting the valuable and too often unknown contributions of Mexican Americans. As a third generation American of Mexican heritage, Hank provides a unique counterpoint to the false dominant narrative that all Latinos have arrived here illegally. I want this book to be required reading for my two daughters—to be reminded of the beauty of their Mexican heritage and to gain a more nuanced understanding of the historical backdrop out of which the current, continued anti-immigrant bias has sprung."

—Roberta A. Rey
PhD, Student Affairs Office, David Geffen School of Medicine at UCLA

"I've read one book in one sitting and this was it. Hank Olguin's *WHO LET THE MEXICAN'S PLAY IN THE ROSE BOWL* is one man's story of finding his place in American society, uniquely told in an interplay of voices; what a story it is. Hank figured out early in life how to fit in but struggled to belong. From his early years in New Mexico to his long journey that led to the Rose Bowl and coming of age, he tells of his quest for and achievement of his identity. His is a story that deserves to be told and needs to be read. "

—Tom Knoles
Retired School Teacher

Who Let the Mexicans Play in the Rose Bowl—
Navigating the Racial Landscape of America
Copyright © 2019 Hank Olguin

E-book ISBN: 978-0-9792661-1-9
Paperback ISBN: 978-0-9792661-2-6

Cover design by Bob Paltrow

Printed in the United States of America

Dedicated to Patricia ~
my wife, my love, my rock.

CONTENTS

PROLOGUE

At first glance, readers may be wondering what the hell kind of title is that? What in the world is this book about? Some may even be asking who ever heard of Mexicans playing in the Rose Bowl? Don't they just play soccer? And who cares anyway?

Choosing that title sprang from my being Mexican and in fact having played on the 1959, University of California Rose Bowl team, along with life-long friend, fellow-Mexican, All-American, and Super Bowl quarterback, Joe Kapp. We weren't granted permission to play in the bowl, as the title may imply. We both earned our way there—but that's only part of the story.

Joe and I not only share a common heritage we share some similar geographical migration patterns. Joe was born in Santa Fe, New Mexico and I, about 60 miles away, in Albuquerque. When Joe was one-year-old, his family moved to Los Angeles and six years later to Salinas. When I was five-years-old, my family moved to Los Angeles and a year later to San Jose, just north of Salinas. We both happily affirm our Mexican background. Joe's father's background was German, but his mother's maiden name is García-Chavez. My mother's maiden name is García-Cosío. Those coincidences are clearly unrelated to our love of playing football but may account for our love of tequila, mariachis, and salsa. All of that minor history aside, I wrote this memoir with a firm objective in mind.

The great American narrative rarely includes positive stories about Mexicans. Many of us are tired of hearing only about immigration problems or of being characterized as foreigners, drug dealers, or criminals. We're hungry for positive, uplifting accounts that tell the whole story.

Actor, playwright, and author of *Latin History for Morons*, John Leguizamo, wrote in an op-ed piece, "The dominant narrative is that we have just 'illegally' crossed the border or are 'fresh off the boat.' People forget that Latinos founded some of America's first cities."

I have no quarrels with tales about recent immigrants, but what about the stories of all of us who are not so recent. If you consider our indigenous bloodlines, we've been around for thousands of years, and our Spanish ancestors have been kicking around this continent for five hundred years or so—not exactly recent.

Although my roots don't go back quite that far, my grandfather first crossed the southern border sometime in the late 1800s, subsequently and easily crisscrossed it many times to work, attend weddings, gamble, party, have kids, and finally stay. His son, my dad, was born in 1893 in a small mining town near Silver City, New Mexico, and I came along in 1936. I'm sure millions of Mexican Americans share a similar chronology, with perhaps many assimilating to the point of losing their Latino identity. I have not. I've been around a while, the whole time navigating the racial landscape of America. Therefore, I want to candidly share one man's experiences while growing up and growing old as an American Mexican.

Years ago, I heard some wise person say that we have to earn the right to speak on a subject. I trust my having lived some 80 plus years— through The Great Depression, World War II, the Red Scare, Civil Rights, assassinations, Vietnam, 9/11, the Internet, and Trump— gives me a small amount of authority to tell my story.

A Note on Labels

On many occasions over the years, I have often found myself in situations with my fellow Mexicans, arguing, close to fisticuffs, about who we are or what to call ourselves. It appears this pattern hasn't changed dramatically. Today, we hear and see Latina/o, Latinx, Hispanic, and other names often used interchangeably. For that reason, I feel it's important to comment on the labels related to the race, ethnicity, background, or nationality assigned to us. For openers, I refer to myself as a Mexican, but that immediately creates a contradiction in getting to an accurate description of the real me. I'm not really a Mexican if that label defines citizenship. I am not a Mexican citizen. I'm an American, an American citizen, a third generation American citizen to be exact. I even enjoy changing it up a bit and sometimes referring to myself as an American Mexican.

We defy accurate description because we easily qualify as a multi-racial, multi-cultural, multi-lingual division of the human species. Maybe we should just be called blendies or mixies. On second thought, that probably wouldn't work either, since those names could apply to all humans and would cause the folks at the Census Bureau to tear their hair out.

Even if it's understood that one was born in the U.S., how many Americans have had to endure being asked, "What are you?" I certainly have on countless occasions. I learned early in my long life that it was a question, depending on the questioner, masking many hidden sub-questions such as: Are you a foreigner? Where should I put you in the pecking order? You kinda look and sound American, but are you really one of us? What do you think about who you are or who you claim to be? Are you proud or ashamed of it?

Depending on when they occurred in my life experience, the questions created a myriad of quick calculations within my own mind: Whoa! Okay, who's asking? What's at stake? What do they want to know and why? What will be the consequences of my response, rejection or acceptance, safety or danger? Choosing the label you use to describe yourself can turn into a critical move. Since I believe I can assign a variety of names and labels to describe myself (most misnomers), I use many interchangeably throughout my story. Hopefully, it won't cause too much confusion.

A Note on Structure

The structure of this book is unusual, but one that should add to the scope and readability of the story. I tell of my youth in chronological order, sharing my first scattered glimpses of memory by attempting to capture how I thought as a child. Subsequently, I describe what I thought, spoke, and experienced as an elementary school kid and, so on, throughout the various stages of growing up. I arbitrarily designated the day I played in the Rose Bowl as the end of my youth. I thought it fitting to mark that date as the beginning of my adulthood, especially since I had gotten married just ten days prior.

I also use a voice appropriate to each phase of my youth by including some of the colloquialisms and vernacular of the period of time I describe, mainly in the '40s and '50s. Words and phrases such as "daddy-o," "the cat's pajamas," and others are sprinkled throughout to convey the feel of the era.

After the chronicling of my youthful experiences in the first half of each chapter, I proceed, "fast forward," to relate in the voice of the adult narrator pertinent stories or events that occurred later in my life. The second half of each chapter includes anecdotes and experiences that help define the evolution of my philosophy and point of view.

Spanish is my second language but one that has played a vital role in the course of my life's journey, making it necessary to include it when appropriate throughout the book. My fascination with language, terminology, and labels drove me to play around in that verbal sandbox. In addition, I've included poems I've written over the years that I felt were relevant to the preceding content of each chapter.

My ethnicity, or whatever people want to call it these days, has always been an inescapable part of my consciousness, pulsing in and out of my awareness like the intermittent beam of a lighthouse. So many of my decisions in life regarding relationships, career moves, and advocacy have come from the influence of that reality—often requiring a delicate balancing act against the backdrop of racial discrimination.

I would like others to gain some insight into that experience. In addition, I certainly want to invite readers to look beyond the labels or presuppositions, to unravel their preconceived notions, to take a second look, and to simply revisit the label "Mexican" with fresh eyes—to even imagine that way back in 1959 a couple of Mexicans could have played in the Rose Bowl. No, I'm not kidding.

Chapter One
The Scent of Earth

My name is "Quiqui," another name for Enrique, although my official given name is Henry. I remember trying to get accustomed to being called many different names.

My mother and father seemed troubled, but what can a small child know of the Great Depression and hardship? No pangs of hunger or thoughts of deprivation appeared to spoil the new experiences of those early years.

My mom would sing as she worked sewing cowgirl outfits made of blue denim and white leather. She sang loudly along with the noise of her foot-pedal-propelled Singer sewing machine. Her little yellow canary sang along with both while reaching to match their volume. It all created a wonderfully exuberant, joyous racket that resonated in my young heart. The hubbub blended and harmonized with the taste of the denim and leather I chewed, making me laugh and gurgle with new discoveries.

I didn't know that my mother sang in Spanish. I didn't know that *Adios Muchachos, Maria Elena*, and *La Paloma* were Spanish songs. To me they felt like rising and falling sounds that came from some wonderful place inside of her. She would open her mouth and out would come those sounds that made my chest tingle.

The magic of the word mijito (my little son) still has no equal in tenderness or in the power to propel me back into my mother's soft, round arms.

On a trip to Santa Fe something called a malt magically entered into my life. I thought how can anything have such a wondrous, glorious taste, and smoothy smoothness? Why must it end? Apples taste good but nothing, nothing like this, and I decided that nothing would ever taste as good again.

Our nearest neighbors, the Hawley's lived way down there at the end of the acequia (irrigation ditch) on Indian School Road, near the edge of my world. Mr. Hawley would walk from that faraway place to visit and talk with my dad. I think they helped each other in some way. I really don't know because they would use so many words I couldn't understand. I sensed the feelings of softness and attention that surrounded me. When Mr. Hawley came around, he patted me on the head, smiled, and winked at me. I knew he was my friend.

Echo Hawley's real name was Ethyl, but she couldn't say Ethyl so would say, "My name is Echo Hawley." I liked the way she said it and the way she wrinkled her nose. I also liked that she was even smaller than me.

My Tía (aunt) María would sometimes slap me because I wouldn't give her a kiss. I couldn't understand how she expected me to kiss her if she slapped me.

One day our dog Blackie ripped the pants off a man who innocently wandered on to our ranchito (little ranch). My father had to help him cover up. Blackie was always nice to me but not to everyone else around there. He liked to chase everything, even skunks, and one day he paid for it. Maybe he paid for ripping that man's pants off.

Rainbows would appear from nowhere to somewhere, floating over the Sandia Mountains like a set of giant colored highway lanes holding up a piece of the sky. Remarkable!

I often wished our mean old rooster and our bigger and meaner turkey didn't live with us. Life would have been a whole lot happier without them. I felt safe when they were locked up in the pen, but when my dad let them out I had to run up the steep acequia to safety. Then I would have to move around the yard carefully to avoid being seen by the two bullies incessantly pecking at the ground with their rock-hard, pointed bills. Sometimes I would let my guard down, get ambushed, and the chase would begin. My flailing little legs could usually get me up the bank of the acequia or in the back door of the house, but if the dreaded monsters got too close my father would have to rescue me from the jaws of death and wipe away a tear as well.

The delicate aroma of alfalfa that grew on our ranchito would envelop me in the early morning coolness. Traces of the deep, sweet greenness and the fresh, clear dew to this day mingle in the elusive air of memory I breathe.

❖ ❖ ❖ ❖ ❖ ❖ ❖ ❖

We all screamed when we heard the enormous bang coming from the long wooden chest we called our pantry. My big sisters Lucy and Irene giggled while I looked at the mess with big, unblinking eyes. The hot root beer had exploded and flying pieces of glass had shattered the jar that once held our supply of syrup. Everything was now free to foam, ooze, and drip all over everything else. I believe my mother thought it was funny, but I'm not sure. My sisters giggled again, the second time a little quieter after my mom's stern glance.

❖ ❖ ❖ ❖ ❖ ❖ ❖ ❖

I often wondered why an unknown mournful sound seemed so strangely familiar? It called to me as it trailed off to somewhere out there in the long, deep darkness. A tugging attraction to steam train whistles engaged my imagination without knowing what they were. Curious.

My sister Lucy and I were surprised and attacked by one of the barnyard bullies. This time it was the rooster. He began to chase us, and we got caught running round and round our house for what seemed like hours. No one would believe this sight: an awkward thirteen year-old girl and a stumbling four year-old boy running side-by-side, both screaming like sirens while pursued by a puffed-up bundle of black and rust-colored feathers no more than a foot-and-a-half tall. To my sister and me, he loomed larger that that. He was the stuff that spawned nightmares. With lumps of raw, red skin dangling from his ugly head, the vicious beast seemed intent on pecking us to death with the murderous sword attached to the end of his nose.

We pumped our frightened legs faster and higher in trying to escape. As we came around to the back part of the house, my mom and other sister Irene held open the kitchen door for us to reach safety. Unfortunately, as we would slow down to turn into the door, we would crash into each other. The rooster would then gain on us, and we would have to speed up once again to avoid his extended beak. If we missed the entrance into the house, we would begin another round. If we missed the door again, another round would begin—on and on. I'm sure I imagined that the chase would never end. Thank god we finally reached safety inside the kitchen only to see my mom and Irene holding their aching sides from laughter. As Lucy and I stood there, gulping extra bites of air to recover from the ordeal, I thought to myself how unfair of them to be enjoying what we have just endured. I'm sure I expected to suffer some bad dreams as a result.

One afternoon my mom and I came back from el centro (the center) of Old Town, Albuquerque. When we arrived home we found that our big mean turkey had retreated into Blackie's doghouse. Apparently, Mr. Hawley's bigger and meaner turkey had escaped from his pen and had come over to our house to challenge our turkey to a fight and obviously win. Our turkey lay in his inadequate hiding place subdued and exhausted. His bloodied, drooping head, looking like a red-soaked sponge, stuck out of Blackie's house just enough for the winner to peck at it whenever he chose.

My old dreaded enemy appeared to be near death, and I couldn't help but feel a bit of "serves you right" in my vindictive young heart. After a while Mr. Hawley came to get his turkey. He seemed angry and not his usual friendly self. I began to feel vaguely sorry for our beaten old bird until my mom said he would probably recover and live. Dreadful visions of being terrorized for the rest of my life returned to haunt me.

The moist and musky scent of earth would erupt when fat droplets of a summer shower would marry with the dusty, dry New Mexican soil. As I inhaled that mysterious fragrance, it formed a oneness with my body I could never describe. It lingers there today, deep within, comforting and forbidding me to forget.

~ FAST FORWARD ~

Returning

Forty-three years later I returned for the first time to the adobe three-room house my father had built for the family. Of course it seemed large when I was a child. Even the old photographs of the house I looked at frequently as an adult revealed its small size but certainly not that of a playhouse. When I returned to discover it had shrunk, almost dissolved, I squinted in disbelief. Everything had shriveled except the trees. The creek, called a conservancy and running alongside the ranchito, the acequia, and the long dirt road leading up to the house had dwindled. Everything had imploded into a kind of miniature land, and I had the peculiar feeling of walking around in the body of a giant longing to be small again.

My visit caused a rush of forgotten sensations and renewed childhood impressions. Imagined, welcomed ghosts appeared, especially of my mom who had died just two years before my returning. Like an erratic camera, my memory's eye first landed on early snapshots of her there on the exact piece of ground on which I now stood. It then spontaneously flashed forward to scenes of the precious relationship we nurtured later in life. The special day I sat her down in front of a tape recorder and microphone to document important parts of her life suddenly shot back to refresh my recollections.

Marie Olguin

She was born María Concepción García Cosío in El Rancho de Gamboa, Zacatecas, Mexico in 1906. Even before her birth, her wealthy grandfather had evenly parceled out his sprawling ranch between his many sons and daughters. Nevertheless, it more than met the basic needs of a large but close-knit family.

In their communal, self-contained ranch they shared and traded cattle, crops, celebrations, births, and losses.

María recalls skipping through the carefree, confident days of her early youth, rushing to her mother or father for them to soothe a bruised knee or to hold and protect her from a cruel word or prank by one of the other children. Their comforting, unwavering arms were always open when her wild spirit required special indulgence. She loved to sing, dance, and pretend. She loved to immerse in the lessons she received from the periodic visits of the traveling maestro (teacher) with the big mustache, little round glasses, and the limp he inherited from falling off a horse. She loved to watch her father and his men riding the big rough horses that he traded, especially at the end of the day when a tight abrazo (hug) would not be far behind. Above all else she loved the kitchen fragrances that lingered on her mother's blouse and apron, her mother's fragile smile and tender ways, and the feel of her supple hands when they cupped María's wind-burned face. As she sprang into her mother's arms, she knew that there she would be safe and shielded from the hidden dangers of the world beyond.

Just before the age of twelve, an unexpected dagger cut into María's world with a cruel swiftness she could not foresee. As she stood in the midnight corridor, she could hear her mother's moans from behind the closed door of the main bedroom off-limits to her. The baby was now dangerously overdue. Aunts scurried about like frightened mice with pans of hot water, sheets, and wide-eyed looks. Before they chased her away from the door, María caught a fleeting glimpse of crimson stains, her mother's soaked and tangled hair, and worse her drained and pale skin. In frozen disbelief María ran back to her room to hide. She threw herself on to her bed in time to hear the moaning stop. Holding her breath, she waited long enough to realize that no other sound would float out from her mother's throat and long enough to feel an icy veil invade her room. A moment later her suspended breath burst forth, and on its heels she heard her own deep-gutted anguish pierce the cruel and empty night.

The death of her mother and unborn sister began the unraveling of María's happy and predictable youth. In the midst of that and other tragic personal events to come, the Mexican revolution struck with a fury into the heart of her world. Two uncertain years followed in which she saw her father sink into a state of waking sleep, leaving behind only remnants of the person she once knew.

One night the sounds of multiple hoofs and the muffled voices of late nightriders awakened her long enough to quickly decide that falling back to sleep would be preferable to discovering the reason for their visit. The following morning Tía Luisa held her hand and told her that a feud had taken place over some bad woman at a neighboring ranch, and that her father was now in his room gasping for life from the bullet in his head that would never be removed.

As before, María bolted from her grief, this time away from the dying house. Across the llano (plain) and down to the dry streambed she hurled her young girl's wounded soul. There she stayed for several numb unthinking hours, remembering only that she saw a thin and frightened fox scurry away for cover into the brush. Her father lasted for a pair of hopeless days. With his burial came the realization that all she had ever treasured was now undeniably lost.

Because her uncle served as a high-ranking general for Pancho Villa, the feared and hunted leader of the revolution, María and her family members faced a particular threat that forced them to hide in the remote and rugged hills to escape detection from government forces. As the revolution raged on, throwing the family-ranch into dangerous disarray, María, her grandmother, and aunts fled to a small town for their protection. At the same time, her brothers and sisters were scattered like lonely pebbles and ended up dispersed among various relatives.

The months that followed turned into endless hungry days, fearful nights, and ever-present dangers. In one instance she remembers cowering as she peered out through her aunt's front window and watched one of her uncle's servants, Fermin, dragged to his death through the streets behind the army soldiers' horses. A kind but frail man, his usual halfway drunken haze no doubt prevented him from escaping with the others. Finally, the death of María's grandmother inexorably closed the door on the peaceful and idyllic life she had known, forcing her into a premature and lonely womanhood. At fifteen she found herself without family, landless, and penniless, working for a distant aunt virtually as an indentured servant.

Desperate to break out of the prison fate had handed her and to seek a better life, María at seventeen found a way to escape to the United States with two other adventurous friends, ending up in the Santa Clara Valley of California. There she and her comrades found work in the fruit and vegetable canneries. While slowly learning English, she began gathering new experiences to hopefully overshadow her turbulent early youth. Making friends with people different from her aroused her interest, and she gravitated toward some of the Italian immigrants with whom she felt an easy camaraderie. Her actions bothered some of her less sociable or adventurous Mexican co-workers. A fiercely independent spirit, fed by earlier more difficult trials, helped her resist the peer pressure to limit her friendships along ethnic lines and disregard the attitudes she considered clannish. The tendency persisted throughout her life, choosing to enjoy the relationships of people that suited her regardless of their background or race.

Unlike many Mexicans who came to this country at the time expecting to someday return to their native land with saved up money and hopes for a better life, María firmly closed the door behind her. She would not go back to live in the shadows of her past losses and grief. She would only look forward and keep searching for ways to displace her sorrow. Perhaps in an effort to reinvent herself and as a symbol of fully accepting her newly adopted country, most of her life she chose to be known as "Marie," the name her Italian friends called her. Although she embraced her new country with hope and confidence, she soon learned that tragedy has no respect for geographic boundaries.

While working in the canneries, she met Francisco Ortega and discovered a love that engulfed her like an irresistible tide. They were married, settled in San Francisco, had two daughters, and strolled through a happy, promising life for a few short years. One evening while changing a tire on a dark road leading into the city, an oncoming car careened into Francisco, killing him instantly. Marie remembers being in church earlier that day and trying to dismiss the fleeting black cloud she imagined drifting overhead. The cloud soon turned into a stark reality, and her life burst into a thousand shards of pain. Once again she felt the need to escape the setting of her sorrow and loss, this time coupled with another pressing reality.

By now the Great Depression had gripped the country, and the U.S.

government was deporting Mexicans, often and illegally, with their American-born children. In the midst of her delirious state, Marie understood the gravity of the situation and decided to take her two daughters and flee to the interior of the country where she had heard the deportation pressure would be less intense. A sister-in-law who lived in Albuquerque, New Mexico had urged her to move there by suggesting that she might feel safer away from the West Coast. Again she bundled up the pieces of her life and attempted to make some sense of continuing to live.

Widowed with two young daughters and in a daze of mourning, she made her way unsteadily to New Mexico and found the Depression devastating the lives of people there as much as in other parts of the country. To be able to take jobs whenever they became available, she placed Lucy and Irene in a Catholic boarding school while she worked as a housekeeper in private homes and hotels. After a short period she inadvertently discovered that her children were the targets of neglect and abuse in the boarding school run by nuns. Reeling in shock, anger, and fear for her girls, she immediately rescued them from the Catholic school. Through the recommendation of a caring friend, she enrolled them in a Methodist boarding school the Harwood School for Girls. She quickly saw the move as a welcomed blessing, one that renewed her faith in the compassion of human beings namely those who provided her children with a safe harbor. All her life she spoke with deep gratitude for the level of kindness, nurturing, and affection Lucy and Irene received by the "angels living on earth at Harwood."

More than anything the experience convinced Marie to finally abandon her Catholic faith. Her decision was prompted not only by the ill treatment her daughters received at the Catholic boarding school but also by her lingering disapproval of the way the poor were treated by the church in Mexico as she was growing up. She remembered, as a girl, sensing the injustice of priests taking money from the poor and faithful campesinos (peasant farmers) in exchange for some blessing. Much to the displeasure of some relatives, she became a Methodist and remained one until she died.

The almost unbearable extent of suffering and sadness she experienced through critical periods of her life made her more compassionate and charitable rather than bitter and angry. She found the way for her generous heart to emerge and share the little she owned with the people in need that crossed her path throughout her life. She claimed she learned that lesson from her father's standing order at the ranch, during more happy and prosperous times, that dictated no one could be turned away hungry from his doors. Her own individual hardships must have also embedded the lesson in her emotional stores.

I can imagine beyond what the woman who gave me life has told us, a period in her life filled with laughter, love, and grace. I can imagine the carefree days of a childhood embraced in the nurturing arms of El Rancho de Gamboa.

SING US YOUR SONG

Sing us your song once more, Marie,
Across the fragile, time-swept years,
When you were safe and wild and free—
Before the fiery storms arrived,
Back in the gleaming morning of your youth,
When life's fair flowers bloomed and thrived.

Sing us your song once more, Marie,
The one about the corn saint's spell
That swirled around the courtyard tree—
Compelling you to run and play,
Secure in the abundance of the house,
All innocent as breaking day.

Sing us your song once more, Marie,
Of horsemen riding thunderbolts
Upon the high plane's dusty sea—
Of how you thrilled to racing herds,
The high, shrill whistles steering them like wheels,
Beyond a thousand, breathless words.

Sing us your song once more, Marie.
Tell of your father's firm, strong hands
That gently held your laughter's key—
Then led you to your mother's arms,
Where evening lullabies embraced your soul,
Far from the sting of war's alarms.

Sing us your song once more, Marie,
Of everlasting childhood dreams,
Spring colors only you could see—
And promises devoid of pain,
Held in the secret silences you kept,
Like healing whispers from the last soft rain.

~ 1985

Chapter Two
A Song in Two Tongues

My mom whispered that there was a dead lady in the big box in the next room. I didn't want to look so I stayed in the kitchen. Candles were burning everywhere and women dressed in black moved around like shadows with long strings of beads in their hands. When they were in the other room, I heard them murmuring the same mournful chant over and over again. I had never seen or heard anything like that before in my life.

Someone named Naty would also walk into that room, sit next to the big box, scream, and cry, "Mamá, Mamá." She would wail on and on but then come back into the kitchen, almost suddenly, smiling and talking very normally and nicely to everyone. After a while she would go back in almost as suddenly and begin to scream again. I hoped I wouldn't have to come to a velorio (wake) ever again. The only good thing about it was that I could grab an empanada (turnover) from the kitchen table and go outside, run, and act crazy with the other kids.

Trudging through the rain-soaked fields of the camposanto (cemetery), I saw several men struggling with the big wooded box. My shoes got heavier with each muddy step, and I could see and hear grown-ups crying like they did at the velorio. I wondered why I was forced to be there. My Tío Nilo and the other men lowered the box with ropes into a hole in the drenched ground, and the cries got louder. I felt scared but didn't understand why.

Irene, her friend Esther Burdick, and I walked from Esther's house to ours. I was in love with Esther. She was the most beautiful girl I had ever seen. We walked through the fields of the neighboring dairy where they gathered and piled the cow manure into neat, cone-shaped stacks. I laughed and ran forward while looking backwards and showing off for Esther. Before I knew it, I had encountered one of the stacks of fresh muck, and by increasingly slowing, agonizing steps found myself stuck waste high in the finest, wettest, and smelliest manure in Bernalillo County. Esther and Irene laughed hysterically. I howled, also hysterically, but only to rid myself of the soaking waste and pungent aura I now exuded. All the way home I kept my arms extended out to my sides like a giant seabird drying his feathers. As we arrived home to my mom's reprimands, I was reduced to a whimper knowing that Esther would never love me now.

My sister Lucy suffered for a long time after allowing our second dog, a little spotted black and white puppy, to eat an apple core. Of course she didn't mean to hurt him, but he choked on it and died anyway. The little funeral and burial service my sisters and I held for Captain Marvel couldn't ease her pain and guilt, and I wished I knew how to tell her it was all right and not to cry.

I was not even one bit afraid of thunder and lightening like my silly sister Irene, who would cover her head with pillows and let out giant squeals with every crack. How funny!

My dad's hands were large and rough, his fingers thick and powerful. He would take my small hand in his, and we'd walk down to the conservancy along our property. He would enter the deep water filled with tall reeds and move through it with great ease and a smile. I remember being afraid, but he would take my hand and everything would feel safe again. I hadn't learned yet that my father's hands were Mexican.

Several of the young men from the Indian school next door would regularly bring us armfuls of the vegetables they grew in their fields. They would stand around, talk, joke and laugh politely with my father and call him primo (cousin). Together they seemed to form a circle of trust and affection. Because my dad liked them I too allowed them to become a part of me. There was an alluring gentleness surrounding them. To me they were strangers but somehow familiar.

I didn't think of those shining young men as Indians. They were just part of the natural flow of our daily lives. When I discovered later what others called them and what they were supposed to be, I lost a part of their essence, their laughter, and, sadly, I lost a part of me.

One afternoon my sisters came home from school all scared. They told my dad that a man under the bridge on Indian School Road had taken all his clothes off. My dad took a big piece of wood like a club, went down to the bridge, and made him get dressed. Then the sheriff came and took him away. I wondered why he would want to undress since it wasn't that hot.

It rained little balls of ice from the sky. My padrino (godfather) came to visit, and we all stayed inside the house until the clattering storm stopped. When we went outside I had fun running around crunching the melting marbles of ice under my shoes. I stopped long enough to say goodbye to my padrino, and I put my hand on the doorframe of his car just before he slammed the door. I screamed, screamed, and screamed from the throbbing, dizzying pain I had never felt before. While they held me down, they poured some watery stuff on my deep-cut finger that made it hurt even more, and then they taped it tightly. My padrino kept saying, "I'm sorry, I'm sorry." I thought maybe he was going to start crying too.

Luminarias (paper lanterns) lined the edges and walkways of our flat-roofed adobe house, simple paper sacks filled with enough sand to hold a single candle and make Christmas in Albuquerque sing with choruses of glimmering lights. As they flickered they tossed shadows on the brown walls and ground for Blackie and me to chase.

I once saw my mother beat a snake to death with a shovel—her obvious phobia of reptiles rendered the irreversible verdict. I had never seen such fury and energy focused on anything in my life. The moment the defenseless creature appeared near our back door it was doomed. A mother's fear can be a devastating and insurmountable force.

Crickets and frogs must have been put on our ranchito to help me sleep warm and well, a benevolent and soothing opiate of nature designed to lull me into feeling my canopy of serenity would last forever.

Abuelito (granddaddy) is the name I was told to call my grandfather Francisco. I had never seen my dad's father until he came to visit one day from a faraway place. He was slender and taller and darker than my father, and he wore crooked copper bracelets that were supposed to cure him of something called arthritis. I didn't know what to think about him. I sensed a strained cord of energy running between him and my dad when they talked. It flowed fairly smoothly until a sudden word would abruptly turn it stiff and brittle. It made me feel as if the next word or look could break the cord and make them walk away from each other.

My grandfather liked to tell stories about scary things but only in Spanish. My sisters and I sat at his knee holding our breath as he talked about evil brujas (witches) or distant fires on the prairie he swore were signs of buried treasure. "Yes, it's true." He would whisper. "And if you ever see one of those fires, you must quickly make the sign of the cross for you never know when el diablo (the devil) may be up to his old tricks."

I didn't always know the difference between Spanish and English. To me the words often formed a continuous melodic line, and I responded not only to the individual notes but to the whole song.

~ *FAST FORWARD* ~

A Troubled Legacy

In spite of all the great tales my grandfather spun, I somehow never easily addressed him with the affectionate term abuelito as a child. A part of me somehow sensed it didn't fit our relationship. My stingy use of the term troubled me until as a teenager I learned that he was something of an irresponsible drifter and gambler. The revealing account came from a gracious, loving white-haired lady, my dad's cousin on his mother's side known to the family as Tía Tana.

She told stories about my dad Si and his brothers and sisters, of how they grew up almost like orphans staying with her family when Francisco drifted away and then being shuffled off to the next relative's home when the situation changed. I recall Tía Tana telling me with tears in her eyes how terrible she felt as a young girl seeing the sad faces of her cousins as they bounced around from place to place. The absence of my dad's mother in the account implied the female subservience that must have been common in that era and family. Sadly, I never asked my dad about his mother, and he never chose to volunteer any information about her. The lack of details left me with an empty page in my mind regarding my paternal grandmother. I could only guess about her role in the family. Hearing Tía Tana's stories, I wondered further if as a child I had detected something hidden about my grandfather that instinctively made me hold back my full affection.

My dad carried with him a shield of hard silence that I never strongly attempted to break through regarding intimate matters surrounding his personal family history. Having me late in his life perhaps contributed to the age-gap rift that existed throughout most of our relationship. His difficulty in expressing emotional issues added to the lack of communication between us. Further, he died early in my adult life. I was only twenty-eight when my father passed away. If he would have lived longer, we might have eventually ventured into the overgrown garden of family secrets and harvested some meaningful connections between us.

The little I knew came partly and sparingly from my dad himself but mainly from other family members and my mom. After my father died the sketchy picture left me wanting to know more about his origins and character. The older I grew the more I longed to examine some of the traits and nuances of personality I might have inherited. The failure to explore together the interconnections of our experiences added to my regrets. I've been forced to piece together the fragments of that and other questions to the best of my ability.

Si H. Olguin

My father was born in Pinos Altos, approximately ten miles north of Silver City, New Mexico in 1893, and his given name was Serapio. My grandfather spelled his last name with an H, Holguin. I never learned the reasons my dad changed his first name to Si, dropped the H from his surname, and made it his middle initial. Since the H in Holguin is silent, I chose to assume that he simply liked the look of his altered handle. He certainly was not trying to pass for White. He spoke almost as much Spanish as English, and often expressed how much he loved the Spanish and multicultural aspect of his beloved native state.

Dad qualified as one of those old-timers from the West who could do everything, a jack-of-all-trades as they say. Miner, carpenter, plumber, farmer, and even court interpreter are some of the occupations he claimed to have mastered. According to my dad's cousin Antonio, he left New Mexico for a time when he was young and worked as a construction supervisor for a company building bridges in California and Oregon. Antonio liked to brag to me about my dad by saying, "Sí, señor (Yes, sir), your dad was a big shot in those days and the boss of a lot of men. Sí, señor." Antonio also remembered when his cousin even served as a U.S. border patrol guard for a short period.

My dad also encountered several interesting and significant people associated with the history of the Southwest. He claimed to have personally known the colorful figure and gunfighter, Elfego Baca; as a little boy to have seen Pat Garrett, the man who shot Billy the Kid; and to have been friends with Ernie Pyle, the Pulitzer Prize-winning World War II correspondent.

I could never confirm the first two claims, but I clearly remember one day when I was nine years old my dad walking into the house with a newspaper in his hand. Quieter than usual he walked straight into the living room where my mom joined him. They spoke in whispers. My mom got up to make dinner, and my dad remained still and staring at the floor in his chair. I went in, sat next to him, and noticed the tears in his eyes that he tried to hide. Probably sensing that his behavior might be confusing and frightening to me, he gave me a quick pat on the head and a tentative smile. Mom later told me that my dad had lost his friend, Ernie Pyle, in the war, that he had been killed by a Japanese sniper's bullet while on assignment in the Pacific.

My dad was also one of the original organizers of the coal and copper miner's union in the state of New Mexico in the days when, as he recounted, "We negotiated with baseball bats." Later he became a delegate to a couple of Democratic National Conventions and remained an ardent supporter of President Franklin Delano Roosevelt (FDR). For as long as I can remember, my dad passionately espoused FDR's philosophy to help the country recover from the Depression. Known as the "New Deal," it fostered government public works for creating jobs and economic opportunity. The approach resonated with his belief system.

From the little I knew of my father's background, I concluded that he spent much of his early life searching for ways to put his compassion and social consciousness to work toward making a difference in the lives of people less fortunate than he. I remember his using a saying that today might be judged as paternalistic but one certainly meaningful to his generation. With a tone of conviction, he would say, "You gotta fight for the little man."

Early in his life he may have believed a way existed to combine one's sense of justice with financial success and that the political process might possibly make the pairing a reality. According to my mom, he later became disillusioned with that idea after a series of personal disappointments,

One such setback involved his close friendship with an Albuquerque attorney by the name of Bob LaFollete, nephew of the famous progressive senator from Wisconsin by the same name. When dad died in 1963, I talked to Bob who reminisced about some of the good times he shared with my dad and how terribly sad he was to hear of "his old pal's death." He also corroborated a story I had heard my dad relate.

Among some of his many occupations, dad especially enjoyed his work as a court interpreter, putting his bilingual skills to good use. His interpreting assignments stimulated his interest in the law. When Bob asked him if he would consider apprenticing in his office, dad seized the opportunity like a hungry kid turned loose in a candy store. At the time a state statute existed that allowed for someone to practice law if they apprenticed with a licensed attorney for five years and could then pass the bar. One day halfway through the program Bob called my dad into his office and showed him a new law that had recently been passed by the state legislature. Dad's shoulders and spirit slumped as he heard that the new legislation required a college and law degree for prospective attorneys. His eighth grade education instantly disqualified him, shoving a hurdle in his path he could not overcome. Bob's heartfelt words of consolation and regret did little to comfort dad's profound disappointment. Mom later revealed that he never wholly recovered from that blow.

Becoming a Family

My dad and mom met in Albuquerque while living in the same apartment building. I know little about their short courtship and eventual marriage. As an adult I suspected that dad felt a deeper love for my mom than she did for him. I often thought the marriage might have been born out of necessity, maybe even my mother's desperation. Nevertheless, she and dad began building in their own tentative way a shared life and family.

Whatever shortcomings their union may have presented, mom remained forever grateful to her second husband for the way he accepted and cared for her daughters. Although he never formally adopted Lucy and Irene, he considered them his little girls and always demonstrated, if not always verbalized, his deep love and affection for them. Since he was the only father they can remember knowing intimately, they reciprocated with equal levels of fondness and affection.

At the beginning of their relationship before mom and dad married, they went to visit Lucy and Irene for the first time while they were still boarding at Harwood School for Girls. Mom packed a picnic lunch, and the four of them spent several hours in a nearby park. The whole time my dad tried his best to make the girls laugh or even smile by telling them fragments of the children's stories he struggled to remember. Meeting this stranger for the first time, Lucy and Irene concentrated mainly on clinging to their mom and venturing away from her side only long enough to bite into a sandwich or take a drink of a soda. My dad's awkward tenderness earned him only cautious looks, polite but quiet nods, and nervous fidgets aimed at confirming their mom's protection. To the best of his ability he attempted to be charming and gain their confidence, but at the end of the day he felt sure he had failed to win them over.

A week later mom and dad returned for a second visit. This time the moment Lucy and Irene came out of the building they instantly began running and smiling. Instead of making the expected stop for hugs and kisses from their mom, they ran past her and flung themselves into my dad's surprised and willing arms. As he attempted to hide his tears, they held on to him like someone they had known all of their lives. As the rest of the gentle day unfolded, he wondered what on earth could have moved those precious little girls to treat him in that manner, a gift he would cherish the rest of his life.

When my mom spoke into a tape recorder about that day, I remembered that the "half" aspect of the kinship with my sisters never entered my mind through the majority of my youth. Even after learning they had a different father they simply remained my big sisters, carrying with the label and relationship all of the ups and downs of normal sibling joys and rivalries. I always knew that my father unquestionably thought of Lucy and Irene as his "real" daughters, a notion that somehow always pleased me. The feeling must have made its way to him from the durable love and devotion they felt for their new dad until the day he died.

After mom and dad married and I was born, another major disappointment arrived to cloud their lives. I have only sketchy details about an incident involving a government contract awarded to my dad for remodeling the plaza in "Old Town" Albuquerque. My dad's company won the contract under the federal Works Progress Administration (WPA), one of FDR's "New Deal" programs created to alleviate the economic suffering resulting from the Great Depression. After the completion of the job, the accusation arose that my dad had misappropriated federal funds while directing the project. A conviction followed that released an avalanche of old fears in my mom and clouded the recent sense of security she had begun to trust. Suddenly life seemed fragile and uncertain again. Before leaving to serve a yearlong sentence at a minimum-security facility called Las Tunas, my mom remembers my dad giving her explicit instructions by saying, "Remember, if anybody asks, you know nothing, nothing, you understand?" Hearing of my dad's admonition caused me naturally to speculate that it implied dangerous political entanglements and corruption.

In keeping with our usual pattern, my dad never discussed the situation with me. My mother on the other hand would never speak about it without the tone in her voice changing into a resentful growl. Her indignation made her sound like an impassioned attorney delivering the summation statement for the defense proclaiming that my dad had suffered a grave injustice and had been blamed for those on the take above him, for those in positions of power. "The only thing he ever got out of that damn project was a couple of measly shirts and a pair of glasses," she would insist. The difficulties our family suffered from my dad's absence locked into her memory like bricks in cement, and she never uttered the word "politics" without preceding it with a sneering and disdainful "dirty."

Although I never learned exactly what took place, I never saw my father cheat anyone or even come close to doing so throughout my whole life. In spite of emotionally missing each other at many critical intersections of our lives, I believed he always conformed to a strict moral code that included honesty and integrity. In the end I found it easy to believe in my dad's innocence.

A Changing World

On the night of December 7, 1941, our family sat outside of our adobe house during a blackout drill. My sisters teased me by saying that a war had started and that some mean soldiers were going to come and get me. My parents ordered the girls to stop teasing and for me to stop crying. Everyone sensed that something irreversible had taken place in our lives. At five years old, I remember hearing on the radio that some people called Japanese had dropped bombs on a faraway American place called Pearl Harbor, Hawaii, a place that no longer seemed so far away.

In the days that followed, our family realized it had accumulated enough reasons to justify a move to California. In a completely new world they might rebuild their lives. In addition to my dad's prison term, other incentives reinforced the decision. My dad's brother and family had already moved to Los Angeles and wrote that the wartime economy of California would be providing good jobs. The time had come to leave behind old disappointments, failures, and betrayals. The time had come to leave the land of enchantment, the place where words with twin-like meanings narrated my playtime dreams.

CHIQUITOLITTLE JUANJACK

Chiquitolittle Juanjack
Bolts through the puertadoor
Of his adobebrick casahouse,
Correruns towards the deep
Verdegreen alfalfaalfalfa field,
To olersmell the lingering scent
Of the afternoon Nuevonew Mexican
Lluviarain.
The newly lavadaswashed piedrasstones
On the tierradirt caminoroad
Sparkle underneath his piesfeet
From the recent aguacerocloudburst.
And as he picks up one small piedrastone
To fling into the rushing arroyocreek,
He sees for a fleeting momentomoment,
Beyond his niñochild's innocence,
Tristementesadly anticipating
The futurofuture loss
Of half the maravillosasmarvelous
Palabrawords
He loves.

~ 1979

Marie Olguin

Si H. Olguin

Chapter Three
Zoot Suits and Foxholes

We took off across the country in a long Greyhound bus that puffed out fumes smelling like burning, oily rags and that burped every time the driver applied the brakes. We got different drivers for different parts of the trip, and the fan next to the driver's seat cooled all of them off but did little to cool the rest of us. I kept wishing I had a fan next to my seat. Then I wouldn't have suffered from the heat that felt like a thick blanket over my head, especially when we drove across places I had never seen before called deserts. As we got off the bus to take a break at a place called Indio, an invisible wave of big, fat hot air almost pushed me back into the bus. I had never felt anything like that back at our ranchito.

The trip took what seemed like weeks, but my mother kept telling me that it only took three days. I didn't believe her. When we arrived in this town called San Jose, I looked around with big wide eyes and saw things I'd never seen before. I had never seen so many trees, row after row of them. I remember hearing my mom and dad call them huertas (orchards). I began to think that I liked being there. I surely liked the tall, old wooden house we moved into with the curved bench next to a round front window. I had never seen a round window before. I mostly enjoyed curling up, looking out through it at the tall green trees, and eating an apple. In our new home I also got to drink Parti-Pak Cola—something else brand new. It came in tall bottles and fizzed funny in my mouth. My sisters always got more than I did which I thought was unfair.

What I liked most of all about where we now lived was walking into the Saint Claire creamery just two blocks from our house. The scrubbed white tile floors, walls, and shiny refrigerator doors of this ice cream heaven sparkled with a clean, delicious fragrance. The magic sweet-milk aroma of vanilla filled the cool air and flowed into the grooves of my tongue—a delectable new treat in my life.

We started visiting my Uncle Sal, my mom's first husband's brother, and his family. Although we weren't related he insisted that I call him uncle. They lived in this big city nearby called San Francisco. It felt like a city made of paved tall mountains with streets going up and down, up and down. Sometimes I thought my dad's car might not make it to the top of one of those streets, and I felt relieved and safe when we could slide down the other side. In my Uncle Sal's neighborhood a bunch of wild, noisy kids rode carts they made out of wooden boxes and old roller-skate wheels. Down the steep hills they would go, faster than I could clap my hands from giddy excitement. I begged my mom to let me ride one of the speeding boxes and she always answered, ¡Jamás! (never!) ¿Quires Matarte? (Do you want to kill yourself?) ¡Jamás!

We didn't stay in San Jose very long and that made me sad. We had to move to another town called Los Angeles. My Uncle Cate, Catarino (he also had two names like my dad) convinced my dad that he could get a better job down there. My mother looked unhappy when he proposed the plan. I didn't think she wanted to go and neither did I. I was just getting to like our new place, just beginning to stop missing the smell of alfalfa.

In Los Angeles we lived over a little grocery store that was owned by some nice people my parents call Españoles (Spaniards). They spoke Spanish but they sounded different than my mom and dad. I started having fun again because I had a lot of cousins near our new home. Henry, Helen, Nano, Gilbert, Mary Lou, Ernest, and Pete. My cousin Fina, who was older and very pretty, sometimes acted like my protector. One time she chased away some kids who had thrown a rock at me, hit me on the head, and caused an egg-like lump to sprout. She hugged me, told me not to cry, and promised that those mean kids would never bother me again. I believed her. It was nice to have older cousins stick up for me.

My mother and father would shop at a big store down on Main Street. This is where I saw Pachucos (Zoot-Suiters) for the first time—young, rowdy Mexican guys. My parents didn't like them saying they were troublemakers and lacked respect. My mother especially didn't like the way they talked, complaining that they didn't speak Spanish correctly.

Lucy and Irene attended Central Junior High School along with a bunch of the Pachucos. They told my parents they were afraid of all those tough boys because they belonged to gangs and were always getting in fights and knifing each other. I was still too young to feel ashamed that they were Mexicans like me. That came later.

A steep, straight, hall-like staircase led from our upstairs apartment to the door that opened to the street below. The banister gave me something to hold on to while I would catapult full-speed, downward taking two and three stairs as I went. It made me feel like I could fly without wings. One afternoon on Easter eve, I was making my usual exhilarating descent when I tripped near the bottom of the steps, lost my grip on the banister, and crashed headfirst into the giant brass doorknob. I howled in pain as the blood spurted from the left side of my head. I hobbled back up the stairs to our apartment expecting the waiting, comforting arms of my parents. Unfortunately, I was conscious, which gave my mother license to smack me on the side of my head that was not bleeding from the collision. At the same time she screamed, "How many times have I told you not to jump como loco (like a crazy man) down those stairs?" Her swat hurt my feelings more than my head and caused my howls to grow even louder. I'm sure I could be heard for miles around.

To look my best for Easter Sunday services at the First Methodist Church, I was supposed to get a haircut. Instead I got a white swath of gauze encircling my head, making me look like one of those wounded soldiers in the war movies we used to see.

My cousin Nano was a teenager who was too sick to go to school. He had an illness that made him very skinny and pale, so he stayed at home in his pajamas and bathrobe most of the time. His mom my Tía Tana sometimes took care of me, and when she did I got to play and build model airplanes with Nano. He was very nice to me. He loved football and wished he could play. He even had some shoulder pads he would put on, but they were too big for him and looked like bulky wings on a stick. With a faraway look in his eyes, he would tell me that maybe someday I might be able to play football for some big college. He made me wonder about that. If that came true I hoped he would live long enough to come and watch me, but a sad, nagging voice floating over my head told me he never would.

My days there were filled up with visiting aunts and uncles (my Tía Tana made the best flour tortillas in the whole world), playing with my cousins (I played only in Spanish with Mary Lou, with Helen, only in English), going to movies, and shopping with my mom and dad. However, something kept telling me that all of that wasn't going to last very long. I heard my mom telling my dad that she wanted to go back to San Jose—just when I was starting to get comfortable and starting to think I would live near all those cousins forever.

America was fighting a war against two countries called Germany and Japan. It seemed that the war was all anyone ever talked about. I heard my parents complain that they couldn't buy certain things they were able to get before the war started.

My cousin David was in the Navy and wore a sailor suit, and my cousin Robert was in the Army and wore a soldier's uniform. I had a uniform they made for little kids so I could look like them. My cousin Ike was also in the Army, someplace far away. I think our family worried about him. Robert showed me some scars on his arms he said he got from using a thing called a flamethrower. I thought maybe I'd be a soldier when I grew up, but after thinking that I might end up with scars like Robert I decided to be a football player instead.

~ *FAST FORWARD* ~

The Mean Summer of '43

Sil Madrigal claimed to be the quintessential Pachuco, and he may have deserved the right to that claim. When I first met Sil in 1968, he was somewhere in his late forties or early fifties. I never asked. I either considered the question impolite or felt intimidated by Sil's self-assured swagger. We worked together for a company providing job training under a government contract for so-called "disadvantaged," Spanish-speaking workers. Sil's confident strut, bulky physical frame, and quick wit worked well with the trainees, many of them street-wise toughs needing a Sil-type-mentor to motivate and keep them in line. His good-humored sarcasm combined well with his genuine ready smile and his commitment to the job. He effectively mixed his street smarts with tough love and a natural understanding of human nature, especially in the foibles department. Always looking for creative ways to inspire his charges to overcome their difficult backgrounds, he would threaten, "I know you vatos (dudes) have had a tough life, but if you don't pay attention and learn what I'm telling you, I'm going to make it a whole lot tougher." All of Sil's flamboyant qualities would emerge during one of his favorite pastimes, sharing stories about his life. I eagerly served as a captive audience.

Sil would brag about being a slick Pachuco in his day, carefully stressing that he wasn't always overweight. The added pounds and beer-fed paunch had not taken away his vanity. He would tell me in his perfect East L.A. English, "Hey, carnal (brother), in those days I was a lean, mean, fighting machine and always made sure I looked fine in my drapes (zoot-suit)." He referred to the fashion that included pegged or draped pants, long fingertip jackets, wide-brimmed hats, long gold watch chains, and double-soled shoes. The look was topped off with ducktail hairdos named for the big crease down the backside of a vato's long pomade-slathered hair.

Sil was a boxer in his youth and made it a point to walk around demonstrating he feared no one. To prove his own individual brand of machismo (manliness), he would visit dances or bars in the best pachuco regalia money could buy— sharkskin drapes and Stacy Adams shoes represented a major investment for a vato. After arriving at the dance or bar and ordering his drink, he would move off into a corner and throughout the evening intermittently smell a small rose held in his clinched fist—a wonderfully inventive and subtle way of saying, "Come on, try me if you dare to think that I'm a flower."

I liked to ask Sil about life in East Los Angeles during the war years, especially since I became interested in the infamous Zoot-Suit Riots of 1943. From what Sil related and I had read, people of Mexican decent were considered less than first-class citizens by the general population during those years. Pachucos became the targets of additional contempt for their outlandish zoot suits and cocky, irreverent behavior.

The style, eagerly adopted by many young Chicanos (Mexican Americans), seemed to represent a kind of badge of defiance against the discrimination and racism suffered by Mexicans at the time. It's as if they were retaliating by proclaiming, "Okay, if you don't like me, I'm going to flaunt what I am and how

I dress even more. I'm going to get in your face about it."

Los Angeles became a training and transit center for servicemen from all over the country, many of them coming from the South where segregation ruled the culture. The White servicemen along with many local civilians were tiring of the presence of what they considered a "Mexican criminal element." During the summer of 1943, the pent-up tensions exploded into a riot sparked by several sailors claiming that a group of Pachucos had attacked them. Over two hundred uniformed sailors responded with a vengeance by chartering taxicabs and invading the heart of the Mexican American community of East L.A. For several nights many zoot-suitors were beaten and stripped of their clothes. Some sailors were arrested but none were ever charged with a crime.

On subsequent nights other uniformed servicemen and some civilians joined the sailors as they rampaged through the streets of East L.A., entered bars or theaters, and assaulted people indiscriminately, not only zoot-suiters. Again the police made no arrests and took no significant action.

The June 21, 1943 issue of *Time Magazine* described the role of police by writing, "The police practice was to accompany the caravans of soldiers and sailors in police cars, watch the beatings and jail the victims." The press in general fueled the hatred of Mexicans, and in the end many of L.A.'s finest citizens saw the rioters as heroes. Few if any ever received any punishment for their role in the mayhem. Reading those accounts as an adult helped me to understand the reasons for the rage displayed by some of my Chicano brothers and sisters.

One day I asked where Sil and his carnales (brothers) would encounter the servicemen, wondering why they would be anywhere near the dances attended by the Mexican kids. I naively assumed that Pachucos were interested in only going to hear Latin bands in their own part of town. Sil chuckled and answered, "What are you talking about, ese (man)? We ran into the servicemen at the mainstream ballrooms, like the Hollywood Palladium, where we went to see Jimmy Dorsey, Harry James, Glenn Miller, and the other great swing bands of the time. We were into the big bands just like the White kids, and the White servicemen hated us being there and the way we dressed, danced, and strutted around."

I soaked in all of the information about the era Sil had to offer and at one point asked him how the whole situation finally became resolved. With a knowing and accepting grin, he said, "Man, it's real simple. They just drafted us all."

With countless other Latinos, Sil put away his zoot suit, put on a uniform, and without protesting went off to defend his country. It seems ironic that so many of the young men who were described as Mexican criminals ended up serving with distinction in the battlefields of World War II and beyond.

The Latino Roll Call

Many years after I had immersed in the experience of listening to Sil's stories, I went to work for an advertising agency, GSD&M, in Austin, Texas. I joined the agency in 1983 as part of a team working to serve clients interested in reaching the growing Hispanic market. In preparing to create a Veteran's Day television spot for one of our major accounts, the Coors Brewing Company, my colleagues and I researched the history of Latinos in American warfare and came away surprised and impressed by their many contributions. I knew some of what old soldiers like Sil and my own relatives had told me but had little knowledge of the full extent of military involvement by Latinos. Most Americans including many Hispanics are barely aware of the dramatic contributions and sacrifices Hispanics have made in wars involving the United States.

As far back as the American Revolution, Hispanics were present in the fighting forces of the U.S. both as officers and in the ranks. They were there again in the war of 1812 and as Texas struggled for independence in the 1830's. In the generations that followed participation in the defense of their country increased even more. When the nation was being torn apart during the Civil War, they fought for both the Union and Confederate armies. A woman by the name of Loretta Janet Velásques masqueraded as a male to fight for the Confederacy, an obscure but intriguing fact in the history of Hispanics as American soldiers.

Countless additional personal stories of bravery and dedication by Latinos flow through the chapters of U.S. military history. During the Spanish-American war, Captain Maximiliano Luna and other Latinos were members of Teddy Roosevelt's famous Rough Riders. For his heroics in World War I, Marcelino Serna was awarded the Distinguished Service Cross, the French Croix de Guerre, the Victory Medal, and Purple Heart. A Department of Defense publication reported that up to five hundred thousand Latinos served in the armed forces during World War II, Sil and my cousins among them. In every branch of the service, in every theater of war, Spanish surnames left their mark in that great conflict.

In Korea and Vietnam as well, Hispanics continued to serve voluntarily or when called. They met every demand placed upon them by playing all of the roles assigned to men and women in uniform during wartime: fighter aces, leaders, casualties, prisoners of war, and heroes. Flying Ace Captain Manuel J. Fernández, Jr. shot down fourteen MIGs and flew one hundred twenty-five combat missions in Korea. Lieutenant Commander Everett Alvarez, Jr. was shot down over North Vietnam and spent a terrible eight and one-half years as a prisoner of war, longer than any other American. In another strange twist involving the crisscrossing of paths, Alvarez turned out to be a close, childhood friend of my Rose Bowl teammate Joe Kapp.

In subsequent conflicts since Vietnam, including the Gulf, Iraq, and Afghanistan wars, Latinos have continued to serve in the military with distinction. Their unquestioned loyalty and sacrifices have been proven time and time again.

In recognition of their valor, Latinos have gathered an impressive list of decorations. As we conducted our research to produce the TV spot for Coors honoring Latino veterans, we learned that they had won an impressive total of thirty-nine Congressional Medals of Honor. Today that number has risen to sixty-one.

In light of that record, I found it natural to reflect on the zoot-suit riots and Sil's flamboyant tales. I concluded that the misled and uninformed young Anglo servicemen involved in the riots probably believed they were assaulting gangs of disloyal, unpatriotic thugs rather than a group of potential fellow combatants. I wondered further if the instance ever occurred on the battlefield when a former Pachuco may have saved the life of one of the rioters. These and other questions inspired me to examine and attempt to capture in verse facets of the larger drama.

THESE SONS

Descendants of Cuauhtémoc and Cortez,
Bolívar, Juárez and Martí,
These sons of Spanish and of Indio blood
Would join those fighting to be free.

Though shifting nations traded them like goods,
They pledged allegiance to this land,
A duty set by history and by fate
To boldly face their flag's demand.

These sons whenever called were there to serve
Without complaint or selfish plea.
Proud names like Pérez, Robles and Marín
Would fight for others to be free.

They fought on land, on sea and in the air
While mothers stayed at home to pray.
To France, Korea and to Nam they went
To battle, sadly some to stay.

Heroic words alone describe their deeds,
No braver men we'll ever see.
And endless decorations tell much more
Of those who fought to keep us free.

Despite imperfect worlds they left back home,
They charged ahead into harm's way,
The place where many took their final breath,
A debt we never can repay.

What's left to do is solemnly observe
The measure of their gallantry,
Extol their sacrifices and recall
These sons who valued living free.

~ 1986

Hank with cousins David and Robert

Chapter Four
Starting Out the Grades

Our family moved back to San Jose, and I had to start looking for another kind of happiness again. At least now I felt I could go to school like my big sisters. In Los Angeles I was supposed to start first grade, but my mother had to work and with her hours she couldn't take me. When we returned to San Jose, I enrolled in the first grade at Horace Mann Grammar School. Going to school and meeting new friends told me I was becoming a big kid. My outgrown pants that hovered embarrassingly high above my shoes told me the same.

Horace Mann smelled like years of crayons, chalk, waxed wood floors, and sweaty kids all ground together. I liked the smell, and it made me feel as if I had been there before. Miss Scott, our first grade teacher, wore a long thin face and short gray hair that made her look mean. Although she was kinda a fuddy-duddy and strict, she treated us all like a nice mom or older aunt and sometimes even allowed us have some fun. Every Friday afternoon before we went home for the weekend, she would put on what she called an amateur hour and invited us to read a poem, tell a story, play an instrument, or sing. Many of the students were too shy and didn't want to get up and perform. I was not and grabbed the opportunity to sing some of my favorite songs like *On Top of Old Smokey* and *Found a Peanut*. For the first time in my life, I got to show off for an audience looking right at me. I also hoped the pretty girl with the blond pigtails, Leslee Rosenquist, liked the way I sang.

It's funny but the place where we lived seemed to be all tangled up with the number three. Three old tall houses stood in a row on Third Street. They all looked exactly the same, and each of them had three floors. My parents and sisters called them Victorian houses, but I didn't know what that meant. We had the entire top floor of one of the houses to ourselves. Man! I had never been around so many threes.

The old house had thick, wooden banisters, lots of windows, and built-in seats right next to the windows. Better yet it had plenty of places where I could play and hide. All of the rooms had high ceilings. A long pole came down from the center of the ceiling in most of the rooms and light fixtures were attached at the end of the poles that looked like giant metal flowers. There were so many rooms in the house that we didn't have enough furniture to fill them all up. I had a room all to myself where I slept and another one where my parents let me build forts and keep all my toys. I guess you could call it a playroom.

Wood, wood everywhere. A wide, wooden staircase on the outside of the house led from the street to the second story and two doors. One of the doors opened to just a staircase, not a room. The staircase with walls on each side led all the way up to the third floor and our part of the house. Everywhere you looked you could see wooden curls just like the ones on my sisters' heads after they took off those round tubes they slept in. The large and small curls decorated the windows, banisters, and even the corners of the building. I imagined the man who put them there long ago wanted to be an artist instead of a carpenter. I think he probably would be sad to see the sixth and seventh coats of paint chipping off all those curls. I liked them just the same.

A thing called a pulley hooked on to the back porch and held a long cord that connected to another pulley attached to a tall pole on the far side of the yard. My mother would hang washed, wet clothes on the cord with wooden clothespins, and the clothes would flap and dance in the wind and sun like boneless dolls as they dried high above the ground. My mom would pull on the cord and the pulleys would squeak with each yank of her hand. She would take the dry, fluffy clothes off the cord one piece at a time and pile them high in a big basket. She always scolded me when I would bury my face in the pile of fresh clothes and try to drink in the crisp, pure-air smell of the sheets and shirts recently scrubbed by Mother Nature's crew.

It was great fun living there because I had kids my own age to play with. Waichin, and his brother Waiful, who liked to be called Spike, lived on the third floor in the big house that was identical to ours right next door. Their last name was Jw (pronounced Ju), and we would spend hours playing and building model airplanes together. Their mother came from China, a country that was fighting on our side in the war. Mrs. Jw was almost as short as I was, and she wore long Chinese dresses that buttoned all the way up to her neck and had a slit on the side. She couldn't speak English or Spanish, only Chinese. She didn't have to speak a language I knew to show her friendliness. She would just smile and bow every time she would see me. I didn't know why her husband didn't live with them. Maybe he was still back in China. Wachin and Waiful's big brother George also lived with them and liked to joke a lot with the younger kids. When I would blow bubbles with my bubble gum, he would squish his nose up and tell me that little bugs were going to jump on my bubble. He would then laugh his head off especially when the bubble would pop and stick all over my face.

Another friend also lived next door, on the bottom floor. Her name was Mary Alesandro. I knew she was Filipino, but was never quite sure what that meant. She had become my best pal, and we would walk to school together everyday. I liked to play with her because she always seemed calm and never said or did anything mean. With the boys, we sometimes had to test each other's toughness and end up in fights. Never with Mary. I was always sorry she didn't have as much time to play because her mom always made her and her older brother Johnny practice the piano. I wished I could play the piano but without having to do all that practicing.

I'm glad my parents got along with my friends' parents. Sometimes they would all stand on the sidewalk in front of our houses and talk, nod their heads, and smile. As always Mrs. Jw didn't talk, she just smiled and bowed. It didn't matter. Everybody liked her anyway.

I also had other friends at school: Ronnie, Jack, and Marilyn. Jack was fat, and I called him fatso one day just playing around. When I did, I noticed that he got a sad look in his eyes. Marilyn got real sore at me for saying that. She stood straight in front of me like the general of an army and said, "Henry, that isn't nice. How would you like to be called dirty names?" At first I got mad back at her, and then I felt something inside of me slowly moving around, like a little face with tears, and I decided not to call Jack fatso anymore. I hoped no one would ever call me any dirty names.

I knew how much I liked my friends because I sometimes felt like crying when they didn't want to play with me. Some of them had brothers and sisters to play with, but I had to play by myself because my sisters were so much older than me. Besides they didn't pay very much attention to me anyway because they went to a place called high school and had lots of books to read at night. After supper, my dad would sometimes tell them he would do the dishes for them because they had so much to read. My mom complained, but he would just wave his hand at her and do the dishes anyway. Lucy and Irene (who now wanted to be called Rene) would hug him, and he would get a grin on his face like a happy, fat, old cat.

An Unexpected Blow

One day, Donny, another kid in our class, called me a dirty Mexican during recess. No one had ever called me that before. At first I felt as if someone had just broken my favorite toy with a baseball bat and that I might start crying. Then my head started to get hot, and I wanted to punch him in his belly because I knew he said it to hurt me. Instead of punching him, I pretended I didn't care and started saying something I'd heard somewhere, "Sticks and stones can hurt my bones, but names will never hurt me." I thought it was sort of a lie, but it was sort of true too. The words didn't hurt as much as the look he gave me, like he wanted to throw me away somewhere in a dirty old ditch, like he hated me. Now I thought I knew how Jack felt.

My mom got angry when she heard about what happened, and she went to school to talk to the principal and my teacher. I didn't know what they decided, but he stopped calling me a dirty Mexican. Donny and I still fought a lot. One day we would be friends, the next day we would not, and then we would be friends again. It was hard to keep track of the whole dumb thing. Mary, Jack, Ronnie, Marylyn, and I were always friends and we never fought. Friends that never fought with me and were always happy to see me were like a nice warm blanket I could put around me to make me feel safe. It almost felt as good as being held in my mom's arms.

I still wasn't sure whether being Mexican was good or bad although I was starting to think about it, letting the question bump around in my thoughts. Although I didn't look very different from everyone else, I began wondering if I should worry about it and if beautiful, blond Leslee Rosenquist would continue to like me if she found out. I knew Donny never had to worry about being Mexican. Maybe he just had to worry about being around Mexicans like me.

We joined the First Methodist Church, and I went to Sunday school with the kids and church services with the grownups. My mom made my dad go. I think he liked church because he wore a big smile during the service. Sometimes while Reverend Farr was talking about God and stuff, my dad would close his eyes but keep on smiling until his chin dropped down to his chest. That's when my mom would poke him in his side. After that he would open his eyes and glance around as if nothing had happened—always with a smile.

Most of my sisters' friends also went to our church and they all seemed to have a lot of fun. They would go to dances, campouts, and other places together. I liked my sisters' friends, and I knew they liked me especially when I could dance the Jitterbug with them. They liked to see a little kid that could dance. Wanting to be like a big kid, I always begged my mom with, "Me too, me too" whenever it was time for my sisters to go out somewhere. I knew Rene felt like hitting me when my mom decided to make them take me to the movies. Rene would tighten her lower lip and grumble, "Why does the little pill always have to tag along with us?" That would get her in trouble with my mom, and I was glad especially when it meant I got to go to the movies with them. I was pretty sure that none of my sisters' friends spoke Spanish at home like we did some of the time. I started thinking that maybe I shouldn't speak Spanish so much anymore.

Sam owned the little grocery store around the corner with a wooden floor that was so worn out it had smooth dents in it where the customers walked. The store's ceilings were as high as our apartment and made of tin with fancy designs. The shelves were high also, so high that Sam used a long stick with claw-like clamps on the end of it to reach and snag packages near the top. He would say that because of the war there were many things we couldn't get, and when we did get them something called rationing meant that we could only get one or two. My parents had little books the government gave out with stamps in them. They had to give Sam stamps when they bought some of the things they needed. When they ran out of stamps, they couldn't buy more things they wanted. I missed bubble gum the most.

One day I was playing on the sidewalk with Mary, and from a block away we saw Wachin running towards us waiving his arms frantically and screaming, "Sam's got bubble guuuum. Sam's got bubble guuuum." When he got to us all out of breath, he told us that Sam just received a new supply of bubble gum but that each kid was only allowed to buy one piece. He told us we had better hurry before it was all gone. Mary and I started jumping up and down, anticipating the first bite of the pink gooey lump of goodness. My parents were still at work, and I worried that Sam would run out before they got home. I was lucky that Mary let me borrow a penny for the gum.

I used to think that nothing could be more delicious than having that heaven-sent ball of sweet chewiness rolling around on my tongue and cheeks. I loved it even more than peanut butter and jelly sandwiches on white bread. I didn't care that the sweetness would go away or that my jaws would get tired. I was going to chew that piece for at least two weeks just like I had done with the last one I bought. I would have to hide it somewhere where my mom wouldn't find it, otherwise she would have made me throw it away before the two weeks were up. I would think to myself that if I had all the bubble gum in the world I would chew a new juicy piece every hour. I dreamed that after the war was over I'd be able to do just that.

Although I didn't like it as much as bubble gum, we always had plenty of fruit to eat. The fruit orchards began right outside of the main part of our town, and like thousands of soldiers in neat, straight lines, the trees would march across the valley for miles. For as far as anyone could see, prunes, apricots, cherries, peaches, and pears grew all around us, bringing vibrant colors and succulent sweetness into our lives.

I loved where we lived. I had my friends, a house with big rooms to play in, and a school that smelled good. I hardly ever thought about our old ranchito anymore, the alfalfa field, or the tall corn my dad planted. I had become comfortable with sidewalks, streets, and cars—far away from mean roosters and Indian School Road. When I remembered the smiles of our young Indian neighbors, I would begin to miss them and wonder why I couldn't have the joys of both now and then.

~ *FAST FORWARD* ~

The Valley of Heart's Delight

Before they renamed it the Silicon Valley, the Santa Clara Valley had another moniker, the Valley of Heart's Delight. The countless fruit orchards, ideal weather, and picturesque surroundings surely inspired the origin of the now old-fashioned-sounding name. During those years, people would come from the surrounding areas and other parts of the state to drive in the foothills above the valley and drink in the springtime explosion of color, compliments of the vast variety of blossoming trees. Many others also came to the valley, not for the aesthetic experience but for the backbreaking work of picking fruit or working in the canneries. Many of those less affluent, itinerant visitors were Mexican.

Because my dad could speak Spanish fluently, he earned a living for a short period hiring pickers for an old German farmer who owned acres of prune orchards along Stevens Creek Road, a two-lane country route leading quietly west out of town. As a crowded multi-lane boulevard, today it streaks west past high-traffic businesses, sleek auto dealerships, and high-end malls. The orchards my dad worked in disappeared decades ago, melted into rebar and concrete.

I can't remember exactly why my dad didn't stay with that sort of work for very long. Maybe he gave it up because he felt a kinship and compassion for the migrant workers who suffered under deplorable working conditions and who often struggled with inadequate housing. Many of the migrant families would create makeshift structures out of the long, flat, wooden trays used to dry prunes in the hot sun. Others would set up tents as shelter during the harvest. I later guessed that dad's empathy for them stemmed from his early union-organizing experiences and passions.

During that period I would tag along to do my own little kid's share of prune picking. My mom liked to proudly announce to friends and family that my summer efforts earned me enough to buy my school clothes and supplies for the following year. For me, the luxury of mixing work together with a fair amount of play made the experience more a minor chore than an unbearable job.

For the migrant children, the harsh reality of their family's survival allowed little time for play. I never forgot the look of disdain my dad shot at me after innocently asking if we could camp out under the trees "like those other lucky kids." Chances are good my father added some accompanying words of disapproval with a look that conveyed his impatience with his son's naïve attitude. Reviewing the incident later in life, I felt fortunate that my dad chose not to include a swat along with the look, although my dad was not big on spanking.

Years later I learned more about the difficulties and the level of discrimination endured by those workers. I also fully realized my own good fortune compared to the children of migrants in simply having grown up in a stable, permanent environment. Attending the same school all year long gave me clear advantages. The absence of that privilege robbed countless Mexican children of fair and reasonable chances for achievement.

The experience of the legendary leader of the United Farm Workers union, Cesar Chavez, provides a pointed example of this hardship. Chavez and his brother Richard attended thirty-seven schools while growing up. Forced to drop out after the eighth grade to help support his family, Chavez found himself swept up by the migrant stream with thousands of other farm laborers.

By the late sixties and early seventies, I like many others had begun to pay greater attention to the plight of the farm workers, mainly due to the courageous union organizing efforts of Chavez and his main co-organizer Dolores Huerta. Their dedication, charisma, and leadership caused me to support their boycotts, empathize with their arrests, and identify with Chavez's fasts—all reminders of the glimpses of injustice I witnessed in my youth.

Coincidentally, my old teammate Kapp also supported Chavez and Huerta. During the height of the farm worker's strikes, San Joaquin Valley growers wondered why in the world Joe Kapp was supporting the likes of the union leaders. They had undoubtedly not read a Sports Illustrated cover story that referred to Joe as "The Toughest Chicano." His surname must have occasionally helped to obscure the issues about which he cared deeply.

Beyond battling to improve the miserable wages and dangerous working conditions faced by farm workers, Chavez and Huerta also fought for their dignity and equal rights. In addition they crusaded against the use of pesticides and other terrible hazards the workers faced in the orchards and fields. In 1975, they helped to outlaw el cortito (the little short one), the short-handled hoe that caused the crippling back injuries of countless workers throughout years of exploitation. A decade later I pondered over the possible reasons growers resisted outlawing such a terribly disabling tool.

WAY UP AND DOWN

I like my "Meskin" workers stoopin' good and low.
That's why I always make 'em use that shortened hoe.

It's so that I can watch and keep a real sharp eye
On anything them lazy "Wets" might wanna try.

Like goin' for that water jug just too damned much,
Or other silly-headed "Meskin" moves and such.

What's more, when they bend over clearly as they should,
Our relative positions sure are understood.

With me up here and all of them a way down there,
We do our jobs a whole bunch better, ain't that fair?

You must admit, some folks were just flat born to rule.
While others, well, were born to sorta be a tool.

For those of us a way up here to get things right well done,
And spread our way of life from here to kingdom come.

~ 1986

Chapter Five
From Hate to Admiration

My mom worked sewing garments in the alterations department at Blum's department store. It was not very far away from where we lived, only two blocks. Sometimes I would go over there after school, and the ladies that worked with my mom would get all smiley, chatty, and touchy. I liked to think of them as my grandmas because both of my grandmothers had died many years before. One of the grandmas, Mrs. Regino, used to be a schoolteacher in a country called France, another country that was sorta fighting on our side in the war. With a kind but stern look she always asked me how I was doing in school. She would nod with approval when I would answer, "Good."

Miss Siemen was from Germany, one of the countries fighting against us in the war. She too would smile but looked down a lot because she was so shy. Whenever my dad would say hello to her, her face would get red as a valentine. I heard my mom say that she had to leave Germany because some of the people there didn't like her family because they were something called Jews. I thought that it had to do with another religion, but I wasn't sure. I didn't understand why anyone would get mad at someone just because they had to go to a different building to talk to God. My mom also said that she didn't think Miss Siemen knew what happened to her brothers and sisters she left back in Germany.

Mrs. Drake, another grandma-like lady that worked with my mom, was born here in America. Her round soft body would always jiggle as her high-pitched voice squeaked out the affectionate names she liked to call me. "Sweetheart boy" and "honey boy" seemed to be her favorites. I didn't mind.

One day when I eight years old, I was playing football with Johnny, Wachin, and Waiful in the gravel parking lot next to our houses. Johnny had the ball, and I tried to tackle him but instead I slipped on the gravel and tackled the big iron fender of a car, not with my arms but with my mouth. The instant loud scream I let out preceded the blood flowing from my torn lip and the realization that half of my front tooth was now missing. Through cloudy, tear-filled eyes I started looking for it by desperately groping around in the gravel.

After quickly assuming it was hopelessly lost in the pebbles of the same color, I automatically started a teary trail toward Blum's and my mother's waiting arms. I sure hoped she wouldn't slug me on top of this injury like she did when I banged my head. As I staggered toward Blum's, the half-tooth that remained intact felt like it was hooked to a chunk of ice, causing a sharp blast of cold air to shoot into my brain when I breathed in through my mouth.

As I stumbled up the stairs of the tailor shop to find my mom, Mrs. Drake was coming down the stairs. She instantly saw my sorry condition, grabbed me, and screeched, "What happened, sweetheart boy? What happened?" She then scooted me up to my mom who instantly became hysterical when she saw her injured little football player, behavior that provided me with little comfort. My three grandmas then gathered around me like a bunch of agitated chickens about to be fed. They began making funny ooh, ahh, and eeh noises as they handed my mom wet towels, pieces of gauze, and peroxide for my battered lip. After they finished cleaning me up, everyone calmed down, and they intermittently hugged me, stroked my head, and told me everything was going to be all right. Sucking in a series of jerky gulps of air after sobbing, I started to feel better until my mom told me that I would have to go see the dentist right away. I imagined even more icy air shooting through me and almost began crying again. Somehow I resisted, and thought to myself that maybe I didn't want to be a football player after all.

When Mary and I would come home from school everyday, I would let Mary's mom Irene know that I was home because she was in charge of me after school. I would then go up to our place, change into my play clothes, do some homework, or come back and play with the kids. Irene took good care of me—almost as good as my mom. On some days Mary and I would come home and Irene would feed us lunch. My favorite dish was her yummy white rice but she always made me eat vegetables I didn't especially like. To me, some of them tasted like crunchy green wax. Irene talked funny and said vegetables with a "b" sound, like "begtables." She kind of held onto the first couple of words in a sentence and then say the last one real fast, "Eeeeeeat, yourrrrrr, begtables." Mary's father sounded the same, but

Mary and Johnny didn't. I concluded that just Filipino grownups talked that way.

Come to think of it, my mom talked English funny too, only different than Irene. My sisters would tease my mom because she couldn't say refrigerator. She said "frigerdator" instead. They didn't dare tease her too much. She mispronounced other words too, but I didn't tease her at all. My dad spoke English just as well as my sisters and I did.

I especially loved Christmas in our big old house with all the wooden curls. Every year we would go to Christmas midnight service at our church. The church sparkled with candles, red flowers, and colorful ribbons everywhere. The smiling faces of the choir sang, actually shouted, the Christmas carols I knew all the words to. I loved midnight service because it gave me the excuse to stay up late.

When we would get back home, I'd sit and stare at our Christmas tree. The blue, green, red, and yellow lights shining in our big window looked like glowing pieces of candy I could almost taste. When I was strangely happy like that, I sometimes felt as if I was somewhere far away or as if I was making it all up. Did I really belong there? Was I really me? Maybe I was just feeling afraid it all might disappear.

The third-floor windows between the Jw's family place and ours were so close together that Wachin, Waiful, and I could pass stuff through them, stuff like comics and glue for our model airplanes. Our moms would also use the windows but to trade food. Mrs. Jw would hand my mom steaming Chinese dishes with names we couldn't pronounce, and my mom would give her enchiladas and Mexican rice. Although they couldn't speak to each other, their exchanges would flow with a sweet, silent understanding that must have been magically born in parts of China and Mexico at the same time. Across those old-fashioned windows high above the ground words seemed unnecessary.

On Saturdays, my movie-going day, I once saw a movie called *Guadalcanal*

Diary with an actor by the name of Anthony Quinn. In the movie he had a Spanish-sounding name, and he said some words in Spanish too. I guessed he was Mexican like me. He was portrayed as a hero just like all the other American soldiers, sailors, and marines I saw tortured and killed in the movies by the dirty Japs. I liked seeing a Mexican playing a hero until they shot him too. That made me cry and hate the Japs even more, made me want to kill them like they killed our brave American soldiers. I thought we were winning the war and that soon we would get even.

One day Wachin and Waiful didn't let me go over to their house. They said I couldn't come in because their brother George was planning a big surprise. All of a sudden I heard people start shouting, "The war is over. The war is over. We've won! Hooray! Hooray!" I was glad that we had already beaten the Germans, and now we beat the Japs, too.

George's surprise turned out to be a load of fantastic firecrackers, spewing out bunches of loud, popping fiery sparks that made us squeal, jump, and hop around as George lit one exploding string after another. That was the most fun I had ever had in my whole life. Everyone on the street was yelling, laughing, honking their car horns, and making a lot of noise. In the evening my dad and I went downtown, walked around, and watched everybody having fun. Soldiers and sailors were kissing girls all over the place. I think my sisters stayed home because they were afraid they might get kissed. Everyone was happy and celebrating just like they do on New Year's Eve. I thought to myself now we can get even with those dirty Japs and buy bubble gum whenever we want it.

~ FAST FORWARD ~

Old Illusions, New Awareness

During the remainder of my days at Horace Mann Grammar School, I can't remember seeing a Japanese person. The war ended in 1945, and my first clear awareness of Japanese classmates did not emerge until four years later when I entered Peter Burnett Junior High School in 1949. By then I had lost much of the blind, hysterical hatred against the Japanese I had accumulated as a child throughout the war years—an attitude largely created by wartime propaganda films designed to turn kids and country against the dreaded enemy. Films such as *Guadalcanal Diary* and *Back to Bataan* conveyed such powerful messages that I'm sure some residual ignorance and prejudices lingered in my young and impressionable subconscious mind.

In the seventh grade I could not ignore the likes of Martha Asanuma, Kenji Yamasaki, and Bob Ishikawa, classmates I easily learned to accept and like. They were all accomplished, personable, and friendly students in spite of the reserved and cautious aura surrounding them. They all seemed to walk around delicately as if wanting to remain unnoticed. I never understood why until the day Yuri Saito stood up in our seventh-grade social studies class to make a report. She spoke of concentration camps, two words loaded with years of terrible images of cruelty and suffering imbedded in my mind by movies, news reports, or live accounts from those who had returned from the war. I immediately assumed she would be talking about the concentration camps Americans and other people on the allied side had endured at the hands of the Germans and Japanese. By then I had begun to learn the tragic meaning those words carried for Jewish people including Miss Siemen, one of my surrogate grandmothers who lost relatives in the holocaust.

To my surprise, Yuri talked about another set of concentration camps. She slowly began to describe the herding of her family and friends into concentration camps located in the United States. As she spoke of the disruption, hardship, and injustice Americans of Japanese ancestry suffered, my brain choked on details too alien to fully absorb. I thought to myself that Americans could not have done anything that cruel. In my innocent, sanitized world view, Americans simply were not capable of committing those sorts of acts. The rationalization that flooded my unreceptive mind could not counteract Yuri's unrelenting argument. She spoke on with an unyielding passion and indignation. Her revelations baffled and astounded me almost to the point of making me angry.

When she finished her report, I timidly asked Elizabeth Kimura, someone with whom I shared several classes and considered a friend, "Elizabeth, did that really happen?"

She gave me a sad look, nodded, and answered with a soft and resigned, "Yes." Her simple confirmation irrevocably altered my point of view regarding the issue. A part of me began to review and question the beliefs I had held as sacred, and I felt a wave of apprehension slowly creeping up from the base of my spine and into my shoulders and neck. I now accepted that some Americans would mistreat people because they looked or spoke a certain way, even to the point of imprisoning them. I pondered if I could ever be on the receiving end of such mistreatment.

Years later after fully accepting the potential in all human beings for bigotry and hysteria, I was not surprised to learn that after the bombing of Pearl Harbor the anti-Japanese sentiment in the country reached a state of near hysteria. It resulted in people of Japanese ancestry, including many American citizens, being rounded up and put in concentration camps euphemistically called relocation centers. Official statements claiming that the action would prevent espionage and sabotage rationalized the extreme move. By contrast people of German and Italian background escaped incarceration in the same large numbers although Germany and Italy had also declared war on the United States.

At first detainees found themselves in makeshift assembly areas, often at racetracks and fairgrounds where the living conditions were chaotic and filthy. Shifted later to remote parts the United States, they soon painfully discovered they would be living in permanent camps located in deserts and swamps. The dust, mud, and extreme temperatures due to the location of the camps, added to the misery and degradation of imprisonment for tens of thousands, guilty only of their ancestral background.

Eager to prove their loyalty to their country, many Japanese-Americans volunteered to serve in the armed services. The volunteers were later joined by draftees to form the 442 Regimental Combat Team. In combination with the 100th Infantry Battalion of the Hawaii National Guard, they formed the most highly decorated regiment in American history. Ironically the 522 Battalion of the 442nd was the unit that located and liberated the Dachau concentration camp. When I learned of this fact, my thoughts immediately returned to a picture of Miss Siemen's shy demeanor and sad smile.

While these men fought and died for their country, their families remained trapped in camps such as Manzanar, located in the harsh desert of east-central California. In the 1970s, I visited a photographic exhibition at the L.A. County Museum documenting the Manzanar camp experiences. At one point I found myself standing behind two petite, older Japanese-American women who had been lingering over a particular photo. As they moved on to the next picture, one of the pair with a slightly bent back shook her head slowly, put her handkerchief up to her face, and with soft tears in her eyes whispered, "Those days, oh, those terrible days." I never forgot the private stab of sorrow and anger I felt at that moment, one that immediately propelled me back to a seventh-grade social studies class and the searing, truthful words of Yuri Saito.

Pete Domoto

When considering some of the coincidences we trip over throughout our lives, they sometimes feel like consciousness-raising devices placed in our paths by some divine playwright. Their neat appearances in the play seem to fulfill the purpose of tying up some loose end or confirming some past question. My friendship with Pete Domoto seems to fit that potential design.

One of the stars of the '58 Rose Bowl team and an All-Coast guard, Pete happened to be a third generation Japanese American, "Sansei." Like Kapp and me, he too would have fallen into the category of an anomaly when we played ball together. Asians like Mexicans were indeed a rarity on college football team rosters in the '50s. Pete became a special friend during our playing days and has remained so for many years. We frequently get together with other members of the Rose Bowl team for reunions and special occasions such as Joe Kapp's induction ceremony into the Bay Area Sports Hall of Fame.

Pete qualified as a star not only on the gridiron but also in the classroom. After Cal he went on to attend the University of California's School of Dentistry where he was voted Student Body President his senior year. I have enjoyed bragging about my friend's accomplishments, such as serving with distinction as the chairman of the Pediatric Dentistry Department at the University of Washington's School of Dentistry for many years. A recipient of several professional awards, he championed the importance of community-based clinical teaching for decades and emphasized cultural competence in the various programs and projects in his department. Given some of the trials Pete faced in his own life, it did not surprise me to discover his natural inclination to serve the entire community, especially those with special needs such as Mexican migrant workers.

One of those trials involved Pete's family who also suffered relocation during the war, not to a camp but far from home nevertheless. Those families with access to residences in the interior of the country could choose to live under special arrangements and conditions. Unfortunately, the vast majority of people did not have that choice especially since they had only a short ninety days to relocate. Because Pete's grandfather managed a highly successful import business and maintained offices all over the U.S., his family located a residence in Dallas approved by the government. Pete, his mom and dad, along with uncles, aunts, and cousins, spent the duration of the war far away from their Berkeley, California home but in relative comfort. Still the family lost a thriving business. Moreover, the men of the family endured severe scrutiny and frequent interrogations especially in the beginning stages of the war.

The subject never entered into our conversations when we were in college. Years later we eagerly exchanged thoughts about our ethnicity and the significance of our personal childhood experiences. During one of our conversations, Pete revealed that although his family avoided the camps, their enforced stint in Texas amounted to being held hostage in plain sight. On one occasion, Pete reflected, "Who can judge whether it's worse to be imprisoned or to be held hostage?"

While Pete and I were still in college, I remember naively suggesting to a couple of the senior members of my fraternity the possibility of pledging Pete. In other words, invite him to join the house. I asked the question before knowing whether or not Pete would even be remotely interested in joining. The instant responses from my fraternity brothers solved the problem. Comments such as, "Are you kidding?" "A Nip?" "Forget it," quickly made me realize that the prejudices of the previous decade had not disappeared, that acceptance and tolerance of all Americans had not yet become a part of the mindset of all my fellow students.

Pete's greatest gift to me came in the form of an accidental litmus test. The attitudes of my fraternity brothers burrowed deep into my psyche, forcing me to consider the potential level of residual poison that might still have been lurking in my system from years of war movies, headlines, and newsreels. My unequivocal disdain for the insensitive comments proved to me that the antidotes of passing time and positive relationships had healed the cancer within me.

Mifune Meets Mexico

For a major part of my life, I have seen myself as an incurable film addict, not only of American movies but of foreign films as well. As a little boy, my parents would take me to see John Wayne and June Allyson one day and then on another day to see Jorge Negrete and María Elena Márquez. The latter were stars of the booming Mexican cinema that attracted and entertained me in the early days of my youth. I'm certain those experiences set the stage for my later interest in foreign cinema and its performers.

In college, I began diving into the works of Bergman and Fellini among others. Then my attention turned to the Japanese directors Kurosawa and Inagaki. *Rashomon, Yojimbo, Chushingura, Duel at Ichijoji Temple, Sanjuro* represent a small sample of the films that began to mesmerize me. The first of many of Akira Kurosawa's films that I discovered, *The Seven Samurai*, instantly left me awestruck and eager to take in more of those cinematic gems.

The mix of chivalry, majesty, honor, villains, and saints woven into these films, suffused with a fresh kind of mysterious beauty, opened the door to a new region of my imagination. This newly discovered Japanese aesthetic took an almost mystical hold of me that has lasted to this day. Part of the aesthetic that has resonated most deeply with me is the concept of Ma, a notion akin to simplicity, emptiness, or space—a minimalism and beauty that has touched me in inexplicable ways.

Other aspects of the aesthetic find expression in a scene that can cut abruptly from fiercely dueling samurai to an isolated, serene pond. While the camera lingers on the peaceful picture, battle cries continue to echo in the distance to punctuate the contrast. I have also experienced a special fascination for the use of sparse but elegant sounds in those films—in the song of a lone bird or the ring of a Buddhist bell laced over a snowy village or pastoral scene. This artistic perspective, with its dramatic contrasts, has stirred my deepest thoughts and emotions, at times leaving me breathless and on other occasions somewhat puzzled.

The question that continues to intrigue me is why as a young man I felt such an instant and profound affinity for the Japanese cinema. I remember often taking friends to see these films, expecting they would love them as much as I only to be disappointed with their impatient or bored reaction to every frame. The Japanese approach to tempo and pacing left some of my American friends feeling trapped on an interminable treadmill while I relished in the meditative aspect of the art form. While watching scenes from some of these films, I sometimes felt overwhelmed by a feeling I could only describe as nostalgia, a longing to return. Occasionally, I have jokingly suggested to friends and family that I must have lived in Japan in a former life.

Of the many marvelous actors and actresses whose performances I have enjoyed and admired in American and foreign films, I would find it difficult to pick one favorite above the others. Like selecting between rubies and diamonds, the task of choosing Olivier over Brando or Hepburn over Streep would present a major predicament. However, if absolutely forced to choose my favorite actor, it would have to be the great star of Japanese films Toshiro Mifune. Starting with Mifune's sympathetic, lovable performance in *The Seven Samurai*, no performer has captivated me more than this giant of the screen.

Perhaps Mifune gains an unfair advantage in my selection process by appearing prominently in some of Kurosawa's best, including perhaps my all-time favorite Kurosawa film, *Red Beard*. Mifune's cinematic stage allowed him to play a variety of memorable characters. His many roles often displaying superb swordsmanship are masterpieces of choreography. Even without understanding the language, I have hung on his every word and gesture for many pleasurable years.

One of Mifune's obscure and forgotten films especially plays into my musings concerning mystical connections. In 1961, Mifune made a film in Mexico called *Animas Trujano*, released in the U.S. with the English title of *The Important Man*. After seeing the film for the first time, my friend Hector Lopez and I left the theater in a joyful daze, stunned by the unlikely combination of artistic elements we had just viewed. Mifune had succeeded in learning the Spanish lines phonetically, but a Spanish demanding an indigenous accent and lilt. Perhaps more astounding, his characterization hit several cultural marks that must have required extensive study and sensitivity. For me this remarkable performance led me into obscure corners of my own reflection. The unusual vision of a Japanese actor playing a Mexican mestizo (half-breed) perhaps brought the cultural dichotomy of my upbringing full-circle. Naturally, the memories of fear and hatred I felt toward the Japanese in my childhood and my subsequent turn of mind and heart must have also played a part in a paradox still difficult to explain. Many years later it prompted me to explore the elements I found so intoxicating in Mifune's art.

BEHIND THE MASK

Mifune moves like silk
Through Kurosawa's
Swirling winds and mists and Ma
Portraying all the shifting shades
Of his unrivaled samurai.

The full proportions of his actor's palette
Paint the screen
With swaggering strides or comic looks
Designed to color epic scenes
Or moments subtle as a sip of tea.

While rising to the peaks of chivalry,
He charges armies, heals the poor,
Defends his honor's code,
All offered with veracity and force,
Propelling conflict to a contradictory height.

But best, he dances
In a duel of lightening swords
Where flashing steel can come to life
And carve a piece of space or flesh
With flawless, whistling grace.

Behind the fury lives the mask of fate,
Appearing as a wooden drum or crickets chirp
Ballets of blood
Against the stillness of a peaceful pond,
To serve the paradox of nature's twists
And elegantly craft
The fleeting stage on which to watch
Mifune move like silk.

~ 1990

Chapter Six
A Mystic Land

Yea! Summer had finally arrived after finishing the third grade. It was time to say good-bye to mean old Miss McDermott, my grumpy third-grade teacher, and to break all of my pencils if I felt like it. I remember ending up with a pretty good report card, but my mom said I had to try harder. She always said that. Again, Mary got the best grades in our class. She was so smart; getting through her lessons was like yawning for her. I thought I was kinda smart, but I hated arithmetic so I ended up in a wrestling match with it all the time.

Lucy and Rene just graduated from high school, class of 1946. They were both in the same grade because my older sister Lucy got seriously sick one year and had to stay back a grade. They too were happy the summer had arrived, mainly because their graduation present was a trip to Mexico to visit some of my mom's relatives. Everyone was happy about the two-month trip, but I wasn't so sure it was going to be that much fun. I didn't know anyone there or who I might be able to play with. I figured I'd also have to speak a lot of Spanish, and I wasn't so sure I'd like that so much. I could feel my family's excitement on top of my apprehension about the trip. My dad had to stay home and work, and I wondered if he would miss us or enjoy the break. As usual he didn't say a word one way or another.

My mom, Lucy, Rene, and I boarded a train in San Jose, and after a couple of days the long chain of cars took us to a place called Nogales, actually two places called Nogales. The towns on both sides of the Arizona border had the same name. There we got off the train and stayed overnight in the American Nogales. The next morning we got on a different train in the Mexican Nogales, and I wondered how two countries existing right next to each other could be so different and so far apart.

I had books, puzzles, and games to keep me entertained, but the trip started out to be pretty boring until this friendly guy they called a porter by the name of Luis started talking to me and becoming my friend. He asked me to help him do things like bring drinks to people and make their beds at night—all kinds of stuff like that. His easy smile filled his smooth dark face, and his deep black eyes beamed out an acceptance of his little helper that made me feel like working for him the rest of my life. Because there were so many Americans on board the train, Luis especially liked that I could speak perfect English to help him find out exactly what they wanted. I think the passengers got a kick out of seeing a little kid helping the porter because they always smiled and said nice things to me when I came around. They also wanted to know my name and where I came from. While I would scoot up and down the aisles of the train for Luis, my sisters and mom would stay in this nice, private compartment they had all to themselves. I liked seeing my mom doing nothing and enjoying herself. She always worked too hard back home.

The train chugged over tall cliffs and mountains through tunnel after tunnel, and occasionally it would stop at little villages along the tracks. It was so far away from my school and friends that I tried to imagine what little kids my age did there everyday. I doubted that they played hopscotch because I didn't see any sidewalks. I imagined that they might have more fun than we did.

The hundreds of trees everywhere made the countryside look like a jungle right out of a Tarzan movie. When we stopped, people came up to the train selling piles of pretty-colored stuff made of straw, wood, and clay. They also sold food. I liked the way some of the vendors would sing out, Hay naranjaaas (we have orangeees). Many of the people we saw looked as if they were real poor, and they all wore huaraches (sandals) made of leather straps with old pieces of tires for soles. Somehow they didn't look as sad as poor people back in San Jose. I asked myself if my mom's family would all be wearing huaraches too.

It took a long time to reach Mexico City, our final destination. I thought getting to places always took longer when you were a kid. As we arrived, we said good-bye to some of the people that had become our friends on the train trip. I had to say good-bye to my best friend Luis back at a town called Guadalajara even before we got to our destination. He had to go work on another train. I didn't know why, but it made me sad when he put his hand on my head, smiled and said, "Adios, mi amiguito. Pórtate bién, ¿Eh?" (Good-bye, my little friend. Behave yourself, okay?) Maybe I knew I would never see Luis again. His natural affection showed me that some people could be as nice or even nicer than your own family. That caused me to miss him even more and to trust the closeness of special strangers.

In Mexico City, we stayed with my mom's cousin María and her husband Alejandro. Their son, a couple of years younger than me, was named Manolo. I thought he was a spoiled brat, but his mom and dad were nice. They had a beautiful big house with lots of colorful tiles on the walls and gardens all over the place that made me think that they were rich. To my surprise no one in my mother's family wore huaraches. They dressed just like we did in America, and they even had nice new American cars.

I guess because they were older, I had to call all my mom's cousins tíos (uncles) and tías (aunts). I didn't mind, but it got a little confusing. My Tía María's mother's sister was a real aunt, my Tía Luisa. She was my grandmother's sister also. I found her to be a jolly lady who liked to hug me, laugh all the time, and move her arms and hands all over the place when she talked. I noticed that she had a lot of freckles on her face and arms, green eyes, and red graying hair. My mom said that she fought in the Mexican revolution, a big war they had down there, right alongside the men. They called those women soldaderas (female soldiers). She sure didn't look that tough or even mean. I couldn't imagine her lugging around a rifle, hiding behind a rock, or shooting at a gang of charging soldiers. She was too nice. I tried to understand how in the world she could switch from that role to a loving, good-humored tía.

I couldn't believe the size of Mexico City; it was much bigger than I expected. Rows of tall buildings poked up at the sky similar to San Francisco or Los Angeles, and cars and people crawling all over the place made it noisy and smoky just like back home. One day we went to a place called a tennis club that my Tía María and Alejandro belonged to. We went swimming in a huge, fancy swimming pool—bigger than any I had ever seen in the U.S. Mexico seemed to be full of surprises.

Swimming pools weren't the only things that were big down there. We went to a house that was even bigger and fancier than my Tía María's. It belonged to her father my Tío Felix and my Tía Pepa who was married to him and was my grandmother's other sister. Oh man, I got a headache from keeping track of all those tíos and tías. My Tía Pepa was very serious and not as much fun as my Tía Luisa. When we walked into a big room to meet my Tío Felix, I saw that he was very old and sitting in a wheel chair. My mom told me that I must treat him with great respect because he was an important general in the revolutionary war and the governor of a whole state. I determined that meant I couldn't jump, run, and laugh around him very much. He didn't seem very lively. I guessed he was too old and sick to tell jokes or anything like that. I was sure he must be the richest person I'd ever met judging from his great elegant mansion.

After we left, I remember my mom telling my sisters that my Tía Pepa was mad at her for leaving the Catholic Church and becoming a Methodist. She loved my tía, but I don't think my mom cared that she was mad.

One of my Tío Felix's sons was named Gilberto. I had to call him tío also, but I didn't mind because I really liked him. He was really neat, and his wife Marta was especially nice and beautiful, with skin the color of coffee and cream and smooth as peaches. I liked hanging around her because she always smelled like fresh flowers. She acted kind of naughty for a grownup because she liked to whisper English cuss words in my ear, ask me what they meant, and then laugh and laugh like a little schoolgirl. Watching all this, my mom would let a little smile sneak on to her face. I was surprised she didn't mind, and I was glad because it was always fun to be around Marta.

Our days were filled with new activities and places I had never dreamed I would see. I loved going to a place they called the floating gardens on a lake filled with hundreds of boats, flowers, and musicians. We also visited an old castle with so many rooms I couldn't even try to count them. My favorites were the dungeons where they once imprisoned and tortured people with all kinds of iron instruments, some with pointed, rusty spikes. We also saw a big carriage covered with dozens of decorative lumps of gold that I'm sure would sink in the ocean as soon as it hit the water. The carriage belonged to a woman named Carlotta who they didn't like in Mexico. They didn't like her because she was the wife of a guy who tried to become like a king, an emperor of Mexico. His name was Maximilian. I learned that they caused another big war down there a long time ago. The castle was their house, but after they lost the war they kicked her out and then executed him. It's funny how sometimes even kings and rich people can end up in dungeons. I don't know why I found those stories interesting, but they sure were different from all the stuff I saw about Mexico in American movies.

One of the most fun things I got to do in Mexico was visit some movie studios with one of my Tío Gilberto's friends, a photographer. Lucy and I got to meet some famous movie stars and take pictures with them. I had seen some of them in Mexican movies back home, and I was excited that I got to meet them in real life. My American friends sure wouldn't be impressed since they didn't know those movie stars even existed.

On another day we went to a bullfight. I guessed that was a pretty big deal with my family down there. My mom went with my Tío Gilberto and Marta, and I went with my Tío Felix's chauffeur, Santiago. He was a guy that drove my Tío Felix around in his big, black car. Before we left everybody chuckled because Santiago and I were going to go sit in a section called sol (sun), and everyone else got to sit in the section called sombra (shade). After a while I realized why they were chuckling. Santiago and I would have to roast in the sun with the poorer fans. My mom, tío, and Marta would get to sit in the shade with the richer people. I really didn't mind because sitting with Santiago made me feel older and more grown up. Besides, I decided the sunny part was more fun than the shady section.

The people in sol ate, drank, laughed, talked to each other, and yelled bad words at the bullfighters, and the whole section moved like one giant pulsing body. The raucous fiesta (party) had a rhythm and joy all its own, one that Santiago and I easily joined. The high-pitched trumpets that played at the corrida (bullfight) added to the excitement of the festivities, and the music awakened my imagination by somehow telling me that a part of me belonged there. With each passing day, I began feeling more comfortable in the land where my mother was born. As the afternoon grew to a close, I sensed that my celebrating neighbors needed to cram in as much fun as possible before the sun set on the corrida. Their overpowering energy caused me to almost forget to watch the graceful, daring moves of the bullfighters, the reason we went to the corrida in the first place. The toreros (bullfighters) displayed their bravery with every dangerous pass of the massive bulls. I even started thinking that maybe I would like to be a bullfighter when I grew up. On second thought I remembered that some people thought bullfights were cruel, so I decided I better be a football player instead.

My Mother's Birthplace

My mom, my Tío Gilberto, Marta and their maid, María (I started to think every woman in Mexico was named María, including my mom) and I went to visit still another uncle, my Tío Rodri, on his big rancho (ranch) located in a place called Zacatecas, the state where my mom was born. My sisters didn't want to go with us because they wanted to stay in the big city and go to nightclubs, dance, and act all grown up. We drove a long way in my Tío Gilberto's shiny new Buick. To pass the time on the trip, Marta in her usual playful way asked me to teach her English songs. I taught her how to sing *Found A Peanut* and other songs, but she had a lot of trouble learning them and couldn't pronounce all the words right. It didn't matter to her. She just wanted to play, giggle, and have fun. I couldn't decide if I liked her more because she was so pretty or so funny. I also decided I didn't just like her. I had fallen in love with her and wished she could come live near us in California.

We stayed at the rancho a long time, for about a month, and it turned out to be the best part of our whole trip—the part that would light my memories forever. Right after we arrived, my Tío Rodri put one of the men that worked for him in charge of me. His name was Antonio, and they called him el caporal (the foreman) because he was the boss of the other vaqueros (cowboys). I soon realized that he was a very important man, and I immediately liked him. His green eyes smiled down at me through a brown, sunbaked face that told me he didn't mind his extra job. For the many days that followed, I spent almost every day with Antonio, and he watched over me just like a father. He showed me how to saddle and ride a horse, something else I had never done before. He also used his machete (large, heavy knife) to cut the tops and sides of the tunas (prickly pears), the fruit of the cactus. He then showed me how to delicately reach in and pluck out the juicy, seedy delicious treat with my forefinger and thumb, leaving them stained purple at the end of the day. Antonio and I became good pals.

During my time with Antonio on horseback, I saw many unusual sights

I never could have experienced back in San Jose. One day a great big coyote appeared out of nowhere, stopped and stared at us, unafraid, for a few minutes, and then casually trotted off. Soon after we saw an eagle flying so close overhead that I could almost feel the wind from its wings. The eagle looked almost as big as the coyote and, it carried a long wriggling snake in its beak. I thought my jaw was going to fall off my face from astonishment.

A large pack of dogs that acted like a gang of wild rats on a ship lived on the ranch. One afternoon as Antonio and I were out riding and checking the cattle, the dogs started chasing a calf. Antonio tried to stop them, even beating them with his whip, but for some reason he couldn't control their frenzy. They kept chasing and biting the calf until they finally killed it. I sat on my horse watching the attack without taking a single breath. Another incredible sight.

When we got back to the big house, I immediately ran up to my Tío Rodri and blurted out the day's murdered calf drama. When he heard the story, it made him angry, and he sternly turned to Antonio and demanded to know what had happened. Antonio stammered around about the attack, but ended up telling him that the calf belonged to a neighboring ranch. That seemed to calm down my tío a little. After the incident, Antonio didn't say anything to me or scold me, but by the way he looked at me I realized that I probably should have kept my thoughts to myself. I was glad he didn't stop being my friend.

María, my Tío Gilberto's and Marta's maid, treated me with a special tenderness, as if she had known me all my life. Although I had never met a maid before, that I know of, she didn't act like how I thought maids should act. She was more like a member of the family, more like another tía—as if I needed another one. She would constantly ask me how I felt or what I wanted to eat. I figured that was probably part of her job as a maid.

Watching her prepare tacos from chicken blood almost made me sick to see her stirring the dark red fluid in a big pan. As she cooked it, she endured my squeals of distaste, yet her confident smile told me she knew something I didn't know. I wasn't too crazy about eating meat anyway so the thought of eating blood made my stomach want to jump out through my mouth. When she finished, the blood now looked like crumbled up hamburger, so I dared to take a tiny taste after Maria's encouragement. Wow! It was so delicious I couldn't even believe it. Who would have ever thought that blood could taste so good? I guess only Dracula.

She also made nopalitos (little cactus pieces) with all kinds of other delicious ingredients mixed in with them. They also tasted great rolled up in a hot corn tortilla that María had made. She liked to say to me, "The next time you come back to see us, Enriquito (little Henry), you are going to be very tall and handsome and I'm going to be very proud of you." Before she even finished telling me that, I began to miss her and hoped I could come back and see her someday—standing there at the stove with her bighearted smile and preparing a special treat just for me.

All of the time I spent on my tío's rancho, I mostly spoke Spanish without even thinking about it. It had become as easy and natural as breathing, and I felt sorry I couldn't do that back home. If I did, nobody would understand me. Worse than that, I knew nobody would like me. At that point, I didn't miss San Jose or any of my friends because all of the people around me in Mexico had wrapped me up in their lives, in their caring, had made me feel as one of their own. I knew I was going to miss that place, and if I ever saw it again I was afraid it wouldn't be the same. Somehow I already realized that nothing could stay the same.

One of my tío's workers, Sebastian, invited my mom, my Tío Rodri's wife, and me to take a ride out to the little house where his parents lived. It was located about an hour's horseback ride from the main house. I think it was on my tío's rancho but I wasn't sure. Like Sebastian, I believed his parents had worked for my tío in the past. He said that he had to take food and supplies out to them because they were getting old and couldn't do it for themselves. We all decided to go.

The next morning we saddled our horses and took off early to avoid the heat. When we got to Sebastian's parents' house, I saw that they only had two little rooms made of adobe (mud) bricks. What I noticed right away was that the dirt floor of their house was so hard and smooth it seemed to shine. My mom told me later that they made the dirt brick-like by wetting and sweeping it over and over for many years. In one corner of their modest rooms, they had an elaborate altar, with saints, colorful candles, and a rough wooden cross. For some reason, I found myself staring at the altar, mystified by a strange tug that drew my attention to it. Mesmerized by the dance of its flickering candles, I found the little shrine more strangely beautiful and soothing than that of any grand church. The two old people seemed to appreciate my curiosity, and with their smiles granted me permission to inspect it more closely—something I could slide into a drawer where special memories are stored.

I knew these people were as poor as anyone I'd ever met, but they didn't act like other poor people I had known. Maybe they just didn't understand how little they possessed. They invited us to sit down and eat, with a courtesy and grace you would expect in a lavish house. All they had to offer us was tortillas and beans from a burned and blackened old clay pot, and when I sat down on a wobbly wooden bench to eat, they made me feel as if they had prepared a royal banquet exclusively for me. Best of all, those were the most savory tortillas and beans I had ever tasted and will ever taste again. I thought maybe they had added a magic potion to them.

Sitting there I tried to understand this new set of feelings seeping in and out of my chest. Why did I feel so sheltered and warm in this tiny, run-down shack of a house? This was as far away from home as I had ever been, and yet I felt as if a part of me had always lived there. Sebastian's parents looked as dark and worn-out as their old clay pot. Their bent backs and gnarled hands revealed the pounding of years filled with endless physical toil, still this man and woman appeared soft and cheerful and talked about everything in their lives with gratitude—their children, the land, their home. To me they seemed like flowers made of weathered, leathery skin, and the light that radiated from their eyes bathed my soul.

I thought how could this be? I had never met them before. I was only ten years old and didn't have all the words to describe the puzzling feelings these strangers aroused in me. Maybe those two old ones were angels in disguise or messengers from another world. Maybe they were sent here to help me see that people and places that previously did not exist always existed somewhere in me.

Before we said our good-byes, they gave us their bendición (benediction): Qué díos los cuide (May God protect you). We rode away and as I turned back for one last look and wave, I hoped that day would stay with me forever, would show up again when I needed to slip into a pool of sustenance and renewal.

In accelerated, blurring beats, we left the little house, my tío's rancho, and Mexico. Before I knew it we returned home to California. The trip of a lifetime had ended abruptly and all too soon.

Back home at the beginning of the fourth grade, I was having lunch with some of my friends, eating a bologna sandwich on white bread with mayonnaise. Two timid, brown-faced boys, new to the school, sat alone at a lunch table. They cautiously pulled out their bean-filled flour tortillas from a wrinkled paper sack. Sitting nearby, my friends snickered under their breath and made fun of them with judgmental glances. I forced a smile as if to go along, and immediately after felt the hidden stab of shame we had just thrust into the hearts our new classmates.

A hidden part of me longed to escape back to my tío's rancho, riding my horse at the end of the day with Antonio and wondering what scrumptious dish María would be cooking for supper.

~ FAST FORWARD ~

To Shame and Back

Balancing the positive experiences of my trip to Mexico with the prejudices of classmates established a recurring pattern I would have to face for many years. Accommodating to the dominant group's negative racial attitudes while attempting to maintain a sense of self—including all I knew to be valuable about my ethnic background and family—became a necessary, frequent occurrence. Coping with a real or imagined danger of rejection began to follow me around, an extra burden to think about and add to the survival kit for growing up. I can recall days from my youth when it was not necessary to attach "dirty" or "lazy" to the word Mexican. The word effectively stood alone as a slur, especially when delivered with the proper contempt and snarl.

I can't remember exactly when I started slowly retreating into a racial closet. I'm sure it began by degrees in elementary school. My white skin and looks, along with the anglicized pronunciation of my name, ALL-gwin (rather than the Spanish pronunciation—Ohl-GEEN), began making it easier to avoid the automatic label of Mexican others endured based merely on their skin color, looks, and surname. The dilemma of how to perform in the face of the prejudices and discrimination against Mexicans I might encounter soon created a built-in warning system for detecting an ever-present sheet of thin ice. Deciding what to say or do when hearing a demeaning remark, whether directly aimed at me or not, presented a tough assignment for a ten-year-old. Who in their right mind would intentionally look for situations that could cause feelings of shame or rejection? For me the problem worsened before it improved, and I felt forced to slug through many unresolved years before finding the peace I yearned for and discarding my bearable but nagging cross.

Ted Williams and Me

Ted Williams is the last major league baseball player to hit over .400, and has been called the greatest hitter of all time. According to a PBS documentary on his life, the Boston Red Sox slugger lived with a shameful secret—having a Mexican mother. Apparently, he not only feared not being good enough, he feared that the prejudice against Mexicans would hurt his baseball career, so he kept his heritage under wraps until close to his death. One writer stated it simply, "He was ashamed."

Ironically, he was a supporter of the early Black players that started joining the major leagues early on. In his Hall of Fame induction speech, he called for the inclusion of African American players that had played in the Negro Leagues before being integrated in the majors.

After his record-breaking rookie year, Williams went back to San Diego as a hero. When he arrived at the train station, a large group of proud Mexican relatives were waiting to greet and applaud him. When he saw them, he made a quick get-away to not be seen with them.

I wonder how many Teds and Hanks, in our long history, have behaved similarly.

Over the years when I had occasion to express or discuss my concerns about ethnicity, people at times suggested that I must be suffering from a terrible identity crises. I don't recall exactly when, but somewhere along the way, I decided and declared that the crises had nothing to do with identity (I knew who I was), that it could best be described as a behavior crises. How should I act in light of the prevalent prejudiced and racist attitudes people held in our society about Mexicans?

Through my young adult years, I slowly discovered that knowledge and understanding could serve as ramrods for breaking open the doors hiding one's complete self-declaration.

Unfortunately, those coping mechanisms were not always readily available to others and me as youngsters. Dr. Beverly Daniel Tatum in her excellent book *Why Are All the Black Kids Sitting Together in the Cafeteria* talks about the embarrassment many young African American students feel when the discussion on the topic of slavery comes up in class. She explains, "They squirm uncomfortably as they feel the eyes of White children looking to see their reaction to this subject."

Many Mexican American kids and members of other groups go through the same ordeal when dealing with other historical occurrences. I can't remember exactly what grade I had reached when I first heard in the schoolroom about the famous battle of the Texas Alamo. Whenever it happened, I'm sure I slid a little lower into my chair as the teacher began speaking about the hordes of Mexicans assaulting the White, brave, and liberty loving likes of Davy Crockett and Jim Bowie. Several of my Mexican American friends have confessed to me that they too felt like becoming invisible when the history lessons came around to that chapter, especially if they had grown up in Texas and could be clearly recognized as Mexican. Who can deny that the battle cry, "Remember the Alamo," meant anything other than let us settle the score by defeating and killing the hated Mexicans.

Accounts and depictions such as movies of the battle and other related historical incidents are often guilty of critical omissions. Prominent roles played in the Texas Revolution by Latino leaders such as José Antonio Navarro, a signer of the Texas declaration of independence, are often forgotten footnotes in the history. As Texas struggled for its independence at the battles of San Antonio (the Alamo) in 1835 and San Jacinto in 1836, men such as Lieutenant Juan Seguín led a force of Tejanos (Hispanic Texans) who fought on the Texas side against Santa Ana, Mexico's dictator. A man by the name of Toribio Losoya was one of several Tejanos who gave his life fighting alongside Crockett and Bowie. He represented one of the few combatants who could actually claim the Alamo compound as his birthplace. Unlike some of the recent arrivals trapped at the Alamo, Losoya was fighting to defend his home.

Today a bronze statue of Losoya stands near the Alamo in honor of his sacrifice. I gained a special satisfaction as part of the GSD&M advertising agency team that facilitated the commissioning and donation of the statue to the city of San Antonio by the Coors Brewing Company. Incidentally, Henry Cisneros, then the mayor of San Antonio (later the Secretary of Housing and Urban Development under President Bill Clinton), provided a brilliant history lesson on Latino contributions at the unveiling of the statue.

The celebration of Losoya's role as an unsung Hispanic hero of the Alamo helped spread a healing balm on wounds of shame some may have felt from historical accounts depicting Mexicans solely as the bad guys. The obscure but important story puts a small but positive spin in the pile of years full of negative perceptions.

Searching for Community

Through the '60s and '70s, calculated career moves on the part of many Latinos played a part in discovering or reinforcing their feelings of self-worth. I too made choices tied to my search for a balance between a financially profitable career and the need to deal with questions of ethnicity. In 1968, I went to work as a talent agent for Pacific Artists, a Hollywood agency representing actors primarily seeking work in advertising commercials. I was hired to establish the agency's voice-over department and within a year produced a house reel that was enthusiastically received in the industry. After a short tenure with the agency, I moved on to produce an award-winning educational project for a leading Hollywood production studio, The Chris Petersen Company. Those successes could have easily pointed me in a career as a voice talent, producer, or some related profession. Instead I chose to focus my energies elsewhere.

While fulfilling my duties in those endeavors, I remained involved in projects or jobs related to the Latino community as a freelance writer. That part-time involvement gave me the opportunity to give back to the community. In 1972, I went to work full-time for a federal program funded by the Department of Labor, SER—Jobs for Progress. It served the special employment and training needs of Hispanics through dozens of projects across the country. Many young, well-educated Latinos, drawn like an army of pilgrims, came to work for the program in the hope of giving back something of their talent and expertise to the community. Along with others, I joined the ranks of the national headquarters in Los Angeles where I worked for eight years, ending my tenure as Communications Director for the program.

I jumped at the opportunity to exercise a voice in the growing importance of Hispanic affairs. Writing and producing everything from press releases and speeches to brochures and television public service announcements gave me that voice. Planning and executing public affairs strategies and essentially operating as the program's in-house advertising and public relations agency also gave me and my colleagues a forum for investigating and debating in detail some of the issues that had begun to engage our attention. Assigned the task of addressing government officials, employers, politicians, community leaders, and program participants, I made it a priority to depict Latinos as proud, capable, and intelligent in all the materials I produced. By counteracting some of the more prevalent stereotypes I had grown to resent, I quietly battled against discrimination in my little corner of the world.

Michael Rey

As my circle of friends grew during those years, it included more and more Latinos. I began feeling as if they were part of a pre-ordained plan, sent to me perhaps as cosmic envoys to fill in some of the empty spaces of my search for meaning and balance regarding my ethnic experience. They provided me with insight and perspective, as well as camaraderie, laughter and a growing supply of affection. My friends became like quarries, allowing me to mine the gems of their experiences that shed light into the dark crevices and hidden tunnels of my own past.

As my involvement in the Latino community grew, I met many outstanding young Hispanics who like me were searching for armaments in what we now considered a fight for justice. My Hispanic friends also would become the living evidence that countless Latinos qualified as gifted, exceptional, and mainstream. Michael Rey stands out in a group of many and remains a friend to this day. Living with low budget constraints for printed materials, such as brochures, presented an ongoing challenge at SER. I certainly could not afford to hire a professional graphic designer. Instead I decided to search for an advanced graphic design Latino student. Luckily, I discovered a promising and willing one at Art Center College of Design in L.A.

I offered Michael expenses, a small stipend, and the opportunity to build his portfolio in exchange for his design work on an important brochure. It soon became clear that I would come out ahead on the trade. As a student, Michael had already begun to display the special intelligence and creativity that would eventually make him an award-winning art director and graphic designer. When I first met him I could not help but doubt that the soft-spoken Mexican kid from the west side barrio (neighborhood) of San Antonio could possibly handle the assignment. I assumed that even graphic design required a measure of assertiveness. I soon discovered that the cover of this particular book not only deceived, it concealed an exceptional talent. Almost immediately I began learning about Michael's penetrating conceptual approach to visual images. The finished brochure reflected Michael's simple but elegant thinking and far exceeded my expectations.

Since that day, Michael has gone on to achieve success in his chosen field. As a young graduate, he moved to New York. He quickly began to make his mark by co-publishing and art directing the trendsetting The Picture Newspaper. The avant-garde publication emerged in the days when the works of Andy Warhol were exerting their influence, and earned a presence in the collection of the Museum of Modern Art. That recognition illustrated the importance of Michael's creations from that era. Later Michael returned to Art Center, earned a Master of Fine Arts degree, and taught at the college. Afterwards, he owned and operated his own design studio, working for clients as prestigious as the J. Paul Getty Museum and the Los Angeles Philharmonic Orchestra. Today he has put his commercial art directing projects aside, and now dedicates his time to his life-long passion for creating fine art.

Aside from a lasting professional affiliation, Michael has remained a trusted friend and respected sounding board on ethnic and spiritual issues.

For more than 30 years, he has participated in Native American sweat-lodge ceremonies he finds so energizing and spiritually uplifting. Along with his beautiful wife and two daughters, Michael has found a quiet, abundant, and grounded rhythm to his life that always soothes or uplifts me whenever we get together.

Leticia Ponce

Leticia bounded into the SER offices displaying a mercurial energy and presence that immediately registered positively on my people meter. To my delight, I soon discovered our complimentary rhythms and set of sensibilities. Assigned to act as a liaison with SER's corporate advisory board, "Amigos de SER," Let used her superb PR and human relations skills to gain the corporate community's support for a variety of projects. Her temperament naturally lead her to turn the assignment into a crusade, a habit of commitment she would find hard to break throughout her professional career. A beautiful, fashionable, and well-educated woman, she received her degree and teaching credential in English, Speech and Drama. Before arriving at SER, she experimented with seemingly unrelated occupations but driven by a compelling common denominator, the love of performing. A couple of examples include trying her hand as a backup singer with a group that regularly opened for the Righteous Brothers and hosting a weekly TV talk show in Denver.

I have always considered Let's healing sense of humor as one of her special gifts. Her comedic talent has kept me laughing through some of our mutual ups and downs. She has even dared to put it on display occasionally at places like L.A.'s Comedy Store during open mike sessions. As a great example of her need for a good laugh, she tells a story about her first teaching job that always leaves me in stiches. As she walked into the teacher's break room for the first time, grabbed a cup of coffee, and sat down, a friendly colleague joined her and politely asked about her new assignment. With a completely serious look on her face, she responded in a feigned Mexican accent by saying, "I'm the new speesh teesher." She quickly erased the stunned look on her fellow teacher's face when she said in perfectly crisp English, "Just kidding, I'm actually going to be teaching English." Two hearty laughs followed, one expressing great relief.

Her ability to creatively mix her funny bone tendencies with a deep curiosity regarding serious spiritual matters has impressed me for years. Being raised Catholic never stopped her from probing the mysteries of alternative paths to spiritual fulfillment. Striving to understand consciousness more fully, she studied and followed the teachings of Indian Swami Baba Muktananda for an intense period. I felt privileged that she introduced me to Swami Muktananda during a gathering and lecture in Santa Monica, California. Our discussions about these matters, intermixed with talk of theater, films, and our mutual ethnicity, have sustained our cherished relationship for many years.

After Let's time at SER, she went on to work as the host for a television magazine show, as a news anchor at NBC, and as a public relations professional for a major aerospace corporation. While at NBC, she won a well-deserved Emmy for a brave investigative piece on the political situation in Nicaragua. On another occasion, I enjoyed watching this bright, attractive Latina feminist in an exclusive television interview playfully and skillfully challenge the Oscar-winning Anthony Quinn on his views about women. All of that behind her, she moved back to her home state of Texas, raised her adopted son, Miguel, and today, semi-retired, still strives to make the world a better place as a spiritual healing consultant.

Many of my colleagues, like Michael and Leticia and I, were caught up by the events leading up to and during the period we worked for SER. Feeling the time had arrived to assert our ethnicity, a new excitement about the possibility of major social changes seemed to be spreading. The Mexican American Civil Rights Movement, including what we referred to then as the Chicano Movement, started in the 1960s and began focusing attention on issues that had been long ignored by the society at large.

The Vietnam War with its disproportionate number of Latino casualties, farmworkers' rights, the land grant movement, and education and voting rights were all topics beginning to gain attention. Support for some of these issues from prominent national figures such as Robert Kennedy had created renewed hope for lasting change. Although a wide spectrum of thought existed among Latinos regarding the era's activism, the debate provided a booster shot of renewed expectations toward controlling and guiding our own destinies.

From East L.A. to Sesame Street

My involvement in the activism of the times had begun earlier, in the late 1960s, due in part to my friendship with Emilio Delgado. Emilio would later become one of the stars of Sesame Street, playing the role of Luis on the show for decades. When he and I first met, I had recently started my job as the voice-over director for Pacific Artists. Represented by the agency, Emilio marched into the office one day to have a serious discussion with the head of the television department, Joan Jones. He essentially told her that she should no longer send him out for any more bandit or gang member roles. After Emilio left, a visibly shaken Joan came into my office, told me what had happened, and asked me to please explain to her what I thought could be troubling Emilio and making him so angry. I answered with a simple, "I guess he's just had it with lousy stereotypic roles."

Emilio's stand impressed me. I sought Emilio out and through our friendship we commiserated on the dearth of positive roles for Mexicans in Hollywood, a situation that unfortunately has not improved significantly to this day. I remember Emilio telling me about visiting a casting director who said to him, "Gosh Emilio, we just don't get many calls for Mexicans." After shuffling some papers around, he added, "For example, I have a call here for an American father but that's about it for now."

Emilio smiled politely and offered, "I guess being American and a father doesn't qualify me for that one."

Emilio and I joined Nosotros, an organization established by actor Ricardo Montalban to improve the image of Latinos in the entertainment industry. I also helped Emilio form the Barrio Theater Ensemble, an informal group of aspiring, young Latino actors from the high schools in East L.A. Emilio conducted acting workshops with these kids and staged a couple of productions. One of them involved a dramatization of the epic poem *I Am Joaquin* written by Rodolfo "Corky" Gonzales, a Denver, Colorado activist prominent in the Chicano Movement. In the poem, Gonzales chronicles the history and struggles of Mexican people in a way that profoundly touched many during that era.

Ironically, the group performed the dramatized poem the day of the infamous "Chicano Moratorium," a major protest march that took place in East L.A. on August 29, 1970. The march staged to protest the Vietnam War and discrimination against Chicanos started out peacefully but turned violent when the police overreacted and began beating, tear-gassing, and arresting people. In the end, three people died that day, including the outspoken *Los Angeles Times* journalist Ruben Salazar who was killed by a policeman's tear gas canister fired into the bar where Salazar had stopped for a beer.

Emilio recalls that as they were performing the poem in the gymnasium of an East L.A. school, they could hear the outside sirens and shouts of the people emanating from the march and the chaotic dispersal by the police. Before they could finish the performance, Los Angeles County sheriffs pounded on the doors of the gymnasium, moved in, and ordered everyone out of the building. Designated as a holding center, the gym served to confine those arrested that day. According to Emilio, the very acts of oppression that the crowds had gathered to protest were clearly demonstrated in the abuse by police that took place that day.

In 1971, Emilio left Los Angeles for New York to begin his successful career as *Sesame Street's* Luis. I went to work for SER with a resolve shared by many young people at the time to change the world. Emilio and I have remained dear friends until this day, and whenever we get together we enjoy reminiscing about some of the individual protests we pulled off during those early days.

I recall one humorous example. Whenever we would walk into a supermarket or convenience store to buy beer or other essentials and the mood came upon us, we would automatically begin speaking loudly in Spanish, often to the chagrin of the people around us— Hispanic or otherwise on either side of the counter. Before leaving the store, we might quickly switch back to an easy flow of colloquial English, a contrast difficult to take for some. In the early seventies, Latinos boldly speaking Spanish in public places outside of their own communities usually turned disapproving heads.

Gestures such as those, however frivolous, allowed my friends and I to make a statement regarding old injustices never redressed. As they were growing up, Emilio and others often suffered ridicule and punishment stemming from long-standing rules against speaking Spanish in school. All too often the same rigid prohibition carried over into the workplace. The practice has always seemed ludicrous to me given the obvious number of states, cities, streets, and natural settings with Spanish names particularly in the Western U.S. Everyone needs to speak Spanish just to get directions to the nearest restaurant.

Over the years Emilio, Leticia, Michael, I, and other friends have periodically gathered to talk about the days, activities, and pranks of our youth and the role they played in the development of our current attitudes and perceptions. More than once, we have also asked ourselves if it was all worth it. Usually coming down on the affirmative side of the question, another one often emerges on its heels, "Are we better off?" A unified chorus usually responds with a loud, "Not yet, not yet."

As a child I luckily escaped the humiliation of punishment for speaking Spanish in school or the indignity of someone assigning a new English name to me. Nevertheless, I learned about the hurt and embarrassment of those ordeals from my friends and many other Latinos and Latinas. I examined the subject in verse around the same time I was hired to write a couple of songs for Sesame Street.

THE CHANGELING

When Juanito started school,
Went off to learn his ABC's,
His mother said, "pórtate bien"
Be good and pay attention please.

The admonition he obeyed,
And did the very best he could
Without the use of English words,
Confined in worlds misunderstood.

The first assault struck like a shot
As he was told he now must change
His name to Johnny
On the spot.

Juanito's lost. How very strange.

~1980

Chapter Seven
The Highwayman Came Riding

We moved to the outskirts of town and away from our beautiful old Victorian house on Third Street because my parents found a house they could rent until they could afford to buy it. Fortunately, I kept going to Horace Mann Grammar School. For just a short while, we lived next door to a place called the Winchester Mystery House. It should be called a mansion rather than a house. Like the castle we visited in Mexico it also contained hundreds of rooms, only this place had ghosts running around in it. It belonged to the wife of the man who invented the Winchester rifle. They say the ghosts belonged to people who got shot and killed by his invention. I guess they hung around the house because they were mad that they died. People would come from all over to visit the house. I liked riding my bike on the grounds with my neighbor Ernie. When I would ride around, I'd look up into the windows and imagine something floating around up there. Sometimes I imagined that I saw a man standing in a window with a bloody hole in his forehead. I never really saw it; I just imagined it. But just in case I wasn't making it up, I would never ride over there after dark.

A man who worked there told me he was Mexican, but that he liked to tell visitors that he was a full-blooded Indian so they'd believe his spooky stories better. Like a kid who gets away with stealing a cookie, he would laugh it up after telling me they believed him. I thought he got away with his white lie because some Mexicans look like some Indians, except that he didn't wear feathers or anything like I saw in the movies.

While we were still living next to the spooky palace, my parents bought an empty lot in yet another part of town, and my dad started building our new house. It looked like our adobe house in New Mexico with big poles sticking out through the front wall. Mainly what I liked about it was the great big back yard loaded with all kinds of fruit trees I could raid whenever I got hungry.

The family that lived across our backyard fence had kids and a girl about my age. I knew her name was Daphne because I heard her parents, sisters, and brother call her that. She used to have friends over to splash around in this little wood and tin pool they had in their backyard. My cousin Pete and I would throw loquats at them from a tree dividing our yards and then duck behind the fence to hide. We would giggle and put our hands over our mouths when we would hear Daphne shout, "Stupid boys!" That made us giggle even more.

I finally started learning to play the piano, taking lessons from my nice teacher, Mrs. Comp. It was easy and fun, but I was not crazy about having to practice so much.

We finally moved to our new house, and I met some of the kids in the neighborhood like Bernie Montoya and Tony Realmonte. Bernie was Mexican like me and like me spoke perfect English. So did his parents. Tony was Italian, and his mom didn't speak much English at all. His dad spoke better English. When I heard them speaking Italian, I could almost understand what they were saying because some of the words sounded the same as Spanish. Tony told me never to call him Tony in front of his dad, that only his dad could be called Tony in their house. Whenever I talked to his parents, I would have to remember to call him Anthony, and I worried about slipping up.

We moved into our new house before it was completely finished. My mom was angry about it, and I didn't like it either. I was pretty sure my dad just ran out of money to buy all the stuff you need to finish a house. I felt embarrassed when Bernie and Tony would come over because not all of the walls between the rooms were done. It wasn't cold or anything like that, we had heat and water, but you could stick your head from one room to the next in a couple of places. Sometimes just for fun and to save a few steps, I'd scoot through an opening to get to the next room. I never understood why my mom yelled at me for doing it. It didn't hurt anything. My dad kept working like mad on the house so my mom wouldn't stay mad at him.

After we moved into our new house, I still kept going to Horace Mann. Bernie, Tony and the girl who lived across our backyard fence went to a different grammar school that was close to our house. I was glad they let me keep going to Horace Mann so I wouldn't lose my friends.

One day Bernie and I were horsing around on his front lawn. His skinny, little, five-year-old brother Patrick was playing with us, and we thought it was fun to swing him around by his arms, round and round in a circle. Bernie then got an idea of how we could make Patrick fly through the air. We would lie on our backs, bend our legs up to our chest, and then have Patrick put his butt on the bottoms of our feet. As we shoved our legs forward and upward, Patrick's thin little body would fly through the air waving and flapping his scrawny arms like a baby bird until he hit the ground five or six feet out. Bernie and I took turns catapulting Patrick through the air, trying our best to extend the distance as we all roared with laughter.

When Patrick landed, after one of his farthest flights, we heard him make a little moan. As he got up and extended his arm toward Bernie, his hand suddenly dropped unnaturally and a bulge appeared at his wrist. We stared wide-eyed at the strange change in Patrick's twig-like limb as his moan started to turn into a squeal. With that Bernie grabbed Patrick's wrist and somehow put it back in place while saying, "It's okay, Patrick. See? It's okay." This momentarily calmed Patrick down and stopped his potential moans from turning into howls. After two more unsuccessful attempts at Bernie's fix, the realization and perhaps the pain made Patrick screech wildly as he ran into the house. Bernie followed reluctantly, and I ran home praying that it had all been a terrible mistake.

Unfortunately, our worst nightmare came true. Patrick's legendary flights resulted in a broken wrist, and Bernie and I caught more hell than I can remember. Of course my parents were horrified that I had participated in this child abuse and doled out the appropriate punishment. For years to come, Bernie's parents did not exactly greet me warmly when they saw me.

I still tried to get good grades in school, but I was becoming more interested in singing in the glee club and playing the piano at assemblies than in history or arithmetic. I also enjoyed acting in little plays and skits throughout the year. I knew I should read more books to get smart and everything, but my pals and I preferred to read comic books. I owned dozens of them, but occasionally my mom would come along and clean them out no matter how much I cried or complained. I did have some hiding places where I could keep my favorites like *Batman*, *Captain Marvel*, and *Plastic Man*.

Miss Baker

As my friends and I were finishing up the fourth grade, we began dreading the possibility of getting Miss Baker as our fifth grade teacher. As we got closer to that day, we got more and more worried. It was bad enough that in the fifth grade you had to study more, but to get old Miss Baker as a teacher would be like getting a tooth pulled and a vaccination all at the same time.

We knew how mean and evil she was from watching her conducting assemblies, taking charge of recess, or drilling the traffic patrol like a general in the army. Just her looks alone told us she wouldn't hesitate strangling us if they let her. Her tall, skinny body, draped in long flowered dresses made her ugly, old-maid shoes stand out even more. Her gray hair wound up in a bun emphasized her angular, wrinkled face. She looked like she was always angry, frowning through the wire-rimmed glasses she constantly pushed back up to a crease at the top of her long nose. Worse than that, she had a hunchback, a lump on her back that told us she might even have a troll for a father.

After summer vacation we returned to school for the first day of fifth grade. A chill ran down my back as I saw my name on Miss Baker's list of students. The instructions read, "Report to Room 16." As I followed the instructions, I felt like I was marching off to one of those torture chambers I saw down in Mexico.

There she was, waiting with her arms crossed and a stern scowl. As we filed into her room, the commands began and in short order we were down to business. Our routine was firmly set, and we realized we were in for a no-nonsense, long tedious year of serious learning.

Yet before we knew it something unexpected happened. Just when we thought the coming nine months would amount to nothing but slavery, Miss Baker took out a book of poetry at the end of the first Friday of the school year, and a surprising smile suddenly crossed her face as she began to read. She read a poem to us called *The Highwayman*. As she read, her eyes sparkled and her hands danced. The stiff old maid became supple and lively. The sounds flowing from her mouth made the words on the page come to life and change into vivid pictures in my imagination. I was in a trance. The old notions about Miss Baker slowly began to disappear. Maybe she wasn't a monster after all. She acted more like a magnifying glass into another world.

At that point a tentative idea began to creep into my mind. I started to think that old Miss Baker and the fifth grade might open doors to strange and mysterious places, much like the adobe house with the flickering altar hidden far away in a corner of Mexico. I wondered if maybe I could be a writer of books or poems when I grew up.

~ *FAST FORWARD* ~

Words for Life

I could not have known the total effect of Miss Baker's startling performances throughout my fifth year of school. Without realizing its lasting influence, I could only feel the thrill of the new music now coming from words. When Miss Baker read Edgar Allan Poe's poem *The Bells*, I knew nothing of alliteration, of sounds that mirror each other to propel sentences and cause the pictures in my mind to crystallize even more. She showed me how words can live, breathe, and be transformed into vivid, indelible images.

Miss Baker's performances stayed with me for many years, periodically appearing to ask if creating my own word combinations could gratify as much as enjoying those of others. Throughout my school days, I only toyed with the idea of becoming a writer without ever fully committing to the possibility, in spite of successfully completing assignments to write scripts for radio shows, skits for school fund-raising drives, or occasional student government campaign speeches. Completing the usual coursework of compositions and reports with some success did not prompt me to seriously consider writing of any sort as a career.

Not until long after I had journeyed through the necessary rigors of writing college essays, papers, and exams did the opportunity to write professionally appear. Acting and the theater, not writing, remained my passion as a young adult. When that option disappeared, I began to dabble with the play of words I dared not call poetry. Nevertheless, the need for some form of artistic expression motivated me to venture into the playground revealed to me by Miss Baker.

Long before I dared show anyone a poem or song, opportunities arose to write practical pieces such as brochures, annual reports, or sales pitches. Reluctant to take on the challenge at first I slowly slipped into this new arena, a move that eventually led to a successful career as a copywriter and creative director in the advertising industry. From somewhere Miss Baker must have smiled to herself watching my gradual evolution. I feel sure she certainly would have smiled to read my tribute to her.

A BARONESS OF BOOKS

We thought of her as curved and cruel.
Her stark, commanding visage
Scaring ten, eleven year-old bodies
Into straight yet squirmy lines,
Distracted rows of playground giggles, grins and groans.

Still ranks of fifth grade urchins
Took in and learned her lessons well.
Hard grammar's rules, arithmetic,
A page from history and much more
Were drilled into reluctant but obedient minds.

She stood in front of us like steel,
A harsh, imposing, icy pole
And stranger to a smile,
Intent on keeping us on edge
For nine, dark, grinding, terrifying months.

And then one day she chirped, "Let's read,"
Caressed the cover of her book,
And gently opened it to start,
While I in awe-struck wonder watched
The magic metamorphosis begin.

The pulled-back hair seemed to shake loose
As phrases redesigned her face
Into a lively picture show
I had not dreamed could breathe or laugh,
A stage where "Bess" and her brave "Highwayman" could meet.

Her crooked hands and frame transformed
With every utterance and move,
Alive with "ghostly galleons," "cloudy seas,"
And all the other countless forms
She could miraculously draw from written words.

She could become a Secret Garden,
Tom and Huck, or parrots, pirates gold,
A Treasure Island full of rhymes,
From trees to bells, from ships to shells.
And I was there to watch the spectacle take place.

That cherished year enlightened me
To see her in another realm,
Accept her as a stately baroness of books
In her imaginary royal court,
And kneel in honor of her noble voice.

~ 1989

Chapter Eight
The Days of Stinking Badges

I started to enjoy playing sports more, football and baseball mainly. I was not the best player but definitely the fastest kid in the school. I won all the races. Benny Gonzales, a classmate at Horace Mann, played every sport real well and won everything. He even won a city marbles tournament and got a beautiful Schwinn bicycle as the prize. I felt jealous and sometimes wished I could play sports better. Robbie Walker, my best friend in sixth grade, was a real good baseball player. Everybody liked guys who could hit, catch, and throw a ball.

Rene didn't live with us anymore. She worked at a place called the Stanford Convalescent Hospital where she also lived most of the time. She wanted to be a nurse. She had always wanted to be a nurse starting when we lived back on our ranchito. She once saved some newborn baby doves that had fallen out of their nest and looked like they were made of wet rubber. She had nursed them back to health. Lucy was now working as a bookkeeper at a flower shop. It seemed as if she always had some boyfriend around. They were all pretty nice so I didn't mind. During those days, I didn't pay too much attention to my sisters. For many years they kinda bossed me around, so I was happier that they weren't around much.

Our next-door neighbors were Al and Jo Huntington. They never had any kids and were almost like another mom and dad to me. Al would take me fishing with him all the time to different lakes, rivers, and even the ocean. I spent a lot of time at their house and even got to go on vacations with them. When Al and I would go deep-sea fishing, we would have to get up early to get our boat at the Santa Cruz pier. At first I hated it because I felt so sleepy in the cold and dark mornings. I was always glad to see the morning sun slowly turn the deep gray sky and ocean into a shiny blue. When I'd hook a flat-eyed halibut and Al would cheer, I promised myself I would never gripe about having to get up before the crack of dawn. I wished my dad would do some of the things Al liked to do. Dad just didn't care about that kind of stuff, and sometimes I thought he didn't care much about me.

I also liked the activities they organized for kids at our church. Mostly I liked singing in the boy's choir. In the fourth grade I joined the Cub Scout troop that met at our church, but I got kicked out for something bad that I did. The bathroom at our church had real high ceilings, so my best church friend Lannie Heffner and I liked to wad up toilet paper, get it sopping wet, and throw it high up on the wall where the wads stuck and were hard to reach. We got a special devilish pleasure out of coming back later and seeing that most of the wads were still securely stuck up near the ceiling. It might have been fun, but too bad for us 'cause we got caught for doing it. Not only did I get thrown out of the Cub Scouts, but my mom gave me a spanking I would probably remember into old age. Moreover, she didn't let me play or go to the movies for a long time, and I missed a great Johnny Mack Brown movie I wanted to see. I decided throwing the wet paper wads wasn't worth it.

In the sixth grade I got a paper route delivering the San Jose Mercury News. It was hard work, especially on Sunday mornings when I had to get up so early to deliver that my eyelids felt like they had boulders tied to them. I made good money, but collecting the money from subscribers was the least fun of all. People didn't always want to pay on time. One time when I went to collect, this guy told me he just didn't have the money right then. When I complained that it was the third time I had come to collect, he said, "Boy, I don't have it. What do you want me to do shit nickels?" I walked away cussing under my breath because I didn't get my money. But the more I thought about what he said the funnier it got, and soon I was laughing out-loud to myself.

Music, Puppy Love, and Movies

As I got older I started to think more about what I'd be when I grew up. I loved movies more than anything, so I thought maybe I'd be a movie star. I sure didn't want to be a fireman, policeman, or even a carpenter like my dad. I hated the thought of doing what my dad did for a living. I loved music too, so I thought about becoming a pianist. To do that though, I'd have to practice much more than I did. Too bad practicing felt like having to climb the same set of stairs twenty times a day.

My piano teacher Mrs. Comp liked unusual piano recitals, so she presented one where all of her students played the music of a composer named Johann Sebastian Bach. We all dressed up in old-fashioned costumes, and my mom made a wig for me like the kind they used to wear in the old days, only mine was made out of cotton. When we finished, all the parents and grownups stood up and gave us a long and loud round of applause. It almost made us feel like we were famous. That's when I thought I'd like to be a pianist, but I still wasn't sure.

This girl in my sixth grade class, Francis Makris, did funny things to my heart. She was pretty and sang great. She even won a talent contest at one of the theaters downtown. I thought for sure that she could be a movie star when she grew up. Fran liked me because I could play the piano and sing popular songs. I'm sure that's why she became my girlfriend.

One day I got mad at Fran for something and called her a dirty Greek. She then turned around and called me a dirty Mexican, and I came close to crying. Later we said we were sorry to each other and made up. When things like that happened, I felt like running, hiding, and even becoming someone else.

At Fran's birthday party we kissed while playing spin the bottle. It was the first time either of us had kissed anyone other than our parents or other family members. After kissing her my heart not only did a flip it almost bounced out of my chest. I tried hard to understand how just touching lips together could cause such an eruption.

I also started playing the cello that year, and I loved the deep mellow sounds that came from the throat of the wood. A student teacher put me in a string quartet with three girls, and we played at school and for a group of her classmates at her college. The college students liked it so much they asked us to come back. I thought it was funny that children playing music always got people all friendly and excited.

As I was riding home on my bike taking my cello home from school one Friday, some kid made fun of me. He yelled out, "Hey, only sissies play big, fat stupid violins." I got off my bike and threatened to beat him up. I didn't let anyone talk about my cello that way.

I not only liked playing music, I sure liked to listen to it on the radio or on my sister's records. Those big swing bands were my favorites. I even liked to listen to my mom's Spanish records. I especially liked Jorge Negrete and Pedro Infante when they sang rancheras (ranch songs), but I sure didn't want any of my friends to know I listened to that kind of music. I knew they wouldn't understand and might even make fun of me.

My mom had a beautiful voice, sang Spanish songs at home and English hymns at church, but my dad could only sing one note. When he was working on the house sawing or sanding wood, he would sing one single note that didn't go anywhere. It sounded just like "Mmmmmm, mmmmmm, mmmmmm," over and over. Man oh man! How boring can you get? Even though my dad could only sing one note, for some reason he would take me to see great pianists like Oscar Levant and Arthur Rubenstein at the San Jose Civic Auditorium. I liked Levant a little more because I'd seen him in movies. He played beautifully, but he was kinda rude. I hoped my dad enjoyed the concert. It was hard to tell with that guy.

My mom changed piano teachers, but I'm not sure why. My new teacher's name was Miss Spitzer. She was nice but a fuddy-duddy. She didn't consider George Gershwin's *Rhapsody in Blue* as classical music. Neither did she want me to play popular songs. I didn't care what she said; I played whatever I liked.

I used to ride my bike across town to Miss Spitzer's house for my piano lesson. The best part of the round trip took place on my way home. I'd stop at a barbershop on Santa Clara Street. It was after dark so the shop was already closed, but they had a television set in the window with a speaker on the outside so that people could hear what was playing. I'd stop there and watch Sid Caesar, my all-time favorite comedian. He was much funnier than Abbott and Costello, Jack Benny, or Bob Hope. Other people from the neighborhood stood in front of the big windows and watched too. We all laughed together when Caesar would make gobbledygook words sound like real languages. Sometimes I'd laugh so hard people would look at me funny.

Movies, movies, movies. I couldn't wait to go to the movies every week. By now I was seeing more American than Mexican movies. I was in love with Esther Williams and June Allison, and I thought Gary Cooper and Jimmy Stewart were great western heroes. Two of my favorite movies having to do with music were *Rhapsody in Blue* about George Gershwin and *A Song to Remember* about another composer named Frederic Chopin. Some of my friends thought those movies were corny and made for old people. I didn't care. I found them interesting, probably because I continued to love classical music along with the more modern stuff. Those movies always made me think I wanted to be a pianist again.

I went to see a movie called *The Treasure of Sierra Madre*, one that I both enjoyed and didn't enjoy. I liked the story, Humphrey Bogart, and some of the other actors, but I didn't like the Mexican bandit in it. He was ugly, mean, and dirty and talked with a stupid accent that everyone laughed at. Everyone liked to imitate him, especially the way he said "...badges? We don't have no stinking badges..." to be exact. I didn't like that a lot of people thought that all Mexicans acted and talked like that. I sure didn't meet anyone like that on my trip to Mexico. I didn't like what some people thought of Mexicans, and I didn't like that some people knew I was Mexican.

~ *FAST FORWARD* ~

The Power of the Silver Screen

Negative stereotypes of Mexicans and other Latinos obviously worried me as a child. At an early age, I understood that it didn't take a genius to realize that movies often showed Mexicans in a less than a positive light. For decades, motion pictures had played a major role in forming the perceptions of ethnic groups in the minds of the public, an enormous influence and power that exists to this day. Countless portrayals of Mexicans as drooling bandits, subservient maids, sleeping peons, loose women, and ridiculous Latin lovers—often in dirty, sleepy village settings—were absorbed by me and my friends as we were growing up. Those and other demeaning images that pounded our psyches for many years remained difficult to erase or counteract. As an adult, I once talked to a Mexican American actor who told me that when he worked in Hollywood the directors particularly liked him because he would chew peanuts before his scenes and then grin to show how filthy and corroded a Mexican bandit could be.

With those one-dimensional perceptions surely transferring into the minds of most Americans, it made sense that I and other Latinos wanted to run away from images associated with the label of Mexican in our youth. In spite of having a broader perspective, a result of positive conditioning from my parents and an enlightening trip to Mexico, I found the preponderance of negative images difficult to withstand. I remember reading about a study that found a substantial number of Native American kids rooting for the cowboys instead of their own while watching Westerns. It would not be terribly surprising to me if Mexican American kids fell into that same trap of shame.

Pictures are powerful—often more so than words. Who can deny that we think in pictures at least part of the time? If we hear the words "sports car," our mind's eye does not see the words spelled out; it sees a picture of a red Corvette, Black Porsche, or some other hot vehicle. I have often wondered what most people picture when they hear the word Mexican. Could it be someone in a doctor's smock, a businessman or woman in a tailored suit, a police officer, or a firefighter in uniform? Even today I doubt those pictures commonly materialize in most individual's minds.

Many of the images of Latinos I took in as a kid have received an overhauled or updated treatment over the years, especially with the advent of television. Today we may not see as many bandits or Mexicans sleeping against cactus plants except in the TV reruns of old western movies. We now more often see pictures of drug lords, dealers, helpless immigrants, and gangbangers. Sadly the images of loose women and maids have persisted. It all adds up to what I refer to as "zoo appeal."

The stereotyping of Latinos in general and Mexicans in particular has remained one of Hollywood's favorite and consistent practices. Countless examples exist to prove the point. Here are a couple of the most striking from my list.

The American remake of one of my favorite films, Akira Kurosawa's classic *The Seven Samurai*, was retitled *The Magnificent Seven* and featured seven gunmen who rescue a village of farmers from a band of bandits. The difference between the two films is significant. In the Japanese version, swords rather than guns are the weapons of choice. More importantly, everyone in the film is Japanese, the good guys and the bad guys. In the American version, both the helpless, inept farmers and the evil, marauding bandits appear as Mexicans. Only the heroes are White (although it's never quite clear whether Charles Bronson portrays a Mexican or not). In subduing the bandits and saving the village against great odds, the seven White liberators display their superior intelligence, courage, and compassion over Mexican bandits and farmers. The racial messages and implications of that scenario are lost only to the most naive.

The portrayal and ludicrous accent of the bandit leader played by a fine actor I generally admired, Eli Wallach, is particularly distasteful. Several years later, Wallach once again played an outlandish Mexican bandit, Tuco in Sergio Leone's *The Good, The Bad and The Ugly*. The accent he applies in both portrayals sounds more like something out of the Bronx than Tijuana. After the release of the DVD version of the film, a review appeared in the Datebook section of the *San Francisco Chronicle*. Reviewer Walter Addiego, wrote, "The film is really Wallach's; his Tuco is supremely nasty, but he's such an absurd little rooster—it's a totally unrestrained performance—that you can't help liking him."

Mr. Addiego couldn't help but like Tuco because he was supremely unaware of the disastrous damage those kinds of portrayals have inflicted on the image of Mexican people. His approval of Wallach's performance perhaps stems from not having carefully reviewed the abundance of similar stereotypic rubbish.

Another film, *The Appaloosa* with Marlon Brando, also reinforced the worst of the bandido stereotypes. In this 1966 Western, John Saxon who also plays a bandit-like character, appears to have taken dialect lessons from Mr. Wallach. His version of the Mexican accent rises to ridiculous heights as well. In the 1964 film *Rio Conchos*, Anthony Franciosa's Mexican character neatly fits into the same general mold. I have often encouraged friends to develop their own list of films and check for the recurring pattern, especially when I've been accused of being hypersensitive.

My mixed reaction as a kid to films such as *The Treasure of Sierra Madre* carried over to others I saw as an adult. Such is the case with a film I consider a brilliant classic on one level and a disaster on another—*Apocalypse Now.* Latinos suffer by omission in this one. Those watching the film today and in the future, long after the nightmare of Vietnam, will undoubtedly walk away believing that the only Americans who fought for the U.S. were either Black or White—a logical conclusion due to the glaring absence of Latinos in the film. In reality, a significant number of combatants and casualties in that war carried Spanish surnames. Martin Sheen, the actor who plays the leading role in the film, openly asserts his Hispanic heritage, an amusing irony related to the film.

Unfortunately, many of the Vietnam era movies failed to depict Hispanics fighting for their country. *Full Metal Jacket* provides one notable exception. It featured Sal Lopez, a fine actor I enjoyed the privilege of working with on several commercials during my advertising days. I have always wished the list included more portrayals that similarly reinforced the truth surrounding that tragic conflict.

A Persistent Pattern

In the '70s and '80s, several Hispanic leaders charged the mass media with either stereotyping or ignoring Latinos. The '90s rolled around, and some felt forced to continue making the same charge. Raul Yzaguirre, President of the National Council of La Raza (since renamed), a Hispanic community-based organization, wrote an editorial for *USA Today* entitled, "Hispanics: Invisible Minority." He started by describing a night of television viewing that led him to conduct, as he said, his own totally unscientific but telling survey. He continued by stating:

As I watched, the question grew in my mind: Where are the Hispanics? Are Latinos not interested in or affected by the economy? Are Hispanics not making news? Are we neither talented nor funny? Then I turned to one of the late-night, "real life" cop shows that are becoming so popular. And, finally, I saw some Hispanics! The screen was filled with images of dark, swarthy people with strong accents being arrested for everything from selling drugs to abusing their spouses.

His observations were apparently confirmed by a Screen Actors Guild study at the time that showed an almost complete absence of Hispanics in film and television and a Center for Media and Public Affairs (CMPA) study that discovered the many existing media portrayals of Latinos showed them as problems—as rioters, looters, gang members, drug dealers, criminals, or illegals. The titles of two CMPA studies hint at their content—"Don't Blink: Portrayals of Hispanics on TV" and "Distorted Reality: Hispanic Characters in TV Entertainment."

The situation has not changed dramatically since I watched countless bandido films in my youth and since Mr. Yzaguirre wrote his piece. Unfortunately, we have seen a limited positive presence of Latinos on television for many years. Published later in 2004, a UCLA Chicano Studies Research Center report analyzing the Fall 2003 network television season showed that despite making up approximately 13% of the U.S. population at the time, Latinos stood as the most underrepresented group in primetime television programming. Latino regular characters showed up only approximately 4% of the time.

The discouraging pattern repeated itself in yet other important areas of the media as well. The annual Network Brownout Report, published by the National Association of Hispanic Journalists in December 2003, took the major television networks to task for their coverage of Latinos. The report found that less than 1% of the sixteen thousand stories that aired in 2002 dealt with Hispanics. The study also found that a full two-thirds of the Latino stories that aired were about crime, terrorism, and illegal immigration. An accompanying qualitative analysis concluded that in spite of the growth of the Latino middle class, negative depictions of Latinos persisted—as criminals, living in poverty, as illegal immigrants, and posing a threat to the country. The 2005 report illustrated that few significant changes had occurred, and a ten-year analysis indicated that the less than 1% representation had remained consistent.

Years later the agonizing practice persisted. USC's Annenberg School for Communication and Journalism published a study concluding that Latinos are still the least represented minority group on film and TV relative to the percentage of the population. Although Latinos made up about 17.1% of the total U.S. population at the time the study was published, they made up only 5.8% of speaking roles. The Latino Media Gap, a report conducted by Columbia University, drew many of the same conclusions: "Today, Latino talent in top movie and television programming is extremely limited. Latino stereotypes are still prevalent in mainstream media and continue to damage the public perception of the group. Latino representation is at its worst in the news media environment."

Moving ahead to the present day, an even later study by USC showed that instead of the situation improving, it has worsened. With the percentage of Latinos rising to 18%, the number of speaking parts in films has dropped to 3%. Talk about moving backwards.

My friend Dr. Federico Subervi, an expert on the mass media and minorities, especially Latinos, published a study on how the national television evening network news programs on ABC, CBS, NBC, CNN covered Latinos and Latino/a issues in the years 2008-2014. The subtitle of the study immediately conveys his findings, "Still Mostly Invisible and Problematic." He goes on to report that Hispanics were often depicted as people with problems or causing problems—same old story.

Real Life Attitudes

Numerous studies conducted through the years, some cited in this chapter, provide powerful evidence that Latinos have been stereotyped, demeaned, or ignored for decades, still are to this day, and will probably continue to be dealt with in like manner for years to come. In spite of the evidence, I often have been challenged on my opinions about the negative perceptions of Mexicans held by many Americans. Challengers have been known to say things to me such as, "Why are you so sure what people really think about Mexicans?" Or: "People don't think all that stuff they see in movies is true in real life."

Aside from the studies and the countless stories told to me, I have often served as an unofficial, secret intelligence-gathering arm of my community, enabled by my ability to pass for White. I'm positive that individuals have used derogatory remarks in front of me they would not have otherwise uttered if they had known I was Mexican. The following serve as a couple personal experiences that make the point.

During my sixteen years of confirmed bachelorhood, I had been known to frequent bars, and one of my favorites was the famous, historic Irish Pub Tom Bergin's, located in the Fairfax area of Los Angeles. For many years throughout much of the '70s, I qualified as what could easily be called a regular at Bergin's. If the staff officially recognized your frequency at the bar, they would put your name on a paper shamrock and paste it on the wall along with thousands of other loyal customers. I was so honored.

Hanging out at Bergin's not only allowed me to develop a cordial group of drinking buddies, it was a great place to meet women. Singles like me gathered at pickup bars at the time (as I'm sure they do today) to hook up with members of the opposite sex. I had my share of success due to my being seen as relatively handsome, having a good time with the other regulars, and enjoying a great rapport with the bartenders. One of my favorite pals behind the bar was Chris Anastasio. As an Italian American and a part time actor, Chris and I could endlessly chat about ethnicity or acting with equal ease. We formed an endearing camaraderie, and I was always glad to see him on duty.

One routine evening, I found myself at the end of the bar on the side Chris was working. At one point he came over to me and said, "Hey Hank, see that good looking girl at the other end of the bar?" After my quick, interested, and affirmative response, he said, "She wants to buy you a drink you old devil. What'll you have?"

I gave Chris my order, and after getting served and catching the young lady's eye, I smiled, lifted my drink, and toasted her from afar. Soon after, I decided to saunter over and thank her in person. We introduced ourselves, and I began the usual small talk attempts to sound hip and urbane. Without feeling overly confident, it didn't take long to detect her serious interest and attraction to me, and I began to anticipate an easy score with a sexy, fine looking woman.

I can't recall what exactly sparked the exchange, but I remember saying something to her like, "You don't have anything against Blacks, do you?"

She quickly answered, "Oh God no. It's Mexicans I hate."

Almost falling off my barstool, I caught myself chuckling in an amused state of shock. Her slightly confused reaction prompted me to say, "Well, (whatever her name was, I've forgotten it), I think you and I might not get along perfectly given the fact that I'm Mexican."

Her own shocked expression was followed by a stammering, "Oh, no you aren't. You are not. You can't be."

I responded with, "Oh, yes I am, and I can prove it. With that, I hailed Chris over and said, "Hey Chris, please tell this lovely young lady, am I a Mexican or what?

Without hesitating, Chris casually said, "Oh yeah, Hank's a beaner from way back." And he quickly returned to his chores. His mischievous use of a derogatory term for Mexicans in my presence indicated that we had established a mutual respect, and that playful language was allowed among trusted friends. Chris's words put an abrupt end to the previously warm exchanges with my now stunned potential date. After some awkward, cursory words, she left.

Chris came over to me and said, "What the hell was that about?" I couldn't answer the question, and we both ended the evening quizzically scratching our heads. I confided in Chris by telling him that I was neither offended nor angered by the young lady's attitude, and I really felt sorry that she was so disturbed by being sexually attracted to a Mexican. Chris concluded, with a chuckle, that in the future she should check IDs before offering to buy someone a drink, and I concluded that a sizable number of people still didn't know what Mexicans looked like.

Here's another similar case in point. One of those years while working for SER, I found myself back in Dallas to provide the local program some PR technical assistance for an upcoming conference. After landing at Love Field I grabbed a taxi and headed for a hotel not far from the program office. Learning that I arrived from California, the chatty cab driver came off as friendly and eager to convince me that Dallas was a great city with a lot of fine people. When my second wife Shirley and I lived there in the '60s, we rented an apartment in what we considered a nice neighborhood, Oak Lawn. As we passed through that part of town, I revealed to the cabby that I had once enjoyed living there and found it comfortable and safe.

With that revelation he began to lament that, yes, it had been a nice neighborhood before all the Mexicans moved in, punctuating his disgust by saying, "…and you know how they are."

Curious to hear more of his perspective, I said, "No, I'm not from here. How are they?"

He then listed all of their well-known, loathsome habits and attributes by saying, " 'Course they're dirty and lazy, don't take care of where they live, get drunk and beat up their wives, and worst of all don't speak English good."

I let the poor guy go on and on with my occasional, "Really? Wow! No kiddin'? Before long we arrived at the hotel, and as he handed me my luggage, I quietly said, with a smile, "You know, I'm Mexican, and I'm not any of those things you described. What do I owe you?" He practically stumbled in shock as he told me the cost of my fare, and with an embarrassed look, clearly conveying he did not expect a tip, turned away with a near inaudible, "Thank you, sir."

I suppose I should have felt sorry for tricking him into showing his cards, but I was hopeful that at least he would think twice the next time he felt like spewing his vitriol. That occurred way back in the '70s, but sadly I still hear of degrading incidents or insensitive slights some people must endure today, sometimes reported to me by my own grandchildren.

Although I have not personally suffered from the persistent negative attitudes about Mexicans, I have often contemplated the potential harm and suffering inflicted on others as a result of blind indifference and the lack of human compassion.

DO YOU NOT WEEP

When you look into the faces
Of our children caged in ravaged city streets,
Do you not weep?

When you learn they have no heroes,
Save their brothers stored in prisons here and there,
Do you not weep?

When you hear their minds are tortured
By a thousand crucifixions every day,
Do you not weep?

Perhaps you simply say, that's life.
That's just the way those people choose to live.
Why should I weep?

~ 1984

Chapter Nine
A Near-Death Experience

Junior High School started out like a bad dream. After only three weeks, a major illness hit me. Dr. Zanger, a serious man with a square body, short hair, and a Hitler-like moustache, couldn't figure out what was causing it. I stayed in bed for ten days and finally got a little better and went back to school. After just a few days back, I got sick again. This time worse. Dr. Zanger came back to visit me at our house. He spent most of the time scratching his head and trying to figure out the reasons for my high fever and why it wouldn't go away. He took my temperature, my blood pressure, poked my body, and stared at me with a furrowed brow. Rene, who was now in nurse's training, told my mom that a fever of one hundred six was extremely dangerous for a boy my age. The fever stayed high for a long time, and Dr. Zanger had to give me a medicine called sulfa to help fight the sickness.

While I was lying in bed, my face feeling like the inside of an oven, I kept jabbering about nothing and laughing. I felt so weak I could barely move any part of my body. Everything seemed to be floating away including my mom standing at the foot of the bed. I remember the worried, helpless look on her face and how it kept changing into these different colors. I thought it was funny, so I continued to jabber and laugh. Then I fell asleep, and the fever broke. While I was still in a daze, I overheard my mom and Rene saying that I could have died. I was surprised to hear that, but at the moment I didn't care one way or the other.

I got well enough to go back to school, but nothing seemed the same. Nothing seemed to work as well as it did before. I felt slow. I'd fallen behind in school, but for some reason it didn't bother me. I had trouble getting things done. It didn't help that everyone at home seemed unhappy. My mom and dad weren't getting along, and they didn't understand my feelings anyway. I felt scared, but I didn't know why—like a small animal trapped in a cage.

To make matters worse, Lucy met a guy from Mexico whose name was Clemente Bedolla, and she liked him a lot. I liked him all right, but he was real dark-skinned and couldn't speak English very well. My mom told me he came to the U.S. to go to college but ran out of money and had to start working. After dating for quite a while, he and my sister decided to get married. They were going to move into their own apartment, but just before their wedding someone stole all the money they had saved for their apartment and a honeymoon. So they had to move in with us. I felt sorry for them, but it was also bad news for me.

I didn't get along with Lucy anymore. She acted like she was my mom, or my boss, or something else, but she was only my sister. That made me mad, and we got into a lot of arguments. My mom would come home, jump in the middle of it, and get all upset. My dad didn't say a word. He just sat there with a sullen look on his face without saying anything. I felt miles apart from my family like I didn't belong there. I didn't understand why everything had changed so much, and I wished I could run away. I was so much happier when I was in grammar school. After my illness I didn't do well in my classes, and I didn't care. I was walking around in a whole different confusing and uncertain world.

I did try to make friends at Peter Burnett Junior High School, but I didn't do a very good job of it. I was still friends with the guys in the neighborhood like Tony, Bernie, and others like Jim Brazda and Eddie Citti. Eddie had come over from Italy just a couple of years before and didn't speak English real well, but everybody liked him.

Eddie Citti's dad, like some of the other Italian men in the neighborhood, made wine from the grapes he grew in his backyard. They all used a big wooden barrel with a crank on it to crush the grapes for their wine. It sat on a trailer that they pulled around from house to house with their pickup trucks. When you stepped outside, the smell of oak and wine soaked the air. I doubted that anyone else's neighborhood in the whole world smelled as good as ours.

One day after school I went over to Eddie's house with Terry Antes, and Eddie asked us if we wanted to sneak a drink of some of his dad's wine. We said, "Sure." Eddie said that we'd better not drink it out of the bottle on the kitchen table 'cause his dad would know that someone had been into it. So we went down into the cellar where his dad kept a large wooden barrel-full of the stuff. We drank a little. It tasted great so we drank some more and then some more. I started getting dizzy, and for no reason we started joking and laughing. After getting almost too dizzy too walk, I decided I'd better go home and go to bed.

When I got home I told my mom that I was sick to my stomach. I wasn't sure if she could tell that I'd been drinking wine because I was too dizzy to see her face very well. The room started spinning around, and I couldn't stop it. Closing my eyes made it worse, made it feel like a small tornado was turning around in my head. Before I could get in bed I barfed all over the floor, and my mom had to clean up the mess. As I staggered into bed, I wondered why she wasn't giving me a beating or punishing me. I couldn't believe it. As I opened and closed my eyes, I thought I saw her laughing at me. I must have been acting goofy or something for her to be cracking up. Just before I fell asleep, I wondered again why she hadn't given me hell. It had to be a dream.

One day I went out into the backyard and saw my neighbor Daphne laying out by her little makeshift pool in her bathing suit. I started to throw some loquats at her, but as I peeked over the fence I got a better look at her. For some reason, I decided not to throw loquats at her anymore. I decided to go in the house and comb my hair instead.

More Mexican kids attended junior high than at my grammar school. Although I didn't feel much like telling people that I was Mexican, I started hanging around with a few of the Mexican guys like Frank Sanchez and Bill Gamez. Frank was a good guy and became a friend, but Bill was a bully. He liked to push me around and pick on me to show how tough he was. Trying to make new friends was like trying to learn to walk all over again. I hung around with those guys because they were good in sports and were popular. I thought that maybe they could help me feel like I belonged somewhere.

The one friend that never went away was Lannie Heffner. We had known each other for so long, through grammar school and church for many years, that I guess I took his friendship for granted. When we were younger we did a few bad things together, but I didn't think Lannie was going to turn into a bad kid. I wasn't so sure about me.

I also made friends with two other Mexican guys who were brothers and a grade ahead of me in school, Peter and Paul Arrichiga. Peter didn't look Mexican at all. He had light skin, hair, and eyes. They had a good friend they palled around with who wasn't Mexican. His name was Frank Genco, and he was Italian. Genco cussed more than my father, swaggered around like a peacock, and was always getting into trouble at school, mainly for talking back to teachers and disrupting classes. Getting detention after school and sitting outside the principal's office was a routine occurrence for him. This guy was constantly cruisin' for a bruisin'. Because he was older he also liked to pick on me, but some of the time he sort of protected me too. Many times I wished I could get stronger so I wouldn't have to depend on guys like Genco.

One day I got into a fight in my gym class with a guy by the name of Fausto Abasolo. I was still pretty skinny and weak from my illness, and Fausto was a tough guy. He looked older but was in my same grade. When we got into it, he punched me in the stomach hard and knocked the wind out of me. After I caught my breath on the ground, I called him a dirty Mexican. Afterwards, I questioned why I had said a dumb thing like that. I guess I was so mad I couldn't think of anything else to call him. Fausto wasn't even Mexican. He was Filipino and Pomo Indian, but I guess you could say he looked Mexican. Some weird thoughts kept popping into my head. Maybe I just got tired of getting pushed around by everyone.

During the summer we would go pick fruit with Peter and Paul's parents. I hated to do it, but it gave me a good way to earn some money so I could buy some of the sharp clothes I liked to wear. When riding to and from work in the back of Pete's dad's pickup, we got disapproving looks from some of the people passing by in other cars, most of them White. I thought they were probably thinking, "There go all those dirty Mexicans off to pick fruit." Moments like those made me wish I could be anything other than Mexican. Sometimes I even wished I had died from that fever because I was so unhappy. I kept saying to myself that I had to find more to be happy about. I started to understand why kids ran away to join a circus or tried to find a place where fun could come more naturally.

Saving Graces

Without music I wouldn't have been very happy at all, in fact, I wouldn't have had much to live for. I still took piano lessons and played cello in the school orchestra led by Mr. O'Reilly. He was a strict old bird, an ex-marine. I also started playing the saxophone and got pretty good at it, enough to join the marching band and the modern orchestra. Lannie played drums in the band, and I looked forward to marching in the downtown parades with him.

I got to know Daphne better after walking home from school with her a couple of times. She started treating me like a friend, and at one point I got a crush on her but didn't tell her. Daphne played in the orchestra too. She played the clarinet. Before we started rehearsing, Mr. O'Reilly would go around the room helping everyone tune their instruments. When he got to Daphne, she would try to blow a B flat, but instead of a tone coming out her clarinet it often just squeaked. She hated it, got all embarrassed, and blamed the clarinet by saying, "This stupid thing won't play." Mr. O'Reilly, as tough as he was, would smile and show his amusement over her excuses while a lot of us giggled under our breath.

All of us boys started getting interested in girls. Lois Wasserman was a pretty cute girl in our class and so was Jeanne Pacheco. I flirted with them, but they were not my girlfriends. I liked Daphne the best, but she was not my girlfriend either. One afternoon Lois and I made out like crazy at the movies during *King Solomon's Mines*. It was kinda fun, but I did it mainly to look like one of the boys.

Some of the kids started liking me more because I could play the piano. I played the theme from a keen movie called *The Third Man*. It was a popular song and playing it sort of made me popular too, especially when I played the piano over at Lois' house. I started asking myself why being liked was so important? I guess I was just afraid I'd be left alone somewhere off in some lonely corner without anyone paying any attention to me.

By now I was kinda getting tired of the music of the big swing bands. I still liked the music of Glenn Miller and Tommy Dorsey, but I felt hungry for something new. Many of the Mexican kids were starting to listen to a new band led by Perez Prado and a new dance craze called "Mambo." The Mexican girls played that music in the gym and boy could they dance, better than any of the White girls. I liked the sound of it too, but I was looking for something else. I wasn't quite sure what I wanted, something that sounded more modern I guess.

A nice Mexican girl that I thought was pretty, beautiful really, sat in some of my classes. Her name, Armida Marichalar, was very Mexican sounding. I liked her, and I thought she liked me, but I didn't want her to be my girlfriend. I could tell she didn't have a lot of money just by the way she dressed. Maybe I didn't want her as my girlfriend because she didn't have a lot of nice clothes like some of the other girls or maybe it was just because she was Mexican. I wondered if I would have chosen her to be my girlfriend if we had lived in another country, like France, Spain, or Mexico. A layer of hesitation surrounded all my actions, always reminding me to make sure I was well liked or never got embarrassed. I could see that was going to become a drag.

I started hanging around with another guy in my neighborhood who lived across the street from Daphne. His name was Bill Gonzales, but he didn't look at all like a Gonzales. He looked completely like a White guy with freckles and blond hair. Bill was only thirteen but his dad let him drive a car. He and I got along great because he was more grown up and showed me how to smoke cigarettes, how to inhale. We'd go down to the creek a couple of blocks from our house and smoke Chesterfields. Smoking made me feel like I was older, so some in the rowdy crowd at school let me hang around with them because I knew how to smoke. Several of us would go off and even dare to smoke during lunchtime. I knew it was dangerous but I didn't care. I sometimes even smoked cigarettes during gym period. It gave me a kind of thrill to sneak off to an unused staircase of the gym, take a couple of puffs, then go back and join the class. I think I did it just because it felt adventurous.

Pants called peggers were in style, gray khaki peggers that we wore real low on our hips. The first pair I bought made my mom go ape, and she ripped them up because she said they were pachuco pants. We had a huge argument and I couldn't believe she would tear up a brand new pair of pants. There were still Pachucos around who wore the real zoot-suit pants, but peggers tapered down just a little. I went and bought another pair, and both my dad and Rene talked my mom into letting me keep them. I knew one thing for sure. I would never let my mom iron my pants. I had to iron them so that the crease was perfect, so they looked neat and I wouldn't be embarrassed.

I think I was the first guy in my junior high to buy suede shoes. They were really different, and everyone said, "Man! Where did you get those shoes?" Another part of our style was to turn up the collars on our shirts, roll up the sleeves on our tee shirts, and stick a pack of cigarettes under the roll. We also wore long hair loaded with Vaseline or pomade and combed it in a ducktail or D.A. (duck's ass) style. I think it was the Pachucos who made up that hairdo. Sharp, daddy-o, sharp!

My mom found out about my smoking and boy did she give it to me. She came after me with the iron cord, chased me out of the house, and made me stay out in one of our backyard sheds for a couple of hours. I had never seen her so mad. After a while my dad came out to the shed and made me promise not to smoke again. He had a little smile on his face when he said it so maybe he didn't think it was all that bad. Around that time, I was getting tired of my mom going crazy over nothing and hitting me with whatever she had in her hands. I even thought that someday soon I might have to stop her from doing that. I knew she went crazy 'cause she thought I was going to get into a bunch of trouble, maybe turn into a some kind of bum, or even a gangster. Sometimes I thought that might not be such a bad idea.

~ *FAST FORWARD* ~

Added Burdens

It's bad enough having to worry about pimples and raging hormones while trying to get through puberty, but also having to worry about the worthiness of your genetic makeup adds to the upstream swim of growing up. Like so many kids in their early teenage years, I expended excessive amounts of energy thinking about appearance, clothes, or what the peer group did or did not approve. My ethnic background presented still another cause for anxiety. The possibility of being rejected, or thought of as somehow substandard, caused me to become preoccupied with questions about looks, skin color, dress, speech, or what to eat for lunch. They could all act as cues or giveaways to pigeonhole me and leave me feeling vulnerable or less accepted.

I didn't know the extent to which other Mexican kids may have suffered the same kinds of apprehensions. While I was worrying about being identified as Mexican, others who could not blend into the mainstream as easily as I constantly faced the sting of overt discrimination. At an early age, the realization that Mexicans were clearly not at the top of the social status ladder locked into my mindset.

Over the years, various people have challenged me by questioning if I had suffered any great amount of discrimination in my life as a result of being Mexican. Their skepticism most likely stemmed from seeing someone that to them did not "look or sound very Mexican." I have readily admitted that I indeed escaped the daily pounding of racial rejection. I had friends whose families had suffered far greater indignities and losses, for example the denial of service in a restaurant, housing, a job, or promotion—insults no one in my family ever endured. Unquestionably, I feel fortunate that in many ways my path had not been nearly as burdensome as that of others.

At one point in my career, I entered into a freelance contract with an association of Hispanic human resources professionals to handle the oral and written documentation of one of their major conferences. The event took place in a large, prestigious Los Angeles hotel. Since they needed to tape-record all of the proceedings in several simultaneous breakout sessions, I met with the manager in charge of the extensive audio-visual facilities offered by the hotel. When I began to ask him questions, his tentative responses caused me to suspect the level of the man's expertise. Finally he felt forced to turn the project over to his assistant Ricardo, a gentleman who happened to be Mexican. I quickly learned that Ricardo really knew his stuff, including the workings of the hotel's state-of-the-art theater and its complex recording capabilities. He quickly got me squared away, and the conference documentation assignment succeeded largely due to his assistance. On a couple of occasions, I went back to the manager for help with some small detail, and each time I received less than thorough answers. I ended up depending heavily on Ricardo's extensive knowledge of the facility.

After the conference ended, I asked Ricardo why he seemed to know so much more than his boss. With a smile of resignation on his face, he told me that he had been on the job for several years. When the time came to hire a new manager, a job he was in line for and felt thoroughly capable of handling, they brought in a White manager over him. He agreed with me that his boss had a lot to learn, and that Ricardo would undoubtedly be the one teaching the boss the ropes for some time. When I asked him why he thought they passed him over, he simply said in an accepting almost stoic way, "I think they felt my looks and my Spanish accent might not be acceptable to some of our clients."

The experience reminded me of my good fortune in avoiding this type of blatantly biased behavior. Somehow that fact did not eliminate the shred of lingering, perhaps unlikely concern, that at some point I might suffer the same fate—might end up the object of rejection or insults because of my background. What never occurred to me for a long time was the possibility of my own children spending even a fleeting moment worrying about the same thing. I was dead wrong.

A Lesson Close to Home

Ten days before playing in the Rose Bowl I married a beautiful girl who had been a friend all through high school. The summer just prior to my '58 football season I went home and fell in love with Pat Cochran. The summer turned into a classic whirlwind romance, and being young and impetuous we plunged into marriage. Due to Cal's Rose Bowl appearance and the wedding occurring just before the game, we found ourselves thrust into the limelight of media attention, including the national press. When we traveled to Pasadena for the Rose Bowl, Pat joined the wives of the coaches and other married players in receiving VIP treatment. It was a delirious, glamorous time for my new bride and me.

For many unforeseen reasons, our marriage did not last very long. Nevertheless, our union produced two beautiful daughters, Laura and Stacy, both loved and cherished by their parents. In the summer of '72 while I was working for SER—Jobs for Progress, they came to visit me for part of their vacation.

Most of my friends during my SER days were Latinos, mostly Mexican. After work we would regularly gather not only to party but also to passionately air our views on political, racial, and social issues. When Laura and Stacy came to visit, I took them to one of those gatherings during which the topics of conversation proved to be no exception. By then all of us had gladly accepted the self-descriptive label of Chicano. It suited us nicely. Because it was slang and irreverent, it served as a powerful political statement, demonstrating our defiance of the status quo. We wore it as a badge of honor with renewed pride in our heritage. Our talks about Chicano power and other such matters flowed as freely and easily as asking someone to pass the butter.

As my girls and I were driving home from the get-together, Laura, my twelve-year-old, sitting in the front seat, asked if she was a Chicano. I was sure she had not heard that term used before—not by her mother and certainly not by her grandmother, my mom, who took several years to fully accept it. (She hated the label, and often referred to it as pachuco or street talk.) I lightheartedly answered Laura's question by saying that since I was a Chicano she must be at least half Chicana (using the correct gender version of the word.) Being the dramatic one, she stuck her chest out and began to brag, "I'm Chicana, I'm Chicana," much to my delight. After just a few moments, my little ten-year-old Stacy moved forward from the back seat and in a quiet, timid voice said, "Daddy, I don't think I want to be Mexican. Everybody's going to hate me." Laura, also being the defiant one, responded with, "That's their tough luck, Stacy," a comment I felt sure did not ease Stacy's genuine apprehension.

I don't recall what I said to try and make Stacy feel better, but I remember feeling sad and angry that my little girl would have to deal with some of the same doubts I faced as a young boy. That she would have to worry in the very least about the possibility of being shamed by her peers, due to one-half of her genetic makeup, shocked and dismayed me.

Ironically, no one would have ever taken Stacy for Mexican. She physically displayed her mom's genes, a woman who qualifies as a typical American hybrid—including Scotch, Irish, Swiss, English, and German DNA. In addition, Stacy was using her stepfather's surname at the time, Dudley, so no one would have guessed from her name the questionable half of her background. She happily returned to using Olguin years later, but her comment revealed an innocent but clear understanding of what people thought of Mexicans in her world as a child—that struck me as stark, painful, and undeniably true.

Many more years later, Stacy lives as a happily married mom of my three thriving grandkids, She's married to Drew, a successful, talented guy whose dad happens to be Finnish. This prompted Stacy to jokingly start referring to their kids as Mexifins. In spite of her lighthearted nickname for them, it doesn't begin to describe the multi-blended nature of their DNA, one difficult to describe in a simple word. They easily qualify as mixes of mixes.

Without trying very hard, Stacy and Drew have taught their kids to respect differences and treat everyone, regardless of race, gender, background, or taste in rock 'n' roll bands, as equals. Their balanced, broad-minded attitudes about people have never seemed to occupy a terribly self-conscious part of their thinking. They simply flow from a comfortable mindset that has naturally transferred to their kids.

My opinion was reinforced when a sports reporter from a local TV station was interviewing my grandson Dalton, voted the most valuable player on his high school football team. When asked to name his number one sports hero, he answered, "Jackie Robinson." The somewhat surprised reporter asked why he admired Robinson, to which Dalton matter-of-factly said, "Because he helped to break the color barrier in major league baseball." I felt particularly proud of my grandson that day for naming someone who had lived in a distant era but who deserved his esteem above many other important sports figures.

In another instance involving my granddaughter Carly, I learned of her intolerance for bigoted comments. During her junior year in high school, she and another girl were on their way to the campus garden to participate in a biology project. As they were walking down an outside corridor lining several classrooms, they noticed a male teacher standing in the open doorway of his room. As they passed by him, he chuckled and said, "You wetbacks getting ready to go labor in the fields?" The fact that the two girls were blonds may have given him added permission to spout his overt racial slur. Several steps passed the doorway, Carly and her friend stopped abruptly and asked themselves in disbelief, "Did we hear him right?"

Not satisfied with ending it there, Carly turned and walked back into the classroom, visibly upset, and asked the teacher, "Excuse me, what did you say?"

He answered, "All I said was are you wetbacks getting ready to go labor in the fields?" No doubt aware of his potentially inappropriate remark, he quickly added, "It was just a joke. Calm down."

His quick, dismissive response angered Carly even more, and she responded with, "That's not funny. My family is Mexican, and I find your comment incredibly offensive."

As she turned to walk away, he continued to imply by his tone and demeanor that she was overacting and reiterated, "Get over it. It was a joke."

Not ready to forget and forgive the transgression, she complained to her biology teacher and when she got home told Stacy, "Mom, you're not going to believe what happened at school today, and you're going to be really mad about it."

Correct in assuming her mom's reaction, it led Stacy to demand a meeting with the principal in which Carly described the encounter. The principal, eager to calm the waters, offered the potential excuse that the teacher had suffered a recent stroke and that might explain his misstep. He then asked Stacy what she needed to resolve the situation. Stacy asked for an apology from the teacher for herself and Carly, but assuming that Hispanic kids from Carly's and the offending teacher's own class might have heard the slur, she argued that he should apologize to both classes. Carly decided she didn't need a personal apology but agreed with her mom that an apology to the classes was fitting.

Stacy received a cursory apology in a subsequent meeting, and Carly was present to hear the teacher apologize to her biology class, but she heard him again rationalize his behavior by insisting that what he had said was a joke, that he shouldn't have said it, and that he didn't mean anything by it. Neither Stacy nor Carly were subsequently informed if the teacher had apologized to his own class. Both are certain that he certainly escaped any major reprimand. It's important to note, that Carly was never convinced that he was truly sorry, and to this day is sure that he meant something by it, something clearly reflecting his racist views.

The incident serves as an example of the ease with which, even recently, individuals as important as teachers feel free to use insensitive, hurtful language about Mexicans and other minorities. Both Stacy's and Carly's experiences, many years apart, have made me realize that my hope for the eventual, unqualified acceptance and equality of Mexican Americans will require a long, continuing, and concerted effort. I'm proud and happy that my daughter and granddaughter are keeping a watchful eye on such unacceptable behavior and stand ready to condemn it.

After dealing with my Stacy's misgivings about the potential consequences of her genetic background, it moved me to write a poem about overcoming the fears of rejection.

WHO SPEAKS?

A thousand questions linger
Stay unanswered, unresolved,
As they await, suspended,
While I ponder harsh-tonged slurs,
Far too frozen to address
The stupefying grip of fear,
The cold unwillingness to risk
Denunciation and rebuffs.

Through murky vacillation,
Testing new and cautious acts,
I finally appear and rise
To take a stand on my behalf,
Defy the probing, judging snarls
And openly reveal my face.

~ 1972

Chapter Ten
Music, Music, Music

Life in junior high school had improved some, mostly because I had jumped into playing music like crazy. I still played cello in the school orchestra and saxophone in the modern orchestra and marching band. Marching in parades downtown during special celebrations put an extra gloss on some of my Saturdays and holidays. Mr. O'Reilly was still pretty grumpy and mean, but I was glad he had invited me to play sax in his modern orchestra. It gave me the chance to do what I liked best, play popular music.

I still loved classical music, so I tried out for the cello section of the All-City Junior High School Symphony. I barely made it into the orchestra as last chair, but I felt privileged to be part of a group that had so many good musicians. Although difficult at times, I loved playing the music we performed and actually practiced pretty hard to get it right. I was interested in popular music more than ever, but I never stopped listening to and enjoying classical music, especially Tchaikovsky, Chopin, and Debussy.

Arthur Rubenstein came to town and gave a recital at the San Jose Civic Auditorium. Again, my old man was the one who took me. It seemed a weird combination. A rough old guy who could only sing one note and his son, possibly on his way to becoming a gangster, sitting together and listening to one of the greatest classical pianists in the world. My eyes and ears were riveted on Rubenstein as he showered the audience with his brilliance, flying over the keys with eyes closed, smiling, and his fuzzy head swaying. After the performance I started thinking I should practice more, but I was pretty sure it was too late to become a concert pianist.

On Fridays I took my instruments home to practice on the weekends. I actually managed to ride my bike hauling a big tenor saxophone and a cello. It was pretty complicated, but I figured out how to hang the sax on my handlebars and rest the cello on the top of my foot as I pedaled along. I must have looked like some mechanical monster pumping down the street. Like before, I occasionally still had to stop and get off my bike, unload the sax and cello, and kick some jerk's ass that had made fun of my instruments and me.

It wasn't easy being a musician and trying to be a tough guy all at the same time.

I still hung around with some fellows that liked to get in trouble. It was as if I had two groups of friends, the bad kids and the good kids. Most of the ones I knew that were involved in music, especially in the symphony orchestra, were good students and well behaved. The others were probably headed for "The Juvie" or reform school. I started smoking again, but this time I was going to be more careful and not let my parents find out.

Things were still not great at home. My parents seemed to always be in a dog-and-cat fight. Lucy was still living with us and had her first baby, which made life worse for me at home. I didn't understand any of my family, and they sure didn't understand me. I was certain my mom still feared losing control over me, and she was probably right. In those days she always acted as if she was mad and yelled at me about everything. My old man walked around as if he was half asleep or bored. He still didn't seem to care about anything, least of all me. He barely talked to me even when we went to a concert together. He would go to work, come home, eat, and either do stuff in the yard or on our house. He had almost finished building it, and it started to look real good. Still, I just stayed away as much as possible.

I got along with Rene best in my whole family. When she would come home from nurses' training to visit, I was always happy to see her. More than anyone she tried to understand what was going on in my life. My mom's brother Phil stayed with us for a while and owned a nice, little Model-A Ford. Sometimes when he and my parents were away for the day visiting relatives, I would swipe the keys, jump in the Model-A, and drive around with some of my friends.

One day Rene was visiting. My parents and Uncle Phil had gone to San Francisco for the day. Lucy and Clemente were also away. I asked Rene if she wanted to go for a ride. She thought it was pretty bad to steal the car but smiled and said, "Okay." I think she considered what we were doing as some kind of naughty mischief, something she wouldn't have dared do when she lived at home. We took off and had a good old joy ride, but on our way back the car stalled. I tried to clean the spark plugs and other stuff but nothing helped. We sat by the side of the road for a couple of hours, and both of us started really sweating it, worried that we were going to get caught and run into some serious trouble. For some dumb reason, the car finally started, and we got back home before my parents and uncle Phil returned. We both breathed a great big sigh of relief. We now had this great secret between us, but my sis never went joy riding with me ever again.

Columbus Park, located in our neighborhood, had a recreation center where I spent many hours when I was not in school. The recreation leader Jerry Melcher liked me and took the time to have some serious, man-to-man discussions with me. I told him about the problems I had at home, and he tried to help me figure out how to get along better with my family. Since he knew I smoked and sometimes hung around with a bad crowd, he encouraged me to try harder in school and stay out of trouble. He even let me drive his car a couple of times.

I guess Jerry should have worried a little more about the bad kids I hung around with. Some of us ran a little business we called the, "The Midnight Auto." We would go out at night, steal hubcaps, and turn around and sell them. Caddie hubs and spinners were the most popular. I sometimes worried about getting caught by the cops, 'cause if it ever happened my parents would have flipped their lids, and I probably I would have become a juvenile delinquent and sent to reform school. Around that time I actually I started doing better in school. I even made the honor roll a couple of times. Of course, I always got good grades in music. I started thinking that maybe I should stop stealing hubcaps.

My behavior must have been real confusing for my mom. On the one hand, I knew she was proud of me for my doing so well in music. On the other, she kept worrying that I might get in serious trouble. I guess that's why she would fly off the handle so easily. One night after I got home late, she got mad at me and reached for the iron cord to give me a smack. I grabbed it away from her, looked her straight in the eye, and in a firm tone of voice said, "Don't you ever do that again." I think I scared her, and it made me feel a little guilty. At the same time, I was glad. I thought she might let me have my way more often from that point on. I thought to myself she better or else.

Johnny Orozco & the Melodiers

A couple of new kids arrived at our school, the Espinoza twins Melchor and Gaspar. We quickly became friends. They were real sharp dressers and used neat words like "daddy-o" and "crazy." Melchor was the first guy I ever heard use the word "cool." They were Mexican, good looking, popular, and very hip.

They introduced me to a guy by the name of Johnny Orozco, a terrific trombone player. Johnny was a couple of years older than me and attended James Lick High School. He decided to put a combo together and asked me to join. I got really excited about it. The other guys in the combo were Gary, who played drums, and Bobby, who played sax. Bobby played with a real mellow style and had a great tone. It was a funny combination of instruments, but we sounded pretty good and picked up a few jobs.

We started playing at dances, parties, and weddings and received some pretty good money for it. I also sang for the combo, songs like "I'm in the "Mood for Love" and "Blue Moon." I liked the applause I got—mainly I liked that the girls went for my singing. So, I definitely decided I should lay off stealing hubcaps for a while.

Older kids attended most of the dances we played at, and some of them were Johnny's friends from high school. After the dances we would smoke cigarettes and sometimes even drink wine or beer that the older kids were able to get. It all felt great, made me feel like a big man.

Johnny and I were getting real tired of most of the pop music we heard. Singers like Frankie Laine, Vaughn Monroe, Bing Crosby, or Patti Page sounded okay, but so many of their songs were corny. We liked Nat King Cole and Frank Sinatra the best. Along with some of the day's pop songs, we kept playing our favorite songs from the swing era, pieces like Glenn Miller's "Moonlight Serenade." That stuff was all right too, but it was more the music of our parents or our older brothers and sisters. We kept searching for our own sound, one that could break the boredom and open us up to new feelings and sensations.

One day Johnny called me on the phone more excited than I had ever heard him before. He told me to jump on my bike and get over to his house as soon as I could, shouting, "I've discovered the sound, man, the sound we've been looking for."

I threw the lawn mower down before finishing my chores. I knew I was going to catch hell for not finishing, but I didn't care. I raced over to Johnny's house. When I got there he played a record by Stan Kenton and his orchestra. I had never heard of this guy, but when the first notes of "Artistry In Rhythm" began pouring out of the round black disk on Johnny's record player I found myself in a hypnotic state, surrounded by unbelievable sounds I never knew existed. We sat completely entranced by driving, swinging rhythms, big deep brass, soaring solos, and orchestral textures that blew over us like a cleansing storm. We listened tirelessly for hours. Being young and unsophisticated, we may not have truly understood the intricacies of the music, but we knew we were listening to something fresh, important, and revolutionary. I had stumbled on an art form that seemed to transcend the mundane concerns of my often-troubled life.

I did get in big trouble for not mowing the lawn, but it was worth it. After that I definitely decided to stop stealing hubcaps. I was just going to spend my life listening to Stan Kenton.

~ *FAST FORWARD* ~

Lasting Musical Connections

Stan Kenton's style, labeled as "Progressive Jazz," truly represented the cutting edge when Johnny and I first heard his magical sounds. His orchestra provided the platform for many great jazz composers, arrangers, and players and allowed for the development of fresh, new concepts in orchestral contemporary jazz. Although it could be said that Stan Kenton remained an innovator for only a couple of decades, for me his music served as the catalyst for my lifelong love affair with all forms of jazz. The Saturday afternoon spent with Johnny began an exciting series of musical voyages adorned with the music of Duke Ellington, Dave Brubeck, Bill Evans, Miles Davis, Chet Baker, Stan Getz and many other great jazz artists.

Long after my junior high era musical experiences, my involvement with music and musicians continued, not only as a pastime pleasure but also while fulfilling some of my professional responsibilities. Writing songs for *Sesame Street* or jingles for advertising campaigns represented two ways that kept me happily engaged. Working for GSD&M Advertising, my duties often called for collaborating with composers and arrangers on a variety of projects. An earlier, gratifying music connection actually began back in college.

Every fall the Cal football team would arrive two weeks before the start of classes for what we called the grueling "two-a-days." The early arrival allowed the team to practice twice a day in preparation for the season. During that time the team would live together at Bowles Hall, a beautiful and old castle-like men's dormitory. It was there I learned that Don Piestrup, one of the team's small but extremely tough, smart lineman, and I shared a great love for jazz and in particular for Stan Kenton's artistry. Don qualified as a well-schooled musician, had studied piano for many years, and like me had also become a fervent jazz buff.

Piestrup had majored in Economics, but after graduation turned his attention fully to music and began studying composition in earnest at Cal's graduate school of music. Within a short period, "Pie" began writing inventive jazz compositions and arrangements and put a rehearsal band together in the San Francisco Bay Area to try out his creations.

While Pie was studying vigorously everyday, he supported himself by working as an insurance adjuster, a job that required investigating claims in the field. His routine involved getting his adjusting work done as early as possible in the day and then going home and studying and writing intensely for hours into the night.

Years later during a period when I thought of making acting my career, Don suggested to me, "Hey, man, get a job as an insurance adjuster and while you're investigating losses you can sneak away and audition for acting jobs." It seemed like a good plan for breaking into films and television at the time. So, I took Don's advice, and in 1963 I went to work for General Adjustment Bureau in Santa Monica, California. The plan never quite panned out. With an ex-wife and two children needing my support back in San Jose, I rarely took advantage of my work schedule for fear of losing my job. I soon determined that the plan was better suited for a single guy with no obligations.

In the early '60s, Piestrup got his first big break as a composer when

Buddy Rich invited him to make a permanent move to L.A. and begin writing extensively for his band. In addition Stan Kenton's Neophonic Orchestra also performed some of Don's pieces in Los Angeles. His relationship with Rich helped establish Don as a serious, in demand, jazz composer/arranger. In the '70s, I would regularly drop into Donte's, a famous jazz venue, to hear Pie's sensational rehearsal band, made up of players who at the time could easily qualify as the Who's Who of the country's jazz elite. His extraordinary career also included leaving an indelible print in the field of music for advertising.

I did not become a professional actor. Still music remained a strong side interest throughout my life and career. Part of that interest allowed me to stay in touch with my old teammate. My work at GSD&M Advertising not only included writing and producing jingles but also directing countless voiceover sessions for several of the agency's clients. In the '80s some of that work came to fruition in a prominent L.A. recording studio owned by Don, Bell Sound. Our relationship had come full circle.

A Noteworthy Side Note

After moving to Santa Monica in the early '60s to begin working as an insurance adjuster, I found myself on a tight budget. I rented an inexpensive flat in the alley behind the building where I worked and a couple of doors down from the Greyhound bus station. To make ends meet, I took in a roommate, a student at UCLA by the name of Andy Engvall. Andy had completed his first two years of college at Harvard and then transferred to UCLA to enroll in the school of cinema. Andy and I became good friends and comfortably and compatibly shared living quarters, cheap wine, and chicken potpies. Andy was a sensitive, thoughtful and compassionate individual, possibly due in part to the influence of his father, a Unitarian minister.

By the time I met Andy in 1963, the U.S. involvement in Vietnam had escalated to a troop level of some 16,000, and Andy had become a passionate, vocal critic of the conflict. I was still of a mindset that advocated supporting our government's commitment to stop the spread of Communism. I listened and argued with my roommate, and finally agreed to attend one of the early teach-ins at UCLA, protesting the war. The arguments I heard proved to be compelling, and I decided that, at the very least, we should be having a vigorous public debate about our war policy. Soon after, I moved over to

Andy's side of the argument.

Andy also introduced me to some of his fellow film students. One of them was Ray Manzarek, a graduate student in film. Ray, his girlfriend Dorothy, and I discovered an easy and compatible rapport. When Ray learned that I aspired to be an actor, he asked me if I would be interested in playing the lead role in his Master's film project. Of course, I eagerly jumped at the chance, and we proceeded to shoot Ray's student film, *Evergreen.* I played a jazz saxophonist who has an affair with a lovely Asian girl, perfectly performed by none other than Dorothy.

After we successfully completed the project, I attended the screening of the student films at UCLA expecting to see myself on the big screen. When they failed to show the film, Ray, my friends, and I were not only disappointed but also confused. It turned out that the faculty refused to screen the film because of a couple of nude scenes appearing in the story. After many years, I saw *Evergreen* again at the Santa Cruz film festival where Ray appeared as a celebrity guest speaker. By today's standards, the minor nudity in the film is laughably tame. Still in 1964, it offended the moral standards of the UCLA professors to the point of censoring it. Ray and I reprised our laugh over the situation when we met again in Santa Cruz.

During the time I knew Ray, his interest in music seemed to match his love of film. Ray always had a music gig of some sort in the works. Whenever he would drop by Andy's and my pad, he would enjoy playing the little Yamaha studio upright piano I had rented for my own musical meanderings. One day he told me that he was putting together a new band with another film student, Jim Morrison. I didn't know Jim very well but had seen him at a couple of parties. When Ray asked if they could use the flat to rehearse their new band, Andy and I easily agreed. Ray liked that the place was located in an alley away from other residences. The location would allow them to turn their amps up full blast and play away. And that they did as The Doors began creating the sound and style that would make them internationally famous— right there in a modest little pad within earshot of the Greyhound station's announcer calling for riders to get onboard for Riverside and points east.

I feel privileged to have stayed in touch with the music scene in one way or another. One of the highlights of my music-related experiences includes the day Pie invited me to attend a rehearsal of Kenton's band. That particular day the band was rehearsing one of Don's compositions. The thrill of meeting one of my childhood idols caused me to silently wish that Johnny Orozco could have joined me that day. I'm sure that Johnny's memory, like mine, would have also catapulted him back to the Saturday afternoon we both uncovered a deep well of unforgettable musical pleasures.

For jump-starting me on a lifetime journey of jazz delights, I found a way to say thank you in verse to Stan "The Man" Kenton.

OPUS FOR STAN

So far beyond the day-to-day
Yet familiar as a friend.

A brash and pulsing tonal wall
Lights cities made of glass,
With signatures in complex times
With trellises of brass.

Far-flung inventions, harmonies
On swinging waves of sound,
Alive as fire, fine as lace,
Breathtaking ups and downs.

The syncopated beats that soar
Or slow to sensual crawls,
Transcend the mundane, worn-out worlds
Of radio's hit list sprawls.

Creating whole new sets of gods
When Kenton points at Shank
Then Maynard, Art, and Salvador
Safranski, June, and Frank.

Dig all those lofty messengers
Delivering tasty flights
Gifts full of incandescent hues
Of phenomenal delights.

~ 1978

Chapter Eleven
Acting Through Dreams

By the time I hit the ninth grade, my old man and I had less in common than ever. Nothing I did including my music made him look up—not even for a minute. Now the only thing that seemed to give him any pleasure was making cedar chests in his workshop. I was sure he wished I was more interested in that kind of stuff, but to me it was just a big, fat drag. The other thing he liked to do was to graft trees with our neighbor Johnny Sinderella. Johnny was a real nice, old Italian guy who lived a couple of doors down from our house. He used to come over and spend hours teaching my dad how to graft the many peach and other fruit trees we had in our backyard. Johnny also loved the opera and classical music and always enjoyed hearing me play the piano. Whenever he would come into our house he would say to me, Enrico (Henry in Italian), Enrico play, play for me." I didn't mind playing for him because he appreciated music so much, and sometimes he would even hum along with it.

Having so many Italian friends, I sometimes wished I had been born Italian rather than Mexican. Although some people made fun of Italians too, it somehow didn't seem as bad as the things people thought or said about Mexicans.

My mom told a story that provided a small escape from the shame of being Mexican. One year, she went to visit a tía in Arizona who was dying. Before she died my great aunt told my mom that she had a shameful family secret she had to get off her chest before she passed away. She confessed that my mom's grandfather was illegitimate and that his father was a Frenchman. According to my mom, the French were hated in Mexico because they tried to take over the country, and for that reason no one in our family had ever admitted that mom's grandfather was half French. I think my mom didn't think it was a big deal one way or another and even laughed it off.

The supposed French side of our family may have been something for my great aunt to be ashamed of, but it gave me a way to avoid being a full-blooded

Mexican. Now when someone asked me, "What are you?" I started saying, "I'm Spanish and French." I even said that to some of my Mexican friends. They would just laugh at me, but I didn't care. One friend, Moises Sanchez, would tell me, "No nieges tú raza, Hank" (Don't deny your race, Hank). I would tell him I'm not, and he would just give me a smile and a knowing look. My other friend, Melcher, once introduced me to a good-looking Mexican girl who asked me if I was a Chicano. I said, "No, I'm Spanish and French." Melcher almost laughed his pants off and said, "Don't you believe it, baby. Hank's a cholo from way back." I decided they could laugh all day long. I wanted to fit in. I just wanted to be an American.

My mom became an American citizen, so she started telling people, "I am an American of Mexican decent." I didn't like that very much either, but it sounded better than just saying that she was Mexican. I often felt real glad my name wasn't Gonzales or Martinez. That would have been a dead giveaway.

Most of the time I tried not to worry about that stuff too much. I tried to stay busy hanging around with my friends and playing piano. Occasionally I would play a little football and baseball. I wasn't great at it, but I was still one of the fastest runners around. Some of my other friends like Frank Sanchez and Tony Realmonte spent a lot of time playing on city recreation teams, but I still didn't want to give sports that much of my energy. Whenever I would join Frank and Tony at Backesto Park for pickup games, I sure wasn't the first one enthusiastically chosen on a side.

I started playing piano and singing with a couple of other trios, not just with The Melodiers. So at the beginning of the ninth grade, I decided to give up the cello and sax and just stay with the piano. I went in and informed Mr. O'Reilly, and he flipped his lid, telling me I didn't appreciate all the music lessons the school had given me. I told him I did but that I just wanted to play piano. He didn't speak to me ever again. I thought of him as a big, old sourpuss, asshole, and I was glad I quit.

I was having more fun at school now. I had stopped hanging around with some of the tougher boys and thought of Lannie, Tony, and Frank as my best friends. Francis Makris, my sixth-grade girlfriend, transferred from Roosevelt

Junior High School to Peter Burnett for some reason. I thought she might have gotten into trouble or something at that school. She was now in my homeroom, and we enjoyed talking about music. I told her she should be singing, but she would just shrug her shoulders and say, "Oh, I don't know." I thought she had a fantastic voice and could be a great jazz singer. I genuinely hoped she would go back to it.

Daphne had become my girlfriend. I wasn't very good looking, but I dressed sharp and had what the kids called a good personality. Now that Daphne was my girlfriend I made a ring for her in metal shop. It was made of brass so she couldn't put it on her finger 'cause it would turn pukey green. She wore it on a chain around her neck instead. It made me feel special to have a pretty girlfriend like her. Even Fran would tell me she thought Daphne was one of the cutest girls in the school. I often wondered why we walked around wearing people like ornaments and why we tried so hard to be admired for that.

Every Thursday they had an amateur hour in between movies at the Victory Theater. It was called Eddie's Adver Show. I asked Bill Gonzales if he wanted to go down there with me, 'cause I wanted to try out for the show. Bill and I walked a few blocks to the theater and went down into the basement where this old fart, Eddie Adver, was smoking a cigar and talking tough like some kind of New Yorker. He asked me what I did, and I said, "I play the piano and sing." He then said, "Let's hear ya." I sang only about four bars of *A Garden In the Rain* before he interrupted me and snapped, "You're on first, kid. Next."

I was surprised it all happened so fast, but it was fine with me. There were four contestants and whoever won would get to come back the next week. I got up on stage, played, and sang. While I was doing it Eddie held the mike for me, hamming it up and making stupid faces the whole time I was performing. I guess it worked out all right because after I finished, I got a great round of applause. When everyone got through performing, Eddie asked people to vote with their applause as he held his hand over each of the contestants. I took second place, getting beat out by a little knobby-kneed, five year-old girl singing some dopey song off-key.

Then I really got a surprise. Eddie told me I had won fifteen dollars worth of groceries. Wow! Bill and I ended up each carrying out two big bags of food that were so full we could barely get them home. When we got back to my house and walked in the door with all that loot, my mom looked shocked and asked me where we got all that stuff, as if we had stolen it. I told her I won it, and Bill told her, "Honest, Mrs. Olguin, he won all of this singing."

My mom eventually smiled, and probably felt as if she'd finally gotten something back for all those piano lessons she had paid for.

The Lewises

After living right next door for years to Daphne's family, the Lewises, they had become a natural part of the ebb and flow of my life. Her parents Val and Pauline always made me feel welcomed. Although he was nice, Mr. Lewis was as strict as a Marine sergeant, so I was always very respectful around him. I didn't know why, he just looked like someone I wouldn't want mad at me. I knew one thing; when he spoke, all his kids stood up a little straighter and paid attention.

I noticed that Mr. Lewis read books like crazy. I would often see him sitting in his big comfortable chair reading a book, with a can of beer by his side, and completely lost in what he was reading. It made me wonder if reading a lot could be more fun than I thought. Mr. Lewis also smoked Kent cigarettes, and sometimes I would sneak one or two out of a little box on a table when no one was watching. Boy! I knew if he ever caught me, he would probably kill me or kick me out of his house and tell me never to come back.

Daphne had a younger brother and two younger sisters, Paul, Valerie, and Monica. I liked everyone in the family, but especially Sandie, Daphne's older sister. She became my friend—actually more like a big sister than just a friend. She talked to me about all sorts of stuff, and, like the recreation leader Jerry Melchor, she really listened. She too must have had the idea that I could maybe get in serious trouble, so she would tell me to behave, try harder in school, and that I could do anything I wanted to do.

Sandie also started introducing me to new things I'd never known about, things that were often hard to grasp. She had a book called *The Prophet*, written by some guy with a strange name, Kahlil Gibran. It was full of ideas I didn't understand, but I was intrigued by them and tried to read it because

Sandie liked it. It was also full of pictures I didn't get, but I kept looking at them over and over again to try and figure them out. She also introduced me to singers I had never heard of, like Josh White and Harry Belafonte, and an album of a Broadway show called *New Faces of 1952*. There was a singer on the album I really liked. Her name was Ertha Kitt. All of those entertainers were different from any of my favorite jazz musicians, but I started finding them interesting too and trying to open up my mind to them.

Sandie also went nuts over an actor named Marlon Brando and a movie called *A Streetcar Named Desire*. I didn't listen much to her oohs and aahs over his looks, but she said so many good things about him that I watched him more carefully and became intrigued by his unusual and rebellious style of acting. Sandie was very interested in acting and that made me want to learn more about it. I even wondered if maybe I could be an actor someday.

I didn't know for sure if Sandie or Daphne knew that I was Mexican or if they did whether they gave any thought to how Mexican I was. Maybe it didn't matter to them. We never talked about it, but I trusted that neither of them would ever say anything to hurt me or make me feel bad. I didn't trust all White people because I knew what some of them thought of Mexicans. Sometimes I heard them say bad things right in front of my face, probably because they didn't know they were talking in front of a Mexican. They would say stuff like, "You know how those dirty Mexicans are." It hurt my feelings, but I decided to just keep acting as if it was not that important to me. I thought that's it; put on an act. That way it might all somehow go away.

For some unknown reason, I felt a special attachment to Mrs. Lewis. She always had a friendly smile for me, but at the same time she seemed distracted, like she was thinking about something else most of the time. She came from Hawaii, so maybe she missed the islands. Sometimes when I would come home late, around sunset, I would see her standing alone at the Hobson Street Bridge that crossed over Guadalupe Creek about a block from her house, smoking a cigarette and looking out over the creek. As the light faded I would ride my bike as far away from where she was standing on the other side of the street so I wouldn't disturb her. I felt her seeing something miles away from the slow stream of water flowing in the creek or the tall crowded reeds growing there—something distant and sad. I would ride by as quietly as I could, and a part of me wondered if she might be looking for something that wasn't there—just like me.

~ *FAST FORWARD* ~

Multiple Roles

Growing up and accommodating to the prevailing negative attitudes about Mexicans necessarily required something of an act. Pretending not to care when hearing racial slurs became one of my various roles. I never felt good in those situations, but I often lacked the courage to confront or disagree with anyone and face possible rejection or disapproval. My real-life performances may have influenced my growing interest in acting and clowning. At an early age I began doing impressions of movie stars and singers. Pretending to be someone else came naturally to me.

In high school I began my involvement in stage and radio acting no doubt due to Sandie's influence, but it was not until I reached college that I began to take it more seriously. In the meantime my childhood friend, Francis Makris, had become the recording artist known as Fran Jeffries and later appeared in several films, including the popular The *Pink Panther.* I hoped that my small nudges in junior high had exerted some small influence toward that end.

After I finished playing football at Cal, I still needed a considerable number of units to graduate. I had bumped around changing majors, and had not exactly dedicated myself to a life of disciplined scholarship. I was also going through some dramatic changes, including the beginning of married life. On top of that, a year before playing in the Rose Bowl, I had also gone through a born-again religious conversion. The very intense experience had left me considering making a career of the ministry. I decided to change my major once again, this time to Rhetoric. I committed myself to getting serious about school and working towards entering seminary. In March of 1960, our first daughter Laura was born. The added responsibility demanded that I work almost full-time while still attending school.

For several months after class, I would jump on my bike in Berkeley and head for KTVU—Channel 2 Television in Oakland's Jack London Square. My job as a floor director, handling the afternoon kids' shows and the evening news, gave me a little taste of show business. It felt more like play than a job. Working with an unusual boss, a talented and interesting man by the name of

Ian Zellick, further enhanced the experience. Whenever we could, Ian and I would engage in lively discussions about music, movies, and theater.

That year marked the inception of the American Football League, formed to compete with the NFL. Through some of coach Pete Elliott's contacts I was drafted to play for the Dallas Texans, a team that later became the Kansas City Chiefs. Professional football players were certainly not getting rich in those days. Nevertheless, I reluctantly decided to play due to the urging of coaches and friends and simply because the opportunity presented itself. In the fall of 1960, I went off to Roswell, New Mexico for training camp.

Designated to play defensive back I gave it my best shot, but in my heart of hearts I knew my passion for the game had seriously diminished. With the meager salaries paid professional football players in those days, it was not likely to be rekindled. About two weeks into training camp, I severely injured my knee, marking the end of my short-lived professional football career. I returned to the San Francisco Bay Area with new uncertainties about life and religion. I worked for a few months as a salesman for Warner Lambert Pharmaceutical and then re-enrolled at Cal.

Some of the new uncertainties included my waning zeal for the brand of evangelical Christianity I had embraced earlier. Challenges seemed to appear at every turn, not only by the subject matter presented in some of my classes but also by the behavior of some so-called loving Christians. I found myself particularly dismayed by members of the faith who professed "loving thy neighbor as thyself," while complaining that "niggers" were attempting to move in to their neighborhoods. The gradual erosion of my religious beliefs left me in a kind of spiritual limbo.

During that time, I enrolled in an Argumentative Discourse class taught by anthropologist Ethel Albert, a caring, thoughtful, and compassionate humanist and atheist. Her enlightened worldview by contrast to the narrow-mindedness of some Christians further challenged my faith.

To partially help fill the void, I pursued my new major with enthusiasm.

In addition I immersed myself in the university's theater activities, perhaps attempting to replace the loss of religious passion with an artistic one. At the time Cal's, ambitious and innovative theater program helped train some of my classmates who were destined to become successful working actors— among them were Stacy Keach and Karen Grassle, who played the mother in television's hit *Little House on The Prairie* series with Michael Landon.

My involvement in Cal's Theater Arts Department became almost obsessive. I enrolled in as many theater classes as I could fit in, including a masters acting course taught by Jean Renoir, son of the famous painter and considered by many as the father of French cinema. Other notable participants in that class included Syd Field who became known as one of Hollywood's screenwriting gurus.

Much of the excitement and interest of my fellow players in the university's theater program came from the challenging and ambitious works its innovative professors dared to tackle. Plays such as Bertolt Brecht's *Galileo* and Ben Jonson's *Bartholomew Fair* not only stretched us as actors but also deepened our appreciation of dramatic art.

During that time, I auditioned and performed in many productions over a period of two years. Although Stacy Keach reigned as the unofficial king of the theater department during that era, and deservedly so, I beat him out one year for the University Theater's outstanding actor award, known as the Sara Huntsman Sturgess Memorial Prize (for outstanding artistic achievement in dramatic art). That little triumph provided me with a satisfying claim to fame, however modest.

My lead in Tennessee Williams' *A Rose Tattoo*, more than others, helped me earn the award. I have occasionally run into Stacy over the years, and feel certain he has forgiven me for stealing a very tiny portion of his thunder.

My total absorption in the theater and acting put a tremendous pressure on my marriage. My spending a significant amount of time away in rehearsals caused Pat to feel removed and estranged from most of my theater friends and subsequently from me. I'm certain the loss of my Christian convictions and my resulting state of disillusionment also added to our estrangement. On the other hand, my involvement with my theater classmates and respected professors, helped to sustain me through some profound soul-searching days regarding the path I might take the rest of my life.

At that point, my ethnicity seemed a remote concern. By then I had assimilated so far into the mainstream that passing for anything but Mexican posed no obvious problem. Other than maintaining a relationship with only one Mexican friend during that period, stark reminders of my background rarely surfaced. The exception involved one of my favorite Theater Arts professors by the name of William Oliver, a fascinating and eccentric man who spoke Spanish with impeccable clarity.

Whenever he ran into me and the spirit moved him, he would enjoy blurting out my surname, giving it the proper and perfect Spanish pronunciation, Ohl GEEN. Raised in Panama by missionary parents, Oliver loved to speak Spanish with a dramatic flair. Although by then I had almost completely disassociated myself from my ethnicity, Oliver's reminders of my background somehow became a welcomed diversion.

He and I would spend time together talking in Spanish about plays and other matters. The struggle to keep up with Oliver's highbrow, scholarly brand of Spanish frequently left me reeling. During the rehearsal of Ben Jonson's *Bartholomew Fair*, Oliver directed me in Spanish to play a scene with the specific kind of comic bravado the great Mexican comedian Cantinflas might have employed. Because of the years spent in my childhood watching Cantinflas, I understood Oliver's direction explicitly and enjoyed knowing that no other cast member could have even begun to grasp it. I took pleasure in those moments with a sense of nostalgia, longing to somehow begin incorporating more of my Mexican side into my artistic explorations.

Before I finished my final semester, Pat and I separated right as our second daughter Stacy was born. Racked by sadness, guilt, and confusion, I staggered through my final classes just in time to learn of my father's terminal cancer diagnosis. During my dad's last few months, I spent time by his side as we tried in our own clumsy way to make peace with one another. After his passing, I had to admit to myself that he exerted a greater effort to connect and heal the past than I—he really tried hard. Ours had not been a close and agreeable relationship through the years, and finding a parting, healing intimacy did not come easily. In the end, I accepted the fact that he had done his best for me given his background and life's challenges.

A Spiritual Aside

With so much of the focus of this book on matters of ethnicity, readers might conclude that spirituality has played only a minor role in my life's journey. Aside from my referring to a "born-again" Christian experience, and admitting that the belief system did not hold up for me, I have said little about spiritual matters.

Several years ago a good Jewish friend of mine told me, "I'm culturally a Jew, but I'm not religious." I found that a good description for me as well: I'm culturally a Christian, but I'm not religious. Therefore, I would have no problem sitting in the pews of a Methodist or Baptist church and "making a joyful sound unto the Lord"—singing a rousing old-fashioned hymn without having to buy into the theology or dogma. I'm sure my friend would be equally at ease and at home while attending a bar mitzvah.

The painful aftermath of losing my Christian faith caused me to become even more interested in issues surrounding religion and to do my fair share of reading about and exploring questions of God and spirituality. In my search I have discovered a number of uplifting teachings that have led me to a place of greater peace and harmony. Way back in 1975, I began practicing Transcendental Meditation and to this day it serves as a path to a deeper centering and serenity—but not the only path.

Seeking to find a deeper meaning to life while dealing with the ordinary issues of relationships, racism, or simply the daily chores of making a living, I've learned how difficult it is to straightjacket spirituality, to put it in a box, and assign it a narrow definition. I believe that it can be experienced in a wide variety of connections with or appreciation for a piece of great music, a special glimpse of nature, expressions of human compassion and empathy, acts of great courage or heroism, heights of human achievement, and much, much more. Additionally, I have often thought of the ways we assess those experiences. For me, tears have often served as a reliable barometer. My sweet mom often referred to me as a chillon (crybaby), since it didn't take much to start the flows of tears from young Hank. That proclivity extended into my adult life until this very day. I have been known to cry over what many might consider frivolous matters: the loss of a hard-fought game, a sentimental scene in a movie, or a kind compliment or gesture sent my way. At other times, the tears flowed often surprisingly as a result of some experience that I could easily label as "spiritual" in nature.

After my mom retired, she volunteered for a program called "Foster Grandparents" in the San Jose area. The program recruited seniors to assist staff at a state hospital with the care and mentoring of handicapped and developmentally disabled children. My mom loved her duties and her co-workers, but mainly she fell in love with the children. She loved all of the kids, but also formed a special affection for a little five-year-old girl by the name of Stacy affected by Down syndrome. She might have been originally drawn to Stacy because it was also her granddaughter's name. When we would talk on the phone, she would chatter on and on about Stacy. I was not only pleased but also happy that she had found a fulfilling activity in which she was so thoroughly engaged.

I was living in L.A. at the time, and one day mom called and informed me that she was coming to visit me by announcing, "Some of my kids are competing in the Special Olympics at UCLA, and I have to go support them." I reluctantly agreed, but reminded her that I didn't do well at those kind of events, not because I considered them sad but because they were so positive and inspiring.

The day of the event arrived, and I took my mom to Drake Stadium, where I had the privilege of competing in Track and Field against elite athletes like Olympic gold medalist Rafer Johnson. The memories of that level of high athletic performance juxtaposed against the aspirations of that day's less-than-perfect competitors, triggered my emotions as expected. While my mom was having a great time hobnobbing with and cheering on some of "her kids," I was having a hard time keeping it together and periodically suggested to her, "Mom, can we leave pretty soon?"

I was doing pretty well, until the gun went off in a 50-yard race for twelve-year-olds. As I watched a little guy on crutches, dragging one useless leg and running dead last, far behind the pack, I was struck by the expression of fierce determination, commitment, and grit on his face, one that matched any I'd ever seen in fellow athletes like Rafer or myself. Yes, the tears quickly engulfed me and, fearing those around me might consider me a little weird, I fought mightily to hold back sobs. Why? I'll never be able to completely understand or define the experience, but I have no difficulty in calling it spiritual—certainly the extraordinary spirit of that child was not in question.

Hope, empathy, gratitude, or compassion perhaps played a role in stirring my soul. My mom just called it love.

She finally consented to leave, and as we walked back to my car we passed by Pauley Pavilion, UCLA's famous basketball arena. Mom couldn't resist, and she convinced me to take a peek inside. As we walked into this temple of athletic prowess, I noticed the impressive hanging banners telling of the many Bruin national basketball championships. What was even more impressive was the eerie silence in that huge hall, one whose walls had heard the deafening cheers of thousands. As we looked down from halfway up the bleachers, we saw imperfect bodies striving for perfection on the floor of the arena, competing in gymnastics by moving through routines on a balance beam only several inches off the mats.

Again, I was moved as before and didn't feel terribly eager to linger. As mom and I were ready to turn and leave, two burly, young men boisterously entered the hall where we were standing. With UCLA Football inscribed on their sweatshirts, I quickly assumed they were major jocks and guessed they had been working out nearby from the sweat on their brows. As they entered and stood next to me, they quickly became subdued and quiet, noticing the serious event taking place below. As we all watched together for a few moments, I think they sensed and respected my deep level of interest and reverent attitude.

They acknowledged me, nodded, and whispered, "Wow! Cool, that's pretty cool." As mom and I left, I agreed with a smile and said, "Yeah, that's very cool." They smiled back, and I walked away thinking that maybe my tears weren't so weird after all.

Over the years I have been fortunate to experience rare but special moments, feelings of oneness, wholeness, or connectedness with life and the universe. The episodes can be called peak experiences, euphoric, blissful, even mystical. Although often unexplainable, I have never felt the need to assign the experiences to some unknown, traditional deity.

If the impulse to worship something beyond us, sometimes referred to as the sacred or divine, has to do with the unknown or, better said, mystery, then I have much to worship, appreciate, and venerate. I stand in awe of the profound mystery and vastness of the universe. I stand in awe of the complexity and tenacity of living organisms. I stand in awe that I am part of the energy and matter formed in the distant reaches of time and space. More importantly, I stand in awe of the precious gift of life, and feel a profound gratitude for each breath that fuels and feeds my spirit and consciousness.

Comic Relief

During the period of my dad's illness, I took on odd jobs here and there. I also tried my hand at a comedy act with Howard Kaminsky, Mel Brooks's cousin. I had met Howard in a play at Cal and moved into a Berkeley flat with him and his girlfriend after my marriage ended. Howard sported a brilliant comic wit, undoubtedly running in the genes, which kept his friends and others around him in a state of constant laughter. One afternoon he tried to talk Stacy Keach and me into joining him in creating a comedy team. Comedy albums were hot then, and Howard was convinced he could write and perform one that would make us all famous. Stacy liked the idea, but finally admitted he wanted to continue focusing on the more serious side of acting. On the other hand, I thought this might be my ticket into the world of show business.

Howard and I went to work and created a two-man comedy act, largely due to Howard's natural and superb ability to write funny stuff. I contributed a good sense of timing and a repertoire of accents and dialects that worked well for the straight man of the team. In a short period we were able to land some gigs, including dates at a Peninsula club called The Embers and two San Francisco venues, Coffee and Confusion and McGowen's West. Although I enjoyed it, I quickly discovered that performing stand-up comedy presented a terrifying challenge. Surviving performances where barely a trickle of laughter came back to us on the stage created a special brand of anxiety I will never forget. Fortunately, we also experienced moments of welcomed laughter and applause.

During the summer of 1963, we decided to move to the Lake Tahoe Stateline area, a kind of mini-Las Vegas on the Nevada side. There we tried to get jobs in the casinos and in our spare time worked on fine-tuning the act. We kicked around for several weeks but failed to land jobs. Giving up our hopes of stardom, I returned to Berkeley, and Howard and his girlfriend headed back to New York.

Broke, and with no immediate prospects for working as an actor, I became discouraged, despondent, and even depressed. I actually stumbled around Berkeley for a while in a state of vacillation and numbness. For a time, I considered disappearing, changing my name, and moving to New York to take a crack at becoming an actor there. In the midst of contemplating the complete abandonment of my ex-wife and children, I realized that action would have certainly caused my family to disown me. I woke up one morning and realized that my kids desperately needed me to go out and land a paying job. In the fall of 1963, I moved to Santa Monica, started my job as an insurance adjuster, and tried to find another path toward fulfilling the precarious goal of becoming an actor.

During some of my more pensive moments, my mind would wander back to my troubled childhood and Pauline Lewis standing at the Hobson Street Bridge—to what I remember as a sense of unfulfilled dreams.

PAULINE AT THE HOBSON STREET BRIDGE

Eyes pleading to a distant sea
As if invoking some lush island to appear,
Sought out among imprisoned reeds,
Who ignorantly anchored in their captive mud,
Could never know the paths
Of radiant colors darting through a coral reef,
Ascending mountains forged by goddesses of fire,
Or bleached soft beaches echoing the ocean's chant.

To wherever you have flown
Off to your phantom, made-up place
I too would like to go.

~ 1979

Chapter Twelve
A Big Leap Forward

It wouldn't have been real difficult for junior high school to end up a whole lot better than it started out. Things were looking up. I was one of the most popular boys in school, and I was doing okay in my classes. I had a cute girlfriend and some pretty good pals. Even better I was having fun and making money playing music. I still didn't play sports as much as my buddies Tony, Frank, and Eddie, but I was no longer as skinny as I used to be either. I'd gotten a lot stronger, and as always no one in the whole school could outrun me.

One day my gym teacher Fred Silva told me about an annual junior high city track meet that was coming up. He wanted to put a Peter Burnett Junior High School team together and enter the meet. He said I should compete in the 100-yard dash and anchor the 440-yard relay team. He also wanted me to enter the broad jump, an event I'd never even heard of let alone tried. I told him I didn't know anything about it, and he said not to worry that he would teach me.

We didn't have a great place to practice, like a real track. Our track amounted to a circle of hard dirt around a field and covered with enough strewn rocks to bruise your feet if you weren't careful. A path through the weeds with a pile of sand at the end of it made up our broad jump pit. As bad as our pit was, Mr. Silva started teaching me how to run down the path and mark my strides so I didn't step past the takeoff board. He told me they called that crow-hopping. He kept telling me I could do well in the event if I tried hard, that I had a good chance of taking first place at the meet. I didn't completely believe him.

I started practicing regularly, but I didn't think I was very good. The ninth grade record was 17 feet, 11½ inches, and I was lucky if I reached seventeen feet on a couple of practice jumps. I kept practicing anyway. I even quit smoking three days before the meet, figuring that would help me get in shape. My friend Tony was also running in the relay, so we practiced passing the baton every day.

The track meet was going to be held at a new high school in San Jose called Willow Glen, so a couple of days before the meet my dad drove me there to try out the track and broad jump pit. When I got on that smooth perfectly flat track, I couldn't believe how it felt under my feet, almost like it was pushing me forward. The broad jump pit was also new and filled with beautiful, clean sand. The springy runway made me feel as if I could fly. It was so different from our crummy practice field I started believing that it might turn out to be more fun than I thought.

Although he didn't say much about it the day of the meet, my old man drove me to the track and stayed to watch. The first event I competed in was the 100-yard dash, and I easily beat everybody. Then it came time for the broad jump. I was a little nervous before my first jump, but I ran down the runway as fast as I could, hit the takeoff board perfectly, and jumped 19 feet, 2 inches right off the bat. Was I surprised. Wow! I had just broken the city record. When it was time for my second jump, I was feeling a lot more confident and thinking nobody was going to do as well. I took off again and this time I hit 19 feet, 6 inches. Now the other boys in the event were all coming up and saying, "Hey, great jump. Man, where did you come from?"

I met this real friendly guy by the name of Frank Ragone from Hoover Junior High. He was also competing in the event and complimented me by saying, "Hey, man, you're good."

When it came time for my third and final jump, I was feeling and acting pretty cocky and bragging out loud, "Maybe I'll go for twenty feet. Yeah, hitting twenty feet would be crazy, man."

I took off, and again I hit the board perfectly and leaped up and out, stretching as far as I could. As I did, I felt as if I was never going to come down. While I was flying through the air, I heard the crowd let out a big, loud gasp. I knew I had jumped a long way, but I couldn't believe my eyes when I came back to see the tape measure, and it read 21 feet, 2 3/8 inches.

The man who was the official for the broad jump event said to me, in a southern accent, "That's a mighty fine jump young feller."

He asked me where I was going to high school and broke out into this big grin when I told him Lincoln High. As he patted me on the back, he let me know he was the track and football coach there and was looking forward to seeing me next fall. My new friend Frank came up to me after taking second place and also breaking the broad jump record. He congratulated me again. As he was leaving, he said, "Hey, I guess I'll see you in high school. Are you going out for football?"

Without even thinking or knowing, I answered, "Yeah, sure."

He said, "Great. I'll see ya."

After that our team also won the relay and took the ninth grade championship. I had never seen Mr. Silva so excited and happy. He kept saying, "I knew you could do it, Hank. I just knew it."

My dad picked me up after the meet and all he said, kind of quiet like, was, "Good job." He was not all excited like Mr. Silva, but he had a look on his face I've never seen before. I think he was proud of me and surprised by what his kid had just done, but he just didn't have the words to express it. I thought it was okay. I was getting plenty of praise from everyone else.

The next day I was over at Columbus Park. As I was standing there, my friend David ran toward me with an open newspaper. As he got closer to me he started yelling, "Man, hang on to your jockstrap. Wait 'til you see this." He showed me the sports page and a huge headline that read, "Olguin Cracks Broad Jump Record in Junior Track." I had never seen my name that big in the newspaper and had never felt that famous in my life, not even when I was playing piano and singing at a big dance. At that moment, I thought that maybe I could become a sports star.

When I returned to school after my big day, many of my teachers, especially the male ones, congratulated me. My classmates thought it was great too, but some of them seemed jealous. Bill Gamez was one of them. He and I had never gotten along real well since the seventh grade when he started bullying me. He hadn't picked on me for a long time so maybe he was wondering if I had gotten tougher.

One day at lunchtime my friend Bill Gonzales got in a fight with a guy named Ismael, a friend of Gamez's. The teachers broke it up pretty fast. But as a bunch of us kids were heading back to the school building, Gamez started shooting off his mouth with stuff like, "That asshole Gonzales started it. It's his fault, and he should get in trouble."

I answered him, "You're full of shit. Ismael started it."

Gamez then said, "Oh, yeah? Well, you want to go at it too?"

I shot back, "Yeah, why not?"

Without waiting I punched him in the nose, and we really got into it. We fought for quite a while, and the same teachers that broke up the other fight finally broke up ours. When it was all over, Gamez had a bloody face, and I didn't even have a scratch on me. I didn't feel one bit sorry for him. It felt like I had gotten even for three years of him pushing me around.

The fight got me in big trouble, and my mom had to go to school to meet with the principal. Since it was just a few days before graduation, it was possible they wouldn't let me participate in the ceremony. It was too bad because I had been selected to perform in part of the program. After thinking it over, I guess the principal and some of my teachers decided to let me graduate, but they punished me in another way. A couple of days before graduation day, we had a final school assembly where they handed out awards to certain students. I was supposed to get an American Legion award, along with certificates and blue ribbons for my three first-place finishes at the track meet. Before the assembly, the principal called me in and told me I would receive my awards, but that she would not present them to me in front of the assembly. Just that fast, there went the glory I expected to enjoy in front of all my classmates. I was disappointed, but I thought the fight was worth it.

For the most part I was looking forward to going to high school, although I hadn't been too sure about attending Lincoln High. There was a part of me that wished I could attend James Lick High, the school my friend Johnny Orozco attended and where they had a great music program. At first I had mixed feelings about my new school, but my record-breaking broad jump and my future coach's reaction to me afterwards made me feel a little more comfortable about going to Lincoln.

Something that worried me a little was that the school was located in a pretty ritzy part of town with a lot of big houses. My friend Lannie said it best, "I guess we're headed for the west side country club now." I was sure a bunch of rich kids with nice clothes and nice cars went there. We definitely lived on the other side of the tracks, and it made me wonder what kind of treatment guys from my neighborhood and I would get. Also I didn't think many Mexicans lived in the area near the high school and wondered if that would affect me. I decided I was not going to let it worry me too much.

Tony Realmonte's father worked as the foreman at Mission Valley Cannery and hired all of Tony's neighborhood pals for the summer, including me. Working in a cannery was a whole lot better than picking fruit, and it paid better money too. With the cash I earned, I bought some neat clothes for high school and looked forward to buying a car. As soon as I turned sixteen, I'd get my learner's permit and then my license. Man, I thought how great that would be to have more freedom than ever before.

I was having a great summer. Going to the movies and the beach with friends who could borrow their parents' cars was fun. Besides, my parents didn't tell me what to do much anymore. I supposed they had given up and felt they had lost control of their son. Daphne was still my girlfriend, and one day Bill Gonzales and I talked her and her friend Marilyn Townsend, whose nickname was Butchie, to go all the way up to San Francisco with us on a date. We wanted to go to Playland, which was a giant boardwalk and amusement park with neat rides, a roller coaster, and other fun stuff. Bill got to use his dad's nice car, and we went up there for a few hours just like the older kids. It made us feel like we were already in high school.

Daphne's parents would never have given her permission to go up there, so she had to lie by telling them that we were going to a movie in town and then out for a malt or something afterwards. A couple of days later Daphne had a serious talk with me. She told me that she was feeling guilty about lying to her parents. She also said that if something would have happened to us that far away from home that it would have really upset her folks, so she decided to never do that ever again. I figured Bill and I would have to find some other dates the next time we wanted to drive to the big city, girls that were rowdier.

Just before the end of summer, I started wondering again what some of the kids at Lincoln might think of Mexicans, especially the rich, White kids. I was pretty sure they probably didn't like them. From time-to-time, I still also questioned if my friends in the neighborhood like Tony and Eddie thought of me as a Mexican. With them I really didn't care. By making a completely new group of friends in high school, I thought that maybe no one would ever guess I was Mexican. I looked forward to not having to think about it.

Off to a Good Start

When we got to high school, almost all of my friends from the neighborhood went out for football. Tony, Eddie, Jim, and Bill were all going to try out, so I decided to join them but with not much confidence that I would do well. My mom had to sign some permission form the school needed that allowed me to play, and for some stupid reason she made a big deal out of it and said she wasn't going to sign it. She said she worried that I would get hurt. It sounded like a bunch of malarkey to me. Rene took my side and really tried hard to talk my mom into signing the form. She had recently married a guy by the name of Nels, had a nursing job, and owned her own house so she didn't have any problem talking back to my mom—not like she used to when she was younger and living at home. My mom kept arguing with us, sounding like an old broken record as she repeated, "What if you get hurt? You're going to get hurt."

Frustrated, I finally got mad, looked her straight in the eyes, quietly and deliberately said, "Take your pick, football or fast cars." She must have believed my threat because she quickly reached for a pen and signed the form.

The head football coach Lee Cox was the man who saw me break the broad jump record and grinned when I told him I would be attending Lincoln High. When I went out for football, he acted happy to see me, but then I barely ran into him again because he was the varsity coach. All the sophomores like me had to start out playing on the junior varsity (JV), and our coach was a nice but tough man by the name of Art Boland.

All those hours spent in junior high playing the piano at dances and listening to jazz sure didn't prepare me to become what I hoped would be a hotshot football player. Even though I wasn't very good at the game and it was hard work, I was going to keep playing and trying to get better. After a couple of weeks, Gonzales quit the team and not long after that quit school. He said he wanted to be a truck driver and make a bunch of money. The money sounded good; the truck driving sounded crappy. I didn't see much of him once he left school.

After arriving at Lincoln High, I had to start making new friends and was happy to see Frank Ragone out for football too. He's the guy I had met at the track meet who was also broad jumping. He was still friendly, and I felt like we would probably become pals. He introduced me to another nice guy, Denny Dudley. These two had known each other a long time because they went to the same junior high school together. Because they had played sports all through grammar school and junior high, they were real good football players and easily made the first string on the junior varsity team. I was just learning how to play so I was way down on the third string. It was a little discouraging, but as always I was the fastest guy on the team and believed I could improve.

It finally came time for our first game. We played the San Jose Tech varsity. Although it was a varsity team, it wasn't a very good one. The players were just older. Since I was a third-stringer, I cooled my heels on the bench for most of the game. It felt lousy because Daphne was watching, and I sure wanted to get in and play to show off. Too bad she left early. Late in the fourth quarter with the score tied, we were backed-up to our own one-yard line. On third down and nine yards to go for a first down, Coach Boland sent me in to tell our quarterback Dudley to punt the ball from deep in our own territory and then hold them on defense.

Because Dudley had become a pal, he decided to let me try getting us out of the hole, so he handed me the ball on a straight running play up the middle. Before I knew it, I was past the line and started dodging guys chasing me like I was a crazy, scared rabbit. I didn't know what I was doing or how I got by so many tacklers, and once I got past the last one none of them were fast enough to catch me. I finished my ninety-nine yard run with a game-winning touchdown and everyone in the stands cheered wildly. When my teammates slapped me on the back and congratulated me over and over again, it all felt like a dream.

The next day at a school rally for the varsity game, Coach Cox announced that this young sophomore had run ninety-nine yards for a touchdown to win the JV game, and that Lincoln had a great future in football. The whole school cheered like mad. I loved the glory and believed a little more that high school was going to turn out to be more enjoyable than I thought. Yeah, I definitely liked the idea of becoming a sports star.

~ FAST FORWARD ~

Coach Lee Cox

Recognizing my natural raw talent and speed, Lee helped me become a competitive athlete during my three years in high school, utilizing a personal brand of instruction, discipline, and, best of all, down-home humor. Hailing from Oklahoma, he never lost his engaging accent and ability to teach some valuable lesson by using colorful language and anecdotes.

One day while returning home from losing a track championship by a slim margin, some of my teammates and I were calculating how we could have won it if just one or two events had gone our way. Coach Cox lifted his impressive six-foot-plus frame into the aisle of the bus and whimsically offered, "You know what you boys remind me of? Y'all remind me of the two hobos under the railroad trestle. One said to the other, 'If we had some ham, we could have some ham and eggs, if we had some eggs.'" He concluded with, "Now, just go lick your wounds, boys." As usual, his boys got the point, and we stopped trying to change something beyond our control—a lesson well learned.

During those years Lee became like a second father to me. Fortunately, it happened at the same time my dad and I were growing further and further apart. Lee's concern for my performance on the field matched his keen attention to my grades and extracurricular activities. I'm sure my mom considered Lee a true godsend, as she and Lee would communicate at critical times throughout my high school years. Certain my mom was now happy she had signed the permission form, I assumed she had found an ally in Lee to help tame her wild teenage beast. Once when Lee got wind that I was considering joining a high school fraternity, an organization clearly outlawed at the time, he offered his opinion and implied admonition in his usual tongue-in-cheek manner. He said, "Although it hasn't happened as yet, and I'm not completely sure it will, I would certainly be deeply disappointed if I heard that one of my star running backs had anything to do with an illegal organization."

His less-than-subtle hint forced me to realize I had but one choice open to me, forget joining the fraternity. Disapproving of the crowd involved, Lee terminated the discussion with, "Remember, son, if ya' lay down with dawgs, ya' git up with fleas."

On many memorable occasions, I heard Lee exercise his wit and distinctive verbal style. Scrimmages seemed to bring out his best expressions, ranging from eloquent abuse to heart-warming praise. When my teammates and I were not shaking in our cleats from his stern castigations, we were struggling not to fall over with laughter. I believed that half of the time Lee made up some of his sayings on the spot as well as the way he chose to pronounce certain words. I think he intentionally played the dumb hick role for effect. For example, he would occasionally refer to a grove of eucalyptus trees that grew at one end of the practice field. I was almost certain Lee would intentionally mispronounce eucalyptus to get the team's attention. Lee would stretch out his long arm, point at the trees and order, "All right, I want you boys to take a great big old, grandma turn around them u-cal-a-PEET-us trees and come back here ready for a dawg-eat-dawg scrimmage."

Coach Cox was big and tough but tender as well. At the beginning of my junior year right after I'd been promoted to first string, I injured my ankle in practice. I tried to run during the warm-up before an important game but could not cut or move well enough to play. The team went out for the kickoff, and I sat alone in the locker room, head bowed and in tears. From nowhere, I felt Lee's large, strong hand on my shoulder as he said, "Your day will come, son. Your day will come."

Lee had stayed behind long enough to help ease my deep disappointment and more importantly to challenge and inspire one of his boys. Several years later as I ran on the field at the Rose Bowl as a starting running back, Lee's inspirational prediction echoed in my mind.

Returning for Lincoln High School games during and after my football playing days at Cal gave me great pleasure. Seeing Lee beam with pride over my athletic accomplishments always reminded me of the day we first met at the junior high track meet, the day when I first saw Lee grin with anticipation over my athletic potential.

Throughout those high school years, I often wondered if Lee knew or even cared about my Mexican background. He certainly had other Mexican players on the team. Good players such as Alvin Valdez, Joel Vasquez, and Don Munoz all received Lee's fair and equal treatment. Discussion or mention of the issue never reached Lee's ears, as was the case with so many other people in my life. I felt such a strong sense of affection and acceptance from Lee that I often wished I could have been more open about doubts and anxieties regarding my heritage. Today I'm almost certain Lee could have offered some form of comforting wisdom to ease my concerns. After all, Lee was an "Okie," the name sometimes used then as a demeaning slur to describe people from Oklahoma or other dust bowl states.

As I entered high school, I had intentionally begun to lessen the possibility of being readily identified as Mexican, a pattern that would persist throughout high school, college, and into early adulthood. Putting the Mexican side of me in the closet became a gradually more important priority. Athletics and my relationship with mentors like Coach Cox served as a welcomed diversion, helping me to feel more a part of the mainstream in spite of another part of me lurking in the shadows.

Many years later, my tribute to Lee clearly transcended ethnicity, focusing only on the respect and admiration I held for my beloved coach.

THE SCRIMMAGE

All right, you lily-livered
Poor excuses for a team,
Time to have a serious scrimmage,
Dawg-eat-dawg style, hard and mean.

Or maybe you'd prefer
To be out dancin' with the girls,
Sippin' Kool-Aid and romancin',
Tippie-toein' little twirls.

Real football players are rougher
Ten times tougher than you boys.
Time to grow up, sweat and suffer,
Time to put away the toys.

No one here should be mistakin',
War and football can be hell.
It's a game of give and takin'.
What you'll take just time will tell.

So let's go, let's see some blockin'.
Cut that run back like a knife.
Never let me catch you slackin',
Lest you want to lose your life.

And when you think you're tired,
Dig down deeper, deep inside.
There you'll find out what you're made of,
Learn the measure of your pride.

Now we're lookin' like a team.
Now we're clickin', yes siree!
That's the effort I've been wantin',
Gather round boys, on a knee.

Well, I reckon that you're ready
For that championship game day.
You've worked hard, deserve to be there.
You've grown up I'm proud to say.

Win or lose, I'm on your side men,
Don't forget that, come what may.

~ 1995

Hank trying to act tough

Olguin Cracks Broad Jump Record In Junior Track

Woodrow Wilson, Edwin Markham and Peter Burnett Recreation Centers won division championships while seven records were shattered and another tied in the San Jose Recreation Department's annual junior track and field meet yesterday afternoon at the Markham Field.

Scoring 22½ points, Wilson copped the seventh grade title. Markham had 24 to annex the eighth grade crown and Burnett tallied 31 to grab ninth grade honors. Record breakers were Bob Sanchez, Rudy Herrera, Joe Stabile, Franklyn Fernandez, Ed Katen, Jack Searfoss and Henry Olguin. Running a dead heat for first, Pat Call and David LaDuca equalled the 60-yard dash standard for seventh graders. Olguin broad jumped 21 feet 2⅜ inches for a new record in the ninth grade class.

Chapter Thirteen
In With the In Crowd

High school was looking like it might turn out to be the cat's pajamas after all. For starters, my ninety-nine yard touchdown run shined the spotlight on me, taking everyone by surprise including me. New friends like Ragone and Dudley started making me feel as if I could belong to this whole new group of kids. Lannie was also attending Lincoln and, of course, remained a buddy. The problem was that he was new too, and he didn't know any many more of these kids than I did.

I also started palling around with three seniors, although I was just a lowly sophomore. I couldn't figure out why these three big-wheel seniors, Bill Bumgarner, Dick Smith, and Bill Thiest, had taken me under their wing and become my friends. They had probably been listening to Sandie who was always saying nice things about me. She was also a big-wheel senior who liked introducing me to her friends, all gushy, by bragging, "This is my friend and next door neighbor, Hank. He's very talented and is going to do great here at Lincoln."

When we were alone she would tell me, "Henry, I'm so proud of you." At the same time she stayed on my case and tried to be stern with me by saying, "By the way, how are you doing in your classes Henry?" When I gave her a quick okay, I often got a kind of doubting look followed by an accepting smile. I didn't mind her butting into my business and sometimes even telling me what to do because I felt she really cared about me.

Hanging around with Bumgarner, Smith, and Thiest was great because not only did they like to take care of the little sophomore they also had cars or could borrow their parents' cars so we could go cat around. They would often playfully pat me on the head to remind me of my subordinate status. Other times they liked to kid me about my long hair by calling me a greaser. I would for sure get all shook up if I thought they were using that word like to call me "Mexican," but I knew they were just talking about guys of any nationality that acted like hoods and wore their hair and dressed a certain way. One day in the gym, Thiest stirred up some trouble for me by saying to a couple of the older guys, "What do you say we give Hank a nice little hair cut?" I put up a pretty good fight, but they finally wrestled me down. In spite of the serious threats, they ended up just clipping a couple of well-chosen strands of my greasy mane. I started thinking that maybe I should get a shorter haircut like some of the other guys, that it might help me fit in more.

Man! I kept thinking my new friends sure were White. They probably hadn't lived around too many Mexicans although there were plenty of them at Lincoln. It didn't take me long to figure out that the Mexican kids at our school fell into four different groups.

The first group was made up of kids that probably hadn't been in the States very long and were not very familiar or comfortable with the way we lived here. That's probably why they walked around acting almost as if they didn't want to be seen, with their heads and eyes slightly lowered. Their behavior made them appear overly shy and polite or as if they were ashamed of something. The clothes they wore, although clean and neat, looked as if they had been handed down from older brothers and sisters, kinda worn out and old-fashioned. Their hairdos also seem handed down. They liked to stick to themselves and didn't get involved in many school activities. Maybe they would have gotten more involved in stuff if they had been invited. I figured they mostly spoke Spanish, but I never heard them because they were so quiet, especially when non-Mexican kids came around.

Although I wasn't friends with any of those students, I got a feeling of what some of them were going through. I didn't like that a lot of the White kids looked down their noses at them because they were different. Sometimes I just felt like walking up to some of them and saying to them in Spanish, "Hey, don't worry about them. You're as good as anyone." Of course I never did. If I had done that, I might have lost some of my popular friends. For some reason I thought that maybe someday I'd gather the courage to do it.

The second group consisted of Mexican kids who had taken on what was left of the pachuco style, including pegged pants, ducktail hairdos, and thick-soled shoes. Their exaggerated swaggers and scowls communicated an attitude of, "Don't get in my way gringo (White person) unless you want trouble." Some of the White kids called them cholos and didn't get anywhere near them. There weren't too many of them at Lincoln High, probably because most of them had already dropped out of school. We would see many more of them when we'd go downtown and drag the main. I occasionally saw a really strange site at dances: a Chinese guy who hung around with the Mexicans and looked and acted just like a real Pachuco. I thought that was pretty weird and wondered where the hell he came from.

Those kids spoke pretty good English but also liked to use pachuco talk with words like Chicano for Mexican, vato and ese for man or guy, and carnal for brother. I'm sure everyone outside their group thought of those boys as troublemakers or juvenile delinquents, although I never saw them get into many fights at our school. They mostly fought among themselves with the gangs over in the slums on the east side where most of the Mexican people in town lived. I was sure they were as tough as they acted, and I wasn't in any hurry to get into a fight with any of them. They were the kind that might pull a knife on you and not hesitate to use it.

The third group included kids that seemed to be more interested in their cars than anything else. They drove these fine custom-cars, lowered, chopped, and channeled, with paint jobs so clean and shiny they hurt your eyes. They all dressed real sharp and in the latest styles, especially when they attended dances where they outdid everyone else on the dance floor with their smooth moves. I especially liked the way the girls in this group, sometimes called "fast girls," looked and acted, although I wouldn't necessarily want one for a steady girlfriend. A lot of them had a loose and sexy style, swinging their asses when they walked down the halls in their tight sweaters and skirts. Every once and a while I thought it might be more fun to go out with some of the "fast girls" rather than the "nice girls" I dated.

The Mexicans that belonged to this group would hang out with all kinds of different kids of all races. I think what they all had in common was staying out late, going to parties, smoking, and drinking. More than wanting to make trouble, I think they were more interested in having a ball twenty-four hours a day. A part of me envied them because they seemed to have so much fun. Since all those kids spoke perfect English, I guessed they did all right in school, but I doubted that many were outstanding students or interested in going on to college.

Kids belonging to the fourth group were more involved in school. You might say they were like everyone else. Some were in sports, others in choir, orchestra, or pep squad. They seemed to be more popular and more accepted than the Mexican kids in the other groups. Guys like Rene DeLuna, a cartoonist for the school newspaper, and Carl Castro, a top student, formed part of this group. Some of those students may have been Mexican but had probably decided not to make a big deal out of it—just like me. There were others that didn't have Mexican names but to me kinda looked Mexican. I imagined there were many ways to hide if you wanted to. Sometimes I couldn't tell from some of their looks, but I wondered what they were all about because of their names. One of these fellows was Kenny Martinez who didn't look or act Mexican one bit. He was one of the big wheels at school, or as we used to say, "one of the boys." I was positive he didn't want to be thought of as a Mexican. At the time I thought I wouldn't be surprised if some day he changed his name. I learned years later that, sure enough, he changed his name to Martin. At times I wished I could have gone up to him and asked what his story was all about, asked what made him tick. Of course, I would never do that but I sure was curious.

I was real glad my name didn't sound Mexican. If it did maybe I would have thought about changing it too. I wasn't sure. Sometimes I got just plain tired of having to think about all that shit. It was a real pain in the ass, and I wished it would magically all go away. Somewhere deep inside me I knew it never would.

Mike Strayer and Nate Hygelund qualified as a couple of the hippest cats I'd ever met at Lincoln. Both were great jazz musicians. Mike played a mean sax, and Nate tore up the vibes. They definitely owned the best jazz chops in school. We'd get together and jam even though they were much better than I at improvising. Sometimes my sophomore English teacher Richard Frost would join us. A tall, skinny cat with horn-rimmed glasses, he played the hell out of the drums. Because he looked as young as some of the students and loved jazz just like the rest of us, I really liked talking to him, sometimes even during class. One day he said to me with a smile, "I don't mind shooting the breeze with you during class as long as you realize that while you're up here the other students are studying, which means that you probably won't earn a very good grade from me." I told him I understood and kept on talking about jazz as long as I could. I was probably headed for a C in the class, but I didn't care. At the same time, I knew that at some point I was going to have to get more serious about my studies.

I had several friends that were just as mad about jazz as I was. We listened to jazz whenever we could, even during lunchtime at school. We also loved going to hear live music every chance we got. We especially looked forward to hitting the Jazz at the Philharmonic concerts where we could see and hear cats like Gene Krupa, Roy Eldridge, Oscar Peterson, and the great Ella Fitzgerald. People used to go wild at those sessions, and during some of the solos the crowd would start yelling in unison to the rhythm of the music, "Go, go, go, go." It was really crazy, man, sometimes a little too crazy. At one of the concerts I attended, some crazy guy threw a bottle from the balcony causing a big pop and the sound of scattering glass right near us. The cops came and took him away.

I was so gassed by those concerts that I decided it would be great to produce one at our high school. We had all the musicians and a school gym big enough to stage it. I proposed the concert to some of my teachers and to Mr. Hunter, the Boy's Vice Principal, and they all agreed to let me produce it. I had never been so excited about a project and jumped right into it, getting Mike, Nate, Mr. Frost, and others to perform.

The concert also gave me the opportunity to play the piano, sing, and backup a vocalist by the name of Sandra Smith. It came off perfectly, and all the kids thought it was the greatest, almost like the real thing. Successfully producing the concert made me even more popular, and I felt like I was flying high. I started thinking that maybe I could become a concert producer when I got older.

Crazy Teenage Stunts

Lots of kids my age got their kicks by doing crazy stuff. Some of the boys, especially the ones that owned hotrods, hit the streets and had drag races with their cars out on country roads. Others played "chicken" by driving their rods right straight at each other at full-speed. The guy who turned away first got tagged as a chicken. I knew I'd have to be real loaded to play that game and never found the guts.

One night during Easter week vacation, I did something that's crazy enough. Chuck Bailey and I stayed at Dick Aniger's folks' cabin in the Santa Cruz Mountains for a few days. A bunch of our friends were staying over in Capitola for the week right on the beach, so the three of us went over to see them in Aniger's souped up '50 Ford. That was some fast car. After drinking more than our share of beer at a party, we came back over the hill on highway 17 at 3:30 in the morning. Aniger asked if we wanted to see just how fast his car would go. After egging him on, he hit eighty miles an hour. He had to take all four lanes of the mountain highway to do it while we laughed and hollered at the top of our lungs. Man, that sure was a blast, but I couldn't help thinking the next morning that we were lucky no cars were coming the other way.

Highway 17 went from San Jose to Santa Cruz and had several sharp, dangerous curves. Since my friends and I headed over to the beach whenever we could, we spent plenty of time on that road. The many wrecks that took place on it proved just how dangerous it was. Bart Fanning, another friend of mine, wanted to try out the new, used car his mom bought him, a cherry Studebaker. He decided the best way to do that was by racing his cousin Lynn over the hill in his Porsche. On one of the curves Bart lost control and ended up on the wrong side of the highway going against all the oncoming traffic. The way he told it, he had two choices: hit the big cement truck roaring down on at him head-on or yank the steering wheel and take his car over the cliff. He chose the cement truck.

They say when the cops arrived Bart was nowhere to be seen near what was left of his mangled Studebaker. They kept scratching their heads and wondering where in the hell he went. Just when they were about to give up on him, Bart came slowly crawling up out of the brush and trees on the side of the cliff that saved his life, groaning, scratched, and bloodied but alive. I guess he made the right choice. If he had gone over the edge, he would have been long-gone forever. The weight of the car would have plunged him to the bottom of the ravine, hundreds of feet below, a fall he could not have survived. Right after that, Bart's mom did not buy him another car and probably never did.

On another occasion, Thiest, Bumgarner, and I decided to jump in Bumgarner's old jalopy and go to a party way up on Loma Prieta, the Spanish name for dark hill—more of a mountain than a hill in a remote part of the Santa Cruz Mountains. After the party we planned to go over to the beach and spend the night in our sleeping bags. We asked Bumgarner if he thought his old car would make it. He said it would but was a little worried that he didn't have a jack in the trunk in case we got a flat tire. We decided it was not that big a deal and headed for the mountains anyway, like on some big adventure.

Halfway to the party, we heard this bump, bump, bump. We stopped the car on a narrow, dark mountain road, took a look and discovered that the right rear tire was flat as a pancake. The three of us realized the pickle we were in and began to figure out what to do. Bumgarner told us he had a small hatchet in the trunk and wondered if maybe we could cut down a tree limb and somehow lift the rear of the car. At first we asked if he had completely lost his marbles. We then decided it just might work and that it was worth a try. Good thing we had the flat in the rear. If a front tire had gone flat, we wouldn't have been able to lift the front end of the car housing a heavy engine.

After trudging around the forest with a flashlight looking to create a jack from mother nature, we finally found a long limb with a curve at the end that would give us the leverage we needed to lift up the car. We then began the tedious job of chopping the limb off the tree with Bumgarner's dull little hatchet. We took turns, and after a lot of huffing, puffing, and cussing we finally got it done. No easy job. We then put the curved end of the limb under the axle, held it in place with a bunch of rocks, pushed down on the limb, and lifted up the back end of the car—a true work of mechanical ingenuity. Bumgarner then took the flat tire off and began to put on the spare.

As he was about to put it in place, the limb suddenly slipped, and the rear fender of the car slammed down on top of the tire. Bumgarner jerked his hands out the way just in time, and looked at us with wide-eyed disbelief and gratitude that the fender didn't chop off his fingers. The tire, amazingly, held up the car even though not perfectly in place. Thiest and I then rushed to lift the rear of the car again while Bumgarner hurried to get the spare on to the bolts and tighten the lugs as fast as he could. When he finished we all collapsed on the dark country road in the middle of nowhere, let out a major sigh of relief and silently offered up a reverent, "Thank you."

As we finally drove off heading for the beach, since it was too late to go to the party, we were laughing and feeling pretty smug that we were able to pull off this miracle. Mainly we felt grateful that Bumgarner still had the means to use a typewriter, comb his hair, or play with his dick.

Very little of my life revolved around home in those days. The place was about as happy as a morgue. I was surprised my parents were still married. Half the time they yelled at each other, and the rest of the time they acted as if the other person didn't exist, even when they were in the same room. I didn't know what the problem was, but I sure didn't want to spend any more time around there than I had to. My mom walked around with this sourpuss, pained look on her face, and my dad grunted more than he spoke to anyone. I think the only time he smiled was when my sister Rene came to visit. She always perked him up. When I was not involved in school activities, I was out of the house hanging out with my friends, and my parents seemed content to let me do it. They must have thought it wasn't worth the effort to get into big fights over what I was up to or where I was going.

Every once in a while my dad would say to me, "Why don't you stick around here and learn to do some man's work?" By that he meant carpentry and the similar stuff he liked. He still liked to build his cedar chests with all this wood he got from all over the world. I was sure he would have liked me to help him with the chests. When I would make the excuse that I was too busy, he would just grunt. One day as I was walking out the door with my track shoes to go work out, he said, "Going out there to run around in circles again, huh?" I actually thought that his comment was pretty funny and I chuckled under my breath. My dad loved baseball and didn't think too highly of track. I thought just the opposite. I'm sure he wished I had been a baseball player, another big difference between us.

I tried to find jobs whenever I could because I hated to ask my parents for money. Again, I worked at Mission Valley Cannery during the summer. It still paid good dough and that helped me make it through part of the year. The rest of the year I also worked on weekends over at the car wash and still played with a combo at dances or parties every once in a while. That gave me the spending money I needed. Rene also would slip me a few bucks now and then. Of my whole family, she was the only one who took a real interest in what I was doing, especially in sports. My mom and dad couldn't seem to find the time to attend any games. Mom used the excuse that she was afraid I'd get hurt, and my sister Lucy was too wrapped up taking care of her husband and son Louie to even give me the time of day.

My mom had been trying to learn how to drive for years, but she just couldn't seem to get the hang of it. Letting out the clutch and stepping on the gas all at once seem to be her biggest problem. Without learning how to do that, she couldn't drive worth a damn. She'd easily get all shook up, and instead of a smooth release of the clutch and an easy pressing of the gas pedal she'd turn it in to a series of leaps and jerks that made the car look like a giant, metal frog bouncing down the road. Anyone who happened to be in the car, sometimes me, got tossed back and forth so hard we were in danger of getting our heads torn off. It didn't help that my dad had no patience teaching my mom to drive or that he sometimes tried to do it in his big, clunky pickup truck. They would start out fine, but always end up in a fight. I tried to help a couple of times, but I didn't do much better.

My dad bought my mom this nice little 1941, yellow Chevy Coupe, hoping she would learn to drive once and for all. Just when my mom started to do a little better, disaster struck. One day I came home after school to see that one side of the cement block wall with the red brick trim that surrounded our front lawn was demolished. Cement blocks and bricks were scattered all over the lawn, looking as if a giant fist had punched the wall in just the right place and sent the pieces flying. I couldn't imagine what could have caused such a mess.

As I walked in the house, my mom didn't hesitate to confess, as if wanting to get the episode over with. She admitted plowing the Chevy into the wall, her haughty, justifying tone of voice making it sound as if the wall had run into her. In her next indignant breath, she implied that it was somehow the mechanical monster's fault and declared that she would never drive another "damn car" again as long as she lived.

I felt sorry for her in spite of her trying to cover it up. I knew how embarrassed she must have felt. I wished that I could go to her and say that it was all right and make her feel better, but I didn't know what to say. She sat silently for a while sensing my empathy, and then said, with an air of detachment, "Now, your dad will probably let you use the car to drive to school."

When she told me that, I almost let out a yelp but managed to control myself. Minutes later I went to my room, and it was all I could do to stop from screaming with joy through my clinched fists and teeth. Man-o-man! I finally had my own car. Wow! I couldn't believe it, but I still felt sorry for my mom. When my dad got home and before he told me I could have the car, I volunteered to help him fix the wall.

~ *FAST FORWARD* ~

Ozzie, Harriet, and the Beats

Getting through high school can be difficult for many students, at times traumatic. The peer pressure to fit-in, conform, and go along with the crowd apparently has not changed much since I attended high school, but perhaps it was greater in the 1950s than it is today. Few would argue that conformity played a major societal role during the post-World War II era.

When I entered high school the country had been involved in the Korean War for two years. In addition, the "Cold War" was raging, and Americans were living at the height of the "Red Scare." On February 9, 1950, Wisconsin Senator Joseph McCarthy delivered a speech in which he claimed to have a list of two hundred five people in the State Department who were known to be members of the American Communist Party. Although the House of Un-American Activities Committee (HUAC) had previously been investigating communist activities prior to McCarthy's pronouncement, especially in the Hollywood motion picture industry, McCarthy chaired his own committee to investigate communist subversion. His finger-pointing actions created an anti-Communist hysteria in the country that lead to what many have called a national witch-hunt, destroying the lives of countless innocent Americans often by mere innuendo.

At the time most teenagers were probably not terribly concerned with the political machinations of the day, including me. I was too busy trying to fit in, trying to be part of the atmosphere of "going along"—one that the spirit of McCarthyism may have partly inspired and fueled. In 1952, Dwight Eisenhower, the commander of the victorious World War II European forces, ran as a Republican against Adlai Stevenson for the presidency of the United States. My father, being a life-long, diehard Democrat and a delegate to two democratic national conventions, greatly admired Stevenson, especially for his role in President Franklin D. Roosevelt's "New Deal" efforts. During the 1952 election, I displayed about as much political sophistication as a turnip. Due no doubt to the majority of my friends saying that they supported Eisenhower, I too went along with the crowd and started mouthing the popular political slogan of the Republican campaign, "I Like Ike."

Although my dad paid little attention to what came out of my mouth in those days, when he heard me parroting the slogan he quickly challenged me by saying, "So, what do you know about it, mocoso (snotty-nosed kid)?" When I could justify my position only with silly generalizations, my dad dismissed his son, walked away, and uttered under his breath, "Goddamned little Nazi." Today the whole incident brings a smile to my face, realizing that my dad knew infinitely more about the issues than I did. At the same time, I regretted that neither of us could find a way to engage in a serious discussion, one that undoubtedly would have enlightened me and made me feel more in line with my dad's philosophy.

Aside from the political influences of the day, many Americans were buying into the "happy-go-lucky" suburban lifestyle promoted by TV shows such as *I Love Lucy, Father Knows Best*, and *The Adventures of Ozzie and Harriet*. Although our family seemed very different from the ones depicted on television, I too wanted to somehow buy into the society's ideal—undoubtedly the result of unrealistic thinking. Many of my contemporaries also admired and emulated the squeaky-clean images of film personalities such as Tony Curtis, Tab Hunter, Doris Day, Cary Grant, Rock Hudson, and Grace Kelly. I also remember longing to look like some of the male idols of the day.

For many Americans a harsher reality of life existed far from Hollywood's and TV-land's ideal. The White middle class may have been experiencing a sense of optimism and opportunity in this decade aptly referred to as the "apathetic '50s," but racism and poverty were keeping many locked in the backwaters of society. School segregation, lack of political power, and institutionalized racism suffered by many African, Latino, Asian, and Native-Americans were issues low on the list of concerns for most Americans. Although somewhat better off, minorities such as Italians and Jews sometimes still struggled to claim their piece of the American dream.

I never forgot the first expressions of prejudice I ever heard against a Jewish person I actually knew personally. I overheard a high school coach, who will remain unnamed (certainly not Coach Cox), referring to one of his players as "a cocky little Jew" for refusing to follow one of his directions. The coach in question failed to see me sitting in the coaches' office when he stormed in and blurted out his comment. When he finally noticed me, he merely chuckled nervously and went about his business as if nothing of any consequence had occurred. On the other hand, I was so naive that I had never considered the demeaned player as someone different. To me he seemed just like any another White kid and a nice one at that. I remember being shocked by the coach's attitude and at the same time grateful that I didn't wind up the target of the same disdain. I often wondered if the coach knew or cared that I was Mexican.

During those years everyone seemed to be living in a kind of dream world, pretending that all was well, playing a game of ostrich. I too was having too much fun to pay much attention to serious matters. I was playing a similar game regarding my ethnicity, pretending to be someone other than myself. My slogan could have easily been, "What they don't know won't hurt them—or me." While I battled with my personal challenges, the society in general began to struggle with its own opposing forces.

Underneath the bubblegum facade of the 1950s, rumblings were beginning to be heard of a gathering "cultural revolution" destined to explode in the '60s. The arts—including film, music, literature, and painting—were slowly beginning to express an underlying dissatisfaction with the conformity and materialism of the era. Nothing in pop art expressed the trend more dramatically than the new against-the-grain acting style and films of actors like Marlon Brando and James Dean, a development that began to reel in my interest.

An early Brando film, *The Wild One*, featured a rebellious motorcycle gang that took over and terrorized a small town. *On the Waterfront,* another Brando film in which he gives an Academy-award-winning performance, looked at the harsh existence of dock workers in New York coping with tenement slums and a corrupt union. In *Rebel Without a Cause*, James Dean played an alienated teenager in a story depicting juvenile delinquency as a problem not just confined to minorities and lower classes living in the inner city but one that also occurred in the affluent suburbs. One of Sidney Poitier's early films, *Blackboard Jungle,* directly confronted the problem of disillusionment and rebellion among youth in a ghetto high school setting. It was also one of the first films to use rock and roll in the soundtrack, a development that must have alarmed, if not terrified, many White middle class parents.

Other works stirring up trouble came from writers of the "Beat Generation," a group of intellectuals highly critical of the blandness and uniformity of American society. By romanticizing their bare bones, bohemian lifestyle, they attacked the "Ozzie and Harriet" notion of American values. Jack Kerouac's novel *On the Road* and Allen Ginsberg's poem *Howl* best exemplified the dissatisfaction of the "Beat" subculture. Involvement with alcohol and drugs, interest in aspects of African American culture such as jazz, and experimentation with new forms of sexual freedom rounded out the subculture's focus. I also remember my obsession with J.D. Salinger's book *The Catcher in the Rye.* Many of us youngsters identified with the honest talk of teen alienation and angst the book dared to explore.

More condemnation of the decade's conformity, specifically regarding the social-climbing values of white-collar corporate executives, came from books such as Sloan Wilson's *The Man In the Gray Flannel Suit* and William Whyte's *The Organization Man.* Even in the world of painting, abstract expressionists such as Jackson Pollock were shattering conventions and pushing the envelope.

To what degree those forces began playing on me would be difficult to assess. I sensed the undercurrents and trends more than I understood them intellectually. Although I certainly bought into the culture of conformity, I didn't feel terribly uncomfortable or threated by the rebellious wave of non-conformity beginning to swell. Although walking around in my own world most of the time, I'm sure I heard liberal and anti-racist comments from my parents, especially from my dad who had fought the establishment in his own way during his union organizing days. My easy acceptance of and admiration for African Americans came from my fascination with the jazz scene. I also considered great Black athletes such as Jessie Owens, Joe Lewis, and Jackie Robinson heroes.

A major challenge to the mores of the establishment occurred with the popularity of rock and roll surging into the lives of teenagers in the second half of the decade. Elvis of course led the way, but countless other artists contributed to the frenzy, notably Chuck Berry and Little Richard. Parents worried that this new form of music would corrupt their children, maybe even lead them into the depths of juvenile delinquency. White teenagers turned on by Black artists must have given countless mothers and fathers across America many sleepless nights.

As rebellious as rock music seemed to parents, my friends and I who were totally into jazz considered Rock & Roll innocent, silly, and unsophisticated. We often referred to the rock instrumentalists disdainfully as "honkers and squeakers," ridiculing the simplicity of the music. Without a doubt we were snobs about our musical preferences and considered the new musical rage as pablum for the younger teens and about as dangerous as a pussycat.

To me the symbols associated with jazz seemed much more defiant and representative of an unconventional underground lifestyle. That may be why the "Beat Generation" naturally gravitated toward jazz forms. On the East Coast legendary players such as saxophonist Charlie Parker, trumpeter Dizzy Gillespie, and pianist Thelonious Monk broke down all sorts of musical boundaries in creating an aggressive, innovative style of jazz called Bebop.

As much as I admired and respected the mainstays of the Bebop era, I identified and immersed more in a style known as Cool Jazz or West Coast Jazz. One of the leading trumpet players of the Cool Era, Miles Davis, actually named an album *Birth of the Cool*. Other great players such as saxophonists Stan Getz and Art Pepper, pianist Bill Evans, trumpet player and singer Chet Baker, popularized the sounds of the Cool Era. I considered this music as part of my soul. Everything about it seemed alluring, mysterious, even intoxicating.

Loving the new cool sounds, I was still hooked on the big band flights of Stan Kenton. One night he came to San Jose to play at the Palomar Ballroom, a night indelibly locked in my memory. I went to the performance alone, stood by the stage throughout the entire evening, inviting the sounds pouring from those horns to take over my mind and being—to send me on a high that only this music could deliver. During those teenage years, I believed that music could serve as the perfect escape from my personal contradictions, could help me find my unique brand of personal contentment.

A Growing Dichotomy

While American society began to cope with the dichotomy of its smug conformity, juxtaposed against an underlying, creeping rebellion, I too struggled with my own dichotomy, one akin to a dual love affair. I loved being American but could not shake my affection for and connection with my Mexican side however hard I tried—a balance difficult to define let alone maintain.

I welcomed the gifts I received from my American membership: exposure to fresh, new musical expressions; a newly-discovered promise of notoriety in sports; growing popularity and praise from my peer group; a sense of newly-discovered freedom; movies; a particularly intriguing book; fascination with the new toy called television; or just flexing my youthful muscles and immersing in good times with friends. Some might see the list as adding up to a love affair.

What I seemed to care about most was being generally accepted as White—or White enough to be accepted. That standing translated into the advantage of White privilege, of being able to live as a White person with relative ease. Never once do I remember my family being refused service in a restaurant or hotel or being denied access to any public function or event because of our background, appearance, or speech. Unfortunately, that was not the case with many Mexican people at the time, including some my friends at the time and in later years. As I have often admitted, I suffered more from the fear of discovery than from any overt expressions or acts of bigotry aimed directly at me. Notably, ours was the only Mexican family in the entire lily-white congregation of San Jose's First Methodist Church, an experience that remains logged in my memory as thoroughly positive.

Although my life remained primarily clothed in a White American costume, a shadow-self followed me around to remind me of another unshakable love affair. No matter how I tried to silence it, my shadow-self continued to tie me back to old bonds. It never stopped whispering that I belonged to something more, something undeniable, mystical, and precious.

Consequently, I continued to listen to the Mexican music I first heard my mother sing, probably before I could speak, but only in the privacy of my room. None of my buddies would ever be invited over to listen to my mother's records of the great charro (Mexican cowboy) singer, Jorge Negrete, her unique Jarocho music from Veracruz, Argentinean tangos, or Flamenco guitars. As much as I loved jazz, this music also continued to move me and stir a special part of my spirit. During much of my youth, the experience would have to remain between me and the walls of my bedroom—underground, a little like the "Beats."

My shadow-self would also often ask how I could survive without my mom's delicious Mexican cooking. In those days few Mexican restaurants existed, nothing like today. Even if more had been around, I doubt I would have taken a blond, blue-eyed date out to eat tortillas and beans. My mom served as the only source for providing me with the joy of enchiladas, tamales, posole, and gorditas, treats she often shared happily with visiting family friends of all backgrounds. Without those meals I'm sure I would have suffered from some rare, mysterious strain of malnutrition.

My shadow-self would complicate the dichotomy by occasionally stoking indelible memories of my trip to Mexico and two unforgettable, ancient saint-like people, my early Mexican-movie-going joys, affectionate tíos and tías, endearing Spanish sayings, hearing my parents express their patriotism and love of this country, and in the same breath their fondness for their Mexican heritage.

The pesky shadow-self, trailing me wherever I went, caused entanglements and dilemmas. Sometimes it arrived as a welcomed guest while other times as a dangerous visitor, threatening to take away the white privilege I believed I possessed. Now and then I would forget about it, especially in the midst of culturally blind accolades from the crowd or carefree camaraderie with White friends, but not for long. Generally, I lived as a happy American kid, whether friends, teachers or other acquaintances knew of my "Mexicaness" or not, and always with my nagging shadow-self as a constant companion. Caught in a complex dual love affair, I longed to find a way to settle, tame, or muffle the contradictions—but that resolution would have to wait.

SELF-PORTRAIT

Hiding behind a light-skin mask
clown white
layered with centuries of papier-mâché nations
cautiously
looking like a myth

Pretended steps
running from
a counterfeit
pursuing spoof
imposed
grinning
foolish

Ignoring
corn wrapped luscious meats
Spanish words revitalized
soaring Mariachi trumpets
faces baking on patches of crops

Venturing through layered mirrored halls
fearing self-reflected glares
stumbling for emancipating outs

Pealing noisy threats
loud laughterloud

Peeling healing time

Welcoming scars
from a torn mask

~ 1967

Chapter Fourteen
The World on a String

Making the varsity football team was bigger than a big deal, and that first game played at night opened up a whole new world to me. I felt like I was in a movie or on a big stage with all eyes on our team and on me. The stadium lights, the marching bands, the cheers all sent a new surging energy through my body. Sometimes it felt like an overdrive took control of my legs. It hit me just before I ran on to the field. The roar from the crowd sent a jolt of energy traveling from my chest, down my spine, through my hips and into my legs, making them feel lighter and faster than ever. Man, could I move. I guess that's what they call adrenaline.

We had a great team. The newspapers said we could win the Peninsula Athletic League (PAL) championship, and we started to prove it by winning the first game easily. After the win we took the bus back to our high school. All showered up, we ran out of the locker room to be greeted by a bunch of waiting, screaming fans, including all the pretty yell leaders and pom-pom girls. They formed a double line, like a corridor, from the door of the locker room out into the crowd, and as we ran out they patted us on the back and told us how great we were. It all made us feel like heroes who had just won a war. Everyone was yelling, "Championship, championship, let's get the championship." The praise didn't stop there. Afterwards, friends came up and said things like, "Great game, Hank," "Way to go, Hank." or "Man, you were good."

It felt great to have the boys say those things, but it felt better if a cute girl said that to me, especially if along with it she gave me a look hinting that she liked me. I got plenty of those. Sometimes, I thought I played football just for the glory of it or for the admiration of pretty girls. I believed what they said in an old popular song, "You gotta be a football hero to get along with the beautiful girls."

After our games, especially night games, we usually had a street dance out in front of the high school. Very few cars drove by the front of the school at night, so all the kids lined up their rods, tuned their car radios to the same station, turned them way up, opened the windows, and enjoyed a wall of music for a couple of blocks—enough to have a real keen dance. Some of the kids drank beer and smoked. The athletes, including me, didn't touch the stuff during football season, but others doing it made it feel like a real bash.

I didn't have a steady girlfriend at the time. I was just playing the field. Daphne and I had broken up a while back. I was sad for a couple of weeks, but I got over it. The street dances after our games gave me the chance to talk to some of the other cute girls at school and strut around feeling like some kind of star. Nothing seemed more important in those days than having girls go for me, although I really didn't have a lot of self-confidence when it came to dating girls. I pretended I did, but deep down inside I wished I looked different, wished that I would have been thought of as "cute" like Rock Hudson or someone like that. I had kinda bold features, big lips, and a nose that was not exactly tiny. The beat-up nose was mostly the result of my busting it a couple of years before when my dad slammed on the breaks on his pickup, and I tried to remodel the dashboard with my face. Later, I also got my nose kicked in a football game. I'm sure it got broken then too. Both times my parents didn't do anything to fix it.

Because my looks weren't exactly in, I didn't think girls considered me very handsome. Still plenty of them flirted and wanted to go out with me anyway. When girls liked you but didn't think that you were very good-looking, they would giggle and say stuff like, "You have such a good personality, or you're so talented." Even hearing those compliments, I would have rather been thought of as good-looking.

I was shocked when a beautiful, smart, and popular blond, named Babs, wrote in my yearbook, "To a wonderful guy. You have a lot of ability and sexy looks so make the most of them." I thought to myself, wow, she thinks I have sexy looks. It was hard to believe, especially since she was a senior and I was only a junior. One of her best friends, Carol, and I dated quite a bit that year. I even took Carol to her Senior Ball. A junior taking a cute and popular senior to her dance of the year was something. I thought Carol was really cute and fun, and I knew she liked me a lot, but I still didn't have a mad crush on her. I don't know why, but I didn't seem to fall hard for any of the girls I had been dating. It could be that I was afraid they'd find out I was Mexican and tell me to hit the road. Maybe I didn 't want to let them have too much of my heart so they couldn't break it. Maybe I just hadn't gotten over Daphne. She knew me. She seemed safer.

In my mind there were two kinds of girls I'd go out with—good girls and bad girls, sometimes called fast girls. When I went on a date with a good girl, it was to have fun, but a lot of the time it was just to show off, to show that a cute girl wanted to be with me, that I was one of the popular boys. It certainly wasn't for sex in those days. The most we could expect from a good girl was a kiss or two, maybe occasionally something we called a cheap feel. Sometimes if you got lucky, you would end up making out a lot, doing some heavy petting. That wasn't always fun if I made out too much and ended up feeling as if a couple of parts of me were going to explode, and I couldn't do anything about it—at least, not until I got home.

If I got real horny, I did go out with a bad girl from time to time but mostly from other high schools or other parts of town   Bad girls let me get a little more and sometimes they'd surprise me with how much. I liked that bad girls could stay out late at night and didn't worry about what their parents thought. It gave me the chance to go places like the beach, take our time, and have fun for as long as we wanted. Some of our other favorite places to go and make out were the new housing tracts that were going up all over the Santa Clara Valley. Located way out in the boonies where it was dark and no one was around made them perfect settings for feeling a little more than just well liked.

Loving Italians

It's hard not to think of Italians as my second family. Growing up in a neighborhood that was so Italian we had a community grape crusher probably contributed to my loving them. I think there were other good reasons too, mainly childhood friends like Realmonte, Citti, and Brazda (who was half Italian—Czech and Italian, to be exact). My mom made great friends with Italians when she first came to this country and continued to nurture some of those relationships. My dad's day-to-day warm friendships with people like our neighbor, Johnny Sinderella; my sisters' Italian friends; our entire family loving, not only Italian food, but the music, the rhythm of the culture and even the language, so close to Spanish—all added to our natural love for them. Having a stack of high school Italian teammates, classmates, and girl friends with names like Ragone, Tranchina, Rodda, Beltramo, Dirienzo, Genco,

Cusimano, Bianco, Gallo, Bengiveno, Citrano, Tognetti, Lanscioni, Vivensi, Farone, and others. Being embraced and treated like one of the family by the Taorminas, Del Frates, and Di Lorenzos. What's not to love?

More good reasons: Going to festive Italian weddings where they didn't just play music that the young people liked, but where they had to play songs that folks from the old country loved as well—just like Mexican weddings. I especially liked it when the old folks got up and sang at the microphone with the drums, violins, one corny, out-of-tune saxophone blaring in the background, and of course an accordion. Man, how Italians loved their accordions. That's why there were so many accordion schools in our town. I got a kick out of seeing them at parades—truckloads of accordion students slowly driving down the street playing like mad while their parents applauded along the sidewalks, cheering proudly for their little bambinos (babies).

I think I also felt close to Italians because I knew that sometimes they too had experienced mistreatment or insults because of their background. Some of the old-timers at the cannery would tell me about having been called dirty wops or dagos. They complained about everyone thinking of them as gangsters or members of the Mafia instead of hard-working, decent people. I didn't blame them for getting mad about that. I didn't know anyone who was a member of the Mafia. On top of that, my friend Eddie was made fun of when he first came over from Italy because he couldn't speak English very well. Other than his Italian friends, he felt most comfortable around Mexicans because he could understand so many of the Spanish words that were similar to the Italian ones.

I've had a lot of them, but I think my two best Italian buddies were Ragone and Harry Rodda, although Harry had half of something else in him, part English I think. I liked to go over to Rodda's house because his mom was a doll and because his house was big and beautiful. I assumed his folks were rich. His dad, actually his stepdad, had this great high fidelity system (we called it Hi-Fi) that made all of our records sound like the real thing, like we were sitting right there at the concert or the club.

I enjoyed going over to Ragone's house too but for different reasons. His house was more like mine, not nearly as fancy as Rodda's. Frank's mom and dad treated me great, but his dad never said much to me, maybe because he was quite a bit older, like my dad, and didn't speak English very well. When

I'd come up to their house, Mr. Ragone was usually sitting on the front porch swing. When he would see me, he would smile, turn, and yell through the screen door, "Eh, Frankie, itsah Hankie."

It almost never failed, after I walked in, Mrs. Ragone asked me if I wanted something to eat. Whether I accepted or not, she always said the same thing to me, "Hankie, you too skeeny. Eat, eat, mangia." It was hard to resist when the food tasted ten times better than any Italian restaurant I'd ever been to. Almost more than the food, I just loved to sit at the table and be part of this family's jubilant, loving uproar. It never failed to make me feel as if I was home.

All of us loved Ragone, mainly because he was fiercely loyal to his friends. Sometimes, if he'd lose his temper and get mad at one of us, we might have to duck a couple of his lethal punches. Frank's big, muscular frame and quick hands were no match for most of us. Even if his punches didn't land, he would end up crying like a baby and falling all over himself to say he was sorry for losing his temper. If they landed, his apology got even more guilt-ridden and sorrowful.

Frank also loved to make us laugh. One day while several of us were hanging around our high school, his beat-up 1942 Ford sedan came flying around the corner, down the wide, quiet street in front of the school. We all assumed he was going to stop, but instead he kept on going. We all fell over dying from laughter when we realized that he was sitting on the passenger side, with one hand somehow steering the car in a perfectly straight line, and pretending to be having an animated conversation with a non-existent driver. He then turned, with a cigarette in his hand, smiled and waved at all of us. As he drove out of sight, he continued to have a lively talk with the invisible man. Even then I knew it was going to be real hard to forget this guy.

All my Italian friends were American just like me, but I'm sure they were more accepted as Americans than Mexicans were. That's because we saw more Italian actors, movie stars, and musicians that were popular, attractive, and well liked than we saw Mexicans—stars like Frank Sinatra, Connie Francis,

Tony Bennett, and Dean Martin. Although some of them were pressured into changing their names, I think we all recognized them as Italian. If we didn't know their backgrounds, some of my Italian friends were quick to point it out. No doubt about it, Americans liked and accepted them. It also helped that they didn't have Italian accents.

So who were the actors we got? Duncan Renaldo, playing a goofy character like the Cisco Kid, and Leo Carillo, playing his dumb sidekick, Pancho—fat, dopey, and definitely not American. The Mexican accents were, of course, always there. I'm sure many Colored people felt the same way about Amos and Andy and Stepin Fetchit as I did about the Cisco Kid and Pancho. They were all so unreal it wasn't even funny. Then we had actors like Fernando Lamas, Ricardo Montalban, and Katy Jurado. They got big roles in movies, but they always had to speak with these thick Spanish accents and never acted like regular Americans. The only exception to the rule I can think of was Anthony Quinn. I happened to know Quinn was Mexican, but I wondered how many other Americans knew or cared about that fact. I suppose some of them may have guessed it when they saw him in the movie *Viva Zapata*.

As much as I loved Italians, I guess I was a little jealous of them. I even wished I could be Italian at times. I think they got a better deal when it came to reputation in this country, way better than Mexicans. Still I knew I would always think of Italians as my famiglia (family). I had a pretty good idea what an Italian/Mexican wedding would look, sound, and taste like. Something told me one of those was bound to take place soon.

Many Roles

One of the classes I enjoyed more than any was Radio Arts. Mr. Kendall, our jowly, constantly smiling teacher, introduced us to the fields of radio production, writing, news- reporting, and acting. I saw him as a balding bundle of warmth, a comfortable old uncle who was genuinely interested in exciting his students about the stuff he taught. Some of the kids thought of him as corny and old-fashioned. In spite of sometimes fitting that description, he knew how to get me all worked up about acting and telling me I had a talent I should develop. He encouraged me to audition for a special radio adaptation of Shakespeare's *Macbeth*, and I landed the lead. I had never performed Shakespeare in my life. At first, I found the words difficult and strange, but with Mr. Kendall's help I began to discover the mystery, magic, and joy of those stories. Because it was a radio production, I also got to play one of the three witches, a role that allowed me to croak, screech, and cackle—great fun. I was hooked.

I did so well in the part, that even my conservative English teacher Miss Ogier was surprised by my performance and complimented me by saying, "You handled the Elizabethan English quite nicely, Henry." She maintained some high standards, so I was flattered. All this helped me decide to take a drama class and audition for the school play.

I landed one of the leading roles in my junior year's school play, *The Night of January the 16th*. The play dealt with a murder trial in which the members of the jury chosen from the audience were asked to untangle the complicated evidence. We prepared and rehearsed two different endings so we could close the play with one or the other depending on the verdict presented by the real live jury. Rene came to the play and was selected as one of the jurors. She thanked her baby brother for the enjoyable experience.

One day a new kid showed up in my acting class, complete with greasy hair and a cocky attitude that for some reason I found appealing. His name was Ves Nolan, and he had just moved to San Jose from a town north of San Francisco called Corte Madera. I discovered later that he came from a rough neighborhood and got in a lot of trouble up there.

Anyway, he and I were assigned a scene to perform in class that called for southern accents, and I soon decided that he was a good actor. He wasn't as interested in acting as I was, but he was crazy about jazz like me. He actually knew a whole lot more about the subject than I did. He raved about unknown players I'd never heard of, especially in places like New York, Chicago, and Kansas City. He also played baseball and the saxophone, the former much better than the latter. Mainly, I liked the guy because he was a pretty cool cat, had a good sense of humor, and best of all dug jazz.

One day we were talking and asking each other that damn, stupid question people always asked, "What are you?" I often wondered why the hell the question wasn't, "Who are you?" That would make more sense. Anyway, I gave him my now usual answer, "Spanish and French." He then came back with a bold, almost boasting, "I'm Irish and Mexican," the Mexican part said without any kind of apology and with the same brash tone as the Irish part. I was floored. I didn't know of anyone walking around in those days bragging about being Mexican. Ves definitely qualified as different. He had his own style, and a part of me envied him. I wished I could declare my Mexican background with the same bravado. I considered starting to tell people that I was Spanish, French, and Mexican. That would have been closer to the truth. I decided against it—too risky.

After Ves and I became friends, I made the mistake of telling him about the Spanish name my family used to call me when I was a little kid, Quiqui, the nickname for Enrique. Although I explained to him that my real name was Henry, he started teasing and calling me Quiqui with a devilish, dumbshit giggle, sometimes even in front of some of our friends. I regarded that as a dirty, lousy, stinking stab in the back. The sonofabitch must have guessed about my Mexican background and was trying to blow my cover. I was left with no way to tease him back except by calling him Sylvester Pussy Cat, the character from the cartoon, and making fun of his lisp. I hated that it didn't get to him very damned much. Lucky for me he didn't call me Quiqui all of the time. It's probably what saved our friendship, that and going to a kick-ass Chet Baker concert together where we were entranced by the unique sounds of the master jazz trumpeter and singer. We both understood what really counted—listening to and immersing in thrilling improvisational flights. One thing's for sure, Ves didn't give a damn that I was Mexican.

I did my best to balance my new interest in acting with sports. The theater usually took a back seat, and by now music had taken a seat even further back. One of my friends, Mark Hammer, who played the district attorney in the school play, also loved acting. He loved it so much, he talked three of his buddies, including me, into doing a one-act play called, *If Men Played Cards as Women Do*, just for the fun of it. We performed it at school and for a couple of service clubs. This funny sketch that everyone liked helped hook me even further into the thing called acting. Playing roles came naturally to me, and I did it well even in real life. Becoming an actor after I finished with sports seemed like a good option.

Maybe this? Maybe that? What role should I play today? I never seemed to stop asking that question. I continued feeling like a character with two personalities, the American me and that Mexican shadow-self. At other times, I felt like I embodied even more selves than that, a bunch of different people trying to stuff themselves into a borrowed or rented body.

I wanted to be a hero, and I wanted to be a rebel. I wanted to be well liked, and I wanted to not give a shit. I wanted to be cute, and I wanted to be rough. More than anything, I wished I could scream out to everyone, "Hey, see this? All these selves you see are the real me." Instead I put on a costume and, depending on who I was talking to, pretended to be what I presumed that person expected. The script called for constant adjustments and realignments. An act, all right. I thought, yeah, maybe I'll become an actor.

~ FAST FORWARD ~

Love, Romance, and Marriage

A preoccupation with girls and the kind of girls that found me attractive persisted beyond my high school and college days. When they became women and I a man, we moved beyond mere light-hearted dating, and I discovered my lack of preparation for lasting, healthy relationships. Three failed marriages glared back at me from the mirror of my life and bore witness to that sad fact. Today, having finally experienced a nurturing, loving marriage for more than twenty-five years, I have often questioned how my struggles with questions of ethnicity may have affected those early failures.

If I had any lingering worries about being acceptable or worthy as a young man, winning the hand of my first wife, an upper middle-class, beautiful White girl, should have dispelled them. Pat knew of my Mexican background, although the subject received little focus or serious discussion during our four short years of marriage. Perhaps our immaturity, marrying too young, or simply our lack of understanding of the level of commitment necessary for a long-term, successful marriage affected us more than any of my shadow boxing moves with ethnicity. I have concluded that I will never know the answer with any certainty.

The question of ethnicity played a far greater and significant role in my second marriage. By 1964, I had been working as an insurance adjuster in Santa Monica for several months. Still toying with the possibility of becoming an actor, but with that possibility becoming increasingly remote, I met a woman who admired my aspirations and would eventually become my second wife, Shirley Humphrey.

We met through a mutual friend after she and Shirley became roommates. I remember the first time I saw this blond, blue-eyed beauty walking in the door of their apartment, carrying with her a casual air of confidence that bordered on arrogance. She had the right to be self-assured. Not only was she attractive, she was smart, articulate, and a University of Michigan graduate. I thought to myself that she would not be an easy catch but decided to take my chances and pursue her anyway. We were soon dating steadily and creating a relationship best described as complicated, turbulent, and at times highly competitive.

In spite of failing to find our piece of psychological and emotional harmony, I always respected Shirley for her intellect and for her social consciousness. She was adamant about her positions on civil rights and social justice at a time when many of the country's eyes were barely beginning to open regarding those issues. She always seemed perfectly at ease making friends and interacting with people of all races. With that part of herself, she was thoroughly comfortable. I soon realized that my being Mexican was a matter of little or no concern to her. Other issues loomed as much larger.

By 1965, I had left my insurance adjusting job after getting involved with a get-rich-quick-scheme, an early pyramid sales program that relied on high-powered sales pitches to large groups of people. Since I knew the owners of the company, I ended up training the salesmen and teaching them how to effectively pitch the deal from the podium. In the process, I met a group of blue-suede-shoe-boys (the name at the time for slick, high-pressure salesmen) who wanted to start their own deal in Dallas, Texas. They invited me to go there and help train their pitchmen. I agreed, and Shirley and I packed up and headed for Big D.

Texas soon taught us how naive we had been regarding prejudice and racism in other parts of America. Although far from perfect regarding race relations, California seemed light years ahead of the Lone Star state when we made our move to Texas in 1966. Shirley and I looked around and realized the severity of the discrimination against African and Mexican Americans in our new home. I quickly decided that working in that part of the country with nothing but White folks would require that I go even deeper underground and pass for White like never before. Shirley was not happy with my decision. She went to work as a social worker for Dallas County.

She soon discovered that government provided one of the few places where people of color could find meaningful employment and where she could comfortably interact with them. Since she was pretending to be married to me (we didn't make if official for another year), she took my name and openly used the correct Spanish pronunciation, Ohl-GEEN, probably as her own private protest. In her usual fashion, she made friends with her Mexican American colleagues and learned in more detail some of the difficulty of life for many "Meskins" (the derogatory label often used to describe Mexicans by some Texans).

Shirley and I met some interesting people during that period: one Mexican guy who was passing for Hawaiian, another who thought it was better to be thought of as Native-American than Mexican, and a woman who referred to herself as a descendant of Aztec royalty. We also encountered several, mostly middle-class people who called themselves Latin, a euphemism no doubt designed to soften the sting of the "M" word.

After about a year in Dallas, I went to work for another similar company in San Antonio, and we headed south. Again Shirley went to work for a government entity where she would meet additional Mexican colleagues in a city that sometimes looked as if it belonged south of the border. Although our personal relationship remained troubled, we plunged ahead into marriage. Using the faulty logic that a commitment on paper might carry over into our daily interactions, we hoped we might magically untangle the snares that kept us from developing a truly harmonious bond.

By the middle of 1968, we were seriously considering returning to California. Time had run out for us in Texas for several reasons. Perhaps we had tired of the stifling racial atmosphere and general intolerance we so often encountered, not aimed against us necessarily, but others. I remember us going out for breakfast the day after we watched the police riot take place on television at the Chicago Democratic National Convention—a significant historical event. We were both appalled by what we had seen the night before on national television but perhaps more astonished by the widespread comments we heard the next day in support of the tear-gassing and beating of students by the police. A waitress's cold and angry sentiments frightened us the most, "Now that they've taught them kids a lesson, they ought to go find their parents and whup up on them too." It was time to leave.

The whole time we lived in San Antonio, Shirley had become more vocal and critical of me for not taking some sort of stand wherever I could against the discrimination, as she would say of "your people." She felt strongly that I should be putting my education and talents for speaking and writing to good use in helping to improve the situation facing many Mexican Americans. My answer to her benevolent nagging often took on a defensive stance, "Look, don't bother me with that shit right now. I'm just trying to make a living, and I know what it takes to survive in this society." She never bought my argument and continued to pound on me whenever the spirit moved her.

I both hated and appreciated her persistence because it was akin to the struggle that had been brewing inside of my own skin for a long time. The Texas experience had unquestionably tipped the scales of my own tolerance for the charade I had been playing for years, for the juggling of selves, and for the roles necessary to accommodate to a racist society. I didn't know for how long I had been preparing and refining, somewhere in a concealed envelope of consciousness, a single person or self to present to the world—one that would encompass all of the selves I had developed out of necessity. I hungered to be confident enough to say, "What you see is what you get even if it looks checkered or unfamiliar to you, even if it doesn't fit into a compartment society accepts." The time had come to take my own unique stand.

Shirley and I moved again, back to Santa Monica, California. Shortly after we returned, I decided to begin taking my stand with a simple gesture. I would experiment by using the Spanish pronunciation of my name as an initial open declaration of my true identity. The difficult first test took place in a fine L.A. restaurant on La Cienega Boulevard. As Shirley and I approached the maitre d', I engaged in an internal debate, saying to myself, "Should I use "ALL gwin or Ohl GEEN, ALL gwin or Ohl GEEN?"

The maitre d' addressed me with a cordial, "Good evening, sir, table for two?"

I answered with a tentative, "Ah, yes."

"And the name, sir?"

I then said it, probably for the first time in my life, "Ohl GEEN."

Continuing with his friendly, respectful manner, the maitre d' asked,

"Yes, and how do you spell that, sir?"

After I complied with his request, he looked up and finished with, "That will be about twenty minutes, sir. Would you care to wait in the bar, Mr. Ohl GEEN?"

I laughingly thought to myself, "I'll be damned. He didn't give me a disapproving look or call me a dirty Mexican." I had passed the first test wearing a piece of my new, genuine costume, but not without experiencing a severe case of sweaty palms, feeling alone in unfamiliar territory, and sensing the formation of new emotional synapses. In retrospect, I found it almost amusing that such a small action could cause such a large psychogenic reaction.

Within a few short months, Shirley and I broke up and eventually divorced but remained friends. Too many psychological incompatibilities condemned us as a love pair. Still, I never lost my respect and admiration for Shirley's care and understanding of others and her gratitude for sticking the needle in me when I most needed it.

A Third Try

After breaking up with Shirley, I remained single for a full sixteen years, concluding that perhaps marriage was best left to others more capable of long-term commitments. During those sixteen years, I lived the life of a confirmed bachelor, enjoying a lot of female friends and lovers but definitely no live-ins. I had determined to be a full-fledged free agent. I had also comfortably settled into living my life as openly and honestly as possible, proudly admitting my ethnicity and actively working in my own way to help "my people," as Shirley had so often suggested. During those sixteen years,

I also happily dated women of many backgrounds, including several Latinas, but never found anyone who could move me to dare try marriage again. When I met Chris Worthington and decided to marry her, some of my Mexican buddies jokingly suggested that marrying another Anglo would be severely frowned upon by our ancestral Mayan and Aztec gods. I smugly replied that they could rest assured that this time ethnicity had absolutely nothing to do with the relationship. Today I'm not so sure about the validity of that claim.

Chris and I were both tired of the dating game and seemed well suited and ready to make a serious pledge toward building a sound marriage. She had a lovely little five-year old daughter, Amber, who perhaps captured my heart even more than her mother, and I felt determined to provide her with a happy family atmosphere and setting. Starting a new career in advertising, we moved to Austin, Texas and began a life together filled with great anticipation and promise.

I spent eleven gratifying years working for GSD&M's Advertising Hispanic division. Our team broke important, new ground in the early days of the corporate world's growing focus on the Latino market. I immersed myself in the challenges of serving my clients but also felt my contributions were helping to build a more positive image of Latinos and Latinas. Countless awards for advertising excellence highlighted our success, including two Clios and a National Addy. I was pleased to find a career allowing me to express my creative side in combination with my desire to be of service to my community. I enjoyed close, warm relationships with many Latino and Latina friends and felt I could be myself in a White world like never before. I had reached a tranquil level of satisfaction with my life. Unfortunately, my marriage began to unravel.

Marriage counseling and therapy seemed to almost exacerbate our problems. The impasses and distance between us had become so great that one therapist literally threw up her arms and said, "I don't see any way to help you get through this maze."

Chris and I eventually divorced and went our separate ways for several years, but later reconnected to form an amicable relationship. Sadly, Chris has since passed away, but I still enjoy a loving kinship with my stepdaughter, Amber.

The reasons I failed are not as important as the manner in which I dealt with the wounds I sustained or the attitude toward marriage I adopted as I walked away for the third time. Having tried hard to make a go of it for eight years, I somehow avoided becoming completely cynical. I managed to retain an obstinate, perhaps stupid hope that somewhere out there a person existed with whom I could create a powerful, loving partnership, one that would allow two people to evolve and discover the best of life together. My Mexican friends' words about Mayan and Aztec gods echoed back to me when I met Patricia Obeso Chalkley and learned about the small but significant percentage of Mayan blood pulsing through her veins.

A Slow but Final Burn

I met Patricia through a mutual friend soon after arriving in Austin. Since the two of us were married, we enjoyed a glass of wine together with our friend and then went on with our lives. Years later, while fulfilling her duties as a city councilman's chief of staff, Patricia called me and asked if I would consider serving as a board member with the Austin Convention & Visitors Bureau. Councilman Robert Barnstone wanted to appoint a Hispanic in advertising to the board, and Patricia contacted the only Hispanic she knew working in advertising. I consented and spent a year in uneventful but dutiful service to the community at large.

At the end of the year while attending a political fundraiser, I ran into Patricia. She displayed the usual friendliness and warmth she had projected throughout the year primarily through phone conversations. When she asked me what I had been doing, I answered with a cursory, "Getting a divorce." She immediately answered with a mischievous gleam in her eye, "Me too."

Although strongly attracted to this lovely, bright, and charming woman, I did not exactly rush to sweep her off her feet. In fact Patricia has often characterized my early courting style as, "a very slow burn." We eventually met for drinks, and six hours later we were both surprised to discover how our easy conversation had caused the time to shrink. Patricia seemed more surprised by my stated willingness to give marriage a fourth try than by the accelerated passage of time. Her attitude toward marriage had become a bit more cynical after her own two failed marriages. Nevertheless, she cautiously allowed herself to get to know me over the next several months.

The slow burn eventually became a durable flame. We came together gradually but inevitably. After buying a house and living together for a short period, we decided to marry. Over the years we have worked through the usual, minor kinks of marriage and moved toward sharing our lives with a mutual respect, supportive friendship, sense of humor, and above all an abiding love. I fell in love with Patricia not only because she was pretty, bright, interesting, thoughtful, and generous, not even because she happened to be Mexican, but primarily because she was a genuine lover. She loved her parents (now passed away), her children, her siblings, her aunts and uncles, her friends, good books, music, life, and me.

Along with a couple of select friends, she understood as well as anyone the journey I had traveled to grasp the meaning and place of ethnicity in my life. She had not grappled with the issue in quite the same way as I, but had experienced enough challenges of her own to understand the importance of facing certain realities.

Patricia happens to come from a remarkable, mainstream Mexican American family. She is the eldest of ten children, all of whom are accomplished. All attended college and all but one have college degrees. Half have earned advanced degrees from excellent schools such as Stanford and Cal. These are people who have knocked down their share of barriers standing in their path toward success, due mainly to the influence of determined, driven, and caring parents.

Patricia encountered such a barrier while attending the University of California at Santa Barbara. One semester she had occasion to visit the office of the Dean of Letters and Science for a routine request. She needed a course change she anticipated would present no major problem. While most students would have been given a routine, rubber-stamped approval, she was escorted into the dean's office. The dean seemed disturbed by having to approve her petition. Patricia naively assumed he was just in a bad mood until he looked up from the form, peered coldly over the rim of his glasses and sneered, "Why don't you go back to the fields with your people where you belong?"

The unexpected words struck her like lightening and left her stunned.

She had never experienced such blatant, insensitive bigotry, and it had a devastating effect on her. For a time it damaged her academic performance and worse her self-image. To this day she regrets not reporting the incident. Fortunately, through the support of strong parents (her feisty mom initially suggested, "Let's go picket the pendejo's [dumbass's] office.") as well as her own inner resources, she was able to deal with the terrible assault. Still, it hurt her deeply and left a wound requiring a creative healing process. If her name had been Smith rather than Obeso, I'm sure the myopic dean would not have dared utter the statement, although a number of Smiths must exist in America who have worked in the fields picking crops. She ultimately was able to handle the effects of the incident and emerge with an even stronger sense of self. Patricia and I have often contemplated how others with a lesser support system than hers might have overcome the incident.

As I looked back through the upheavals and uncertainties of some of my relationships with women all the way back to high school—including the madness, sweet moments, and the good and bad times—I feel grateful to have finally found a caring partner and friend who can graciously accept all that has gone before.

THE SUM OF LOVE

Back in the dimming, distant light of my young life,
I tentatively reached for love with timid hands,
Believing that the gods had only granted me
A firmly fixed amount of it to give and get.

While stealing into love's uncharted troves,
I tightly parceled out or hoarded my supply,
Disbursing bits and pieces of the precious stuff
When satisfied the swap would clearly favor me,
Afraid an unfair trade might leave me wanting more,
Might find me on the short end of a love exchange.

And then one night I dreamed I woke alone and spent,
An empty ledger as my only means of sustenance.
Watched phantom love float out away from my locked safe,
While moaning back alarms and warnings to my bankrupt soul.

Before awakening to morning's healing light,
I heard the gentle stirring of love's consciousness,
Enlivened to restate its ancient rule:
"You cannot hope to hold the wind
Though it may kiss your face.
It only comes to see if you can trust in its return,
To see if you have learned true treasures lie
In letting gold slip from your open hands."

~ 1998

Chapter Fifteen
Senioritis

I would have to say that everything went along smoothly my senior year. Everything seemed to be cool except for the epidemic of senioritis, a serious disease many of my classmates and I caught. The symptoms included slacking off, believing you're the greatest, acting like you're on top of the world, that you are the center of the solar system, not wanting to study or take any more exams, feeling invincible and immortal, believing you know infinitely more than your parents and sometimes even your teachers, wanting your frivolous high school days to last forever, and masking your fears and doubts about the future with swaggers and devil-may-care remarks. It was an illness I was sure would pass, but many of us suffered through a pretty good case of it.

In sports, my junior year was a blast, but my senior year began with one major disappointment. The previous year we had won the league's football championship just like everyone predicted. Beating out a couple of the senior halfbacks and becoming first string early in the season put an extra strut in my step, and lettering in track helped put the icing on the previous year's personal sports cake.

My senior year we missed winning the championship by one lousy touchdown, one I happened to score. It was called back because one of our linemen got a penalty for illegal use of hands. Putting his mitts where they didn't belong cost me a touchdown and the rest of the team a championship. As a result, we just had to take our colorful coach's usual advice after losing a tough one, "Boys, just go home and lick your wounds." Lee always said the right thing, but the bleeding and the pain from the wounds didn't stop for weeks after the season ended.

Whenever the subject came up, Ragone, Dudley, Rodda, or I broke into angry explosions of sour grapes and frustration. It was not uncommon for one of us to punch something during the release—walls, lockers, dashboards, and even beach blankets on the sand served as common targets. My compensation for our downfall came from playing with a bunch of great guys and for a one-of-a-kind coach, ending up the leading scorer in the league, and being selected for a couple of all-star teams.

Up until then, I hadn't thought seriously about college. I guess I'd been too busy having fun. Now schools were talking to me about possible football scholarships—Cal, Stanford, San Jose State, and College of the Pacific. I started believing I had a chance to play big-time college football somewhere. The Cal athletic department looked at my transcript and gave me the good and bad news. They told me my grade point average was pretty good, but that I hadn't taken all the right college-prep courses to get into Berkeley. That meant I'd have to spend a couple of semesters at a junior college to qualify. I sort of knew that, having purposely avoided taking any kind of math class since the eighth grade. I escaped sitting through all that boring, exhausting algebra and geometry, but it also confirmed my shortsightedness.

For a while I thought of taking Spanish in high school, but since I had to go to junior college anyway I decided to wait and take it there. Maybe I avoided taking it because my classmates would have learned that I could speak it well and that I had been hiding that fact. I chose not to rock the boat. Whenever I decided to eventually jump into it, I'm sure getting an A would be no sweat. Funny, avoiding doing something you know you can do well seemed awfully stupid. I decided that I was not going to be able to avoid all the academic stuff if I wanted to play football with the big boys. A part of me wished I hadn't goofed off so much and paid more attention to my studies sooner.

Trying to make up for lost time, I took Physiology to complete my science requirement and actually enjoyed it. I liked my teacher Miss Fauquet. In spite of her strict, business-like style and well-starched attire, she had a sweet smile that haloed into her eyes. With pointy-edged glasses that rested on her equally pointy nose, she seemed frail but displayed surprising energy, especially when she tried to be cute and funny. In the male anatomy, the vas deferens is the duct through which sperm travels from the testicles to the prostate. In teaching this fact, Miss Fauquet, with a naughty hint in her high-pitched voice, explained, "Don't forget students, the 'vas deferens' between the male and female reproductive organs." She then chuckled gleefully, probably believing her corny pun to be as funny as any Bob Hope joke. We all moaned quietly but made sure to grin politely.

Dissecting rats that had been soaking in formaldehyde for what seemed like ten years must have sounded like a drag to most people but I found it interesting. Taking the course made me feel good, even smart, especially when Miss Fauquet lavished warm praise on me for completing an assignment well. Informing me that I was maintaining a solid A in her class, she followed it with, "Henry, you're doing extremely well. I'm especially proud of your fine rat anatomy drawings. Keep up the good work." Man, I never thought I'd be complimented for drawing accurate pictures of rat guts.

My dad decided to go away for a while. He took a government job in Guam as a construction supervisor for a government-building program. My mom and dad's marriage boat hadn't totally capsized quite yet, but it was certainly approaching the rocks. Maybe he felt that going away for a while might help restore it. I was just guessing. I wasn't sure if he even thought in those terms, with that strong, silent demeanor covering up whatever might have been slapping him around inside.

A part of me still felt sad that we had continued to drift apart, but I had to admit I was glad he was off to parts unknown. From a long distance, he tried in his own way to start an awkward conversation with me. A letter offering me five bucks for every class I got an A in and every touchdown I made surprised me. The touchdowns cost him dearly. The A's not so much.

With him gone my mom and I discovered that the air we breathed was clearer, the atmosphere less contaminated with missed opportunities, unspoken hurts, and unresolved conflicts. It gave us a chance to know each other better. Since she had totally lost parental control, our relationship no longer involved any attempt on her part to impose her will on me or even to guide me.

Like a frightened doe waiting for her fawn to return to the safety of the forest, she seemed to be quietly waiting for the danger of my wild youthful phase to pass. Perhaps she was praying. I was sure she had seen glimpses of some positive direction in my otherwise carefree kicking around. I think she was most pleased that my football fantasies were pointing me toward a college education. She even revved up the courage to go watch me play in a couple of games, putting aside her obsessive fear of my being injured. She did feel a moment of apprehension when dehydration and the lack of salt caused me to go down and hobble around from leg cramps. It all passed quickly, and I could almost hear her sigh of relief all the way down from the stands.

All of those changes softened my attitude toward her. With my dad gone our roles had taken some unexpected turns. No longer did I feel the need to instantly put up my emotional defenses when she offered advice or automatically dismiss what I had described in the past as her hysterical rantings. I now almost felt protective of her. I had begun to allow myself to feel the threads of her life's pain and disappointments, to tentatively unzip my youthful, defensive cloak and step out towards her with arms open as never before. More than anything, I enjoyed making her laugh. I loved to see her throw her head back, let out a hearty carcajada (guffaw), and playfully dismiss my deliberate antics or silly jokes with, "¡Payaso!" (clown). I decided we were going to be all right.

My sister Lucy, who had long since moved away, was wearing an indelible groove into her life of unquestioned servitude to her demanding husband and family (she now had a daughter).

Occasionally asked how I was doing but remained too burdened to give her younger brother very much energy or thought. My natural love and affection for her helped me not take her lack of interest in my life too seriously, and I accepted that her self-imposed cross preoccupied her days.

Rene, on the other hand, had become my ardent fan, getting out to every football game she could, sometimes with her husband Nels. She also made time to hit as many of my track meets as possible. She seemed totally excited about my decision to try playing college ball and constantly offered me advice and encouragement. She sometimes played it tough with me and gave me an extra push, but I didn't mind. I knew she was on my side one hundred percent. I never questioned that. I appreciated everything about her, from her winning personality to her support of all I tackled. The one thing we never discussed was anything to do with being Mexican. I think she had found a way to not let that interfere with just living her life as a regular American professional woman. I'm sure she didn't know how much energy I assigned to it. Nevertheless, I loved and respected my sis.

I knew she had to be tough working as an operating room nurse. Several times I had heard her telling my mom stories of sad things that took place at the hospital without crying. One day while I was visiting her at one of our family gatherings, she arrived home after a long day at the hospital. As she walked in the door, I noticed her moist eyes. When I asked her what was wrong, she whispered softly, "I'm sorry. We lost our patient today after four long hours in the operating room." As she quietly walked away to gather herself, I saw her rare, vulnerable side and realized that her toughness occasionally deserted her. I didn't like to see her sad.

I wasn't sure my dad would be back before my senior year was over. He seemed to be enjoying himself over there on that island. He bought a 35mm camera and went ape taking pictures of water buffalos, buildings, plants, and beaches. He even started cattin' around the island wearing flowered, Hawaiian shirts. I found that very strange, uncharacteristic behavior for him. Maybe he'd change into a whole new man when he returned, but I doubted it. I didn't give my parents' marriage much of a chance to make it. Sad, but probably true. I just thought I'd wait and see. It made me wonder where a guy is supposed to learn about successful marriage if not from his parents— certainly not from some dopey, unreal TV show like *The Adventures of Ozzie and Harriet*.

Guarded Anticipation

The last days of high school involved trying to hold on to the carefree days while looking forward to new challenges and opportunities. Daphne and I were going steady again and enjoying our last days at Lincoln together. I assumed I was in love with her. I was still not very clear on what that all meant, and found it hard to believe that I had known her since I was eleven-years old. All I knew was that we were having loads of fun going to parties, dances, movies, the beach (getting our kicks at the Santa Cruz boardwalk ranks right up there), snow and water skiing, concerts (the one with the Four Freshmen turned out to be the greatest) or just plain goofin' off.

In the spring of 1955, I found myself walking on the Cal campus with my coach Lee Cox. We were there to compete in a regional track meet. As we passed a cathedral-like grove of Redwood trees on our way to compete on Edwards Field, Cal's track stadium, I felt an almost imperceptible quiver passing through me. It led me to look beyond the aging bricks, the winding paths, the lofty trees; calling me to breathe in the tradition, the spirit of what had gone on before on those grounds; asking me to embrace a thought that had never lived within my imagination.

I felt strangely at home and quietly almost reverently said to Lee, "I think I'd like to come here coach."

He answered with a gentle smile and understated tone, "It's all up to you, son. Just make up your mind." I believed him.

We knew it was all coming to an end, and I guessed that some of us were a little scared of what the future held. The only kids that seemed to be confident were the real smart ones, the ones we sometimes jokingly called bookworms. Kids like Stan Goodman, Nancy Beard, and John Gates seemed to know exactly where they were going. Among them were my buddies, Lannie and Rodda. Harry was heading for Stanford, so I figured we were going to be rivals. I was not as cocky as they were, but I was feeling like maybe my future might have a rainbow or two in it due mainly to my excelling in sports. I ended up as the top sprinter in the league and won our school's Outstanding Sportsman of the Year award. I was pretty happy coming up on graduation.

The Senior Ball, the last big-deal dance of the year before we all said good-bye on graduation day, was upon us. I scrimped, saved, and even hocked a few things for this important day. It took plenty of bread to rent a dinner jacket, buy a corsage, and pay for dinner at the Brookdale Lodge, a beautiful restaurant in the Santa Cruz Mountains with a real brook running through the middle of it. Daphne and I double-dated with Daphne's good friend Pat and my pal Dudley. Feeling completely grown up, sophisticated, and on top-of-the-world, we started the evening with a cocktail party at Johnny Wilson's house then headed for Brookdale. After dinner we danced at the ball until 1 a.m., hit several parties until dawn, and ended up eating breakfast at our favorite drive-in restaurant. We then all went home, changed, and headed for the beach where we spent the day, mostly sleeping. Now that's what we called livin'.

Summer, bathed in a soft sadness after graduation, came and went before we knew it. The time had come to move on. With Daphne going off to faraway Chico State, other friends heading in separate directions, and my staying behind in San Jose to attend junior college, I was left with a strange feeling of loneliness and vague isolation. Perhaps those feelings of uncertainty about the future would pass and be replaced with the confidence to find the fiber, the toughness in me to truly cut it and end up at a great university. One thing I knew for certain, I would never let being Mexican stand in the way of my fully participating in college life.

~ *FAST FORWARD* ~

Believe It or Not

My worrying for so many years of what others might think if I openly declared my Mexicanism today seems like a colossal waste of energy, especially in light of so many positive experiences that occurred after I began to do just that. An incident challenging my declarations of self-acceptance occurred in the early 70s in L.A. A close African-American friend and former roommate, Darryl Dillingham, and I were having coffee with a couple of Darryl's White buddies from high school. They had known each other since their youth, and Darryl's friends felt the freedom to indulge in some light-hearted racial kidding. It seemed Darryl wasn't in the mood for jokes that day so he cleverly moved the conversation toward a more sober discussion on civil rights and racism in America. The discussion took on a serious tone, and I found myself completely siding with Darryl's arguments. At one point, I offered, "Well, I think I can understand Darryl's position on that issue because as a Mexican I've had some similar negative experiences."

The two guys looked at me with shocked expressions on their faces, and one of them asked, in a subdued tone of voice, "Gee Hank, are you really Mexican?—'cause you don't look it."

My response instantly popped into my head out of nowhere as if I had rehearsed it for years. It came out accompanied by a smile as, "Yes, I do. You just don't know what we look like. We go from black to blond and everything in between and sometimes even in the same family."

The other guy haltingly joined in with, "Ah, well yeah, but you must be Spanish, right Hank?

I mean, you don't have any Indian blood in you, do you?" As if to say I hope you don't have cancer.

My answer again came to me unexpectedly when I said, "I hope I have Indian blood in me. I'd hate to feel cheated."

The two guys became less comfortable and the conversation decidedly less animated following the exchange. Shortly thereafter they left, thanking me for helping them to understand something they hadn't thought about much. I assumed that they must have felt disappointed that I didn't take the comment about my being Spanish as a compliment. Maybe they were just unaccustomed to having their stereotypic notions challenged.

What I found ironic is that my boldly asserting my ethnicity seemed to make them uncomfortable. They acted somehow as if they didn't want me to be Mexican, as if they were eager and willing to soften the blow of such an admission. Over the years, I have answered the same question the same way on literally countless occasions. Unfortunately, I'm still often forced to deliver the same stock answer decades later. The pattern can get discouraging if I let it get to me. In earlier days, I truly believed that by the time I hit my sixties the need for such rhetoric would long be over. I wished I could see the day when it would be unnecessary for me to sing the thousandth verse of the same song. Good thing that here in my eighties I haven't lost my voice for the next time I have to sing another verse.

Several years after my encounter with Darryl's friends, I received a phone call from an executive search firm in Dallas, Texas. The firm was putting together a list of candidates to form GSD&M Advertising's new department, a Hispanic advertising team. I gladly interviewed for the position of senior copywriter with the headhunter, a charming, friendly woman. When she discovered that I also had a solid amount of public affairs experience to complement my writing skills, she said, "Well, Hank, I think you're more than a copywriter and someone the agency would find quite valuable." In the very next breath, she then asked in her twangy, Texas drawl, "Incidentally Hank, are you really Hispanic 'cause you don't have an accent?"

I blurted out a knee-jerk answer in my perfectly delivered west coast English, "Why should I? I'm a third generation American." As soon as the words left my mouth, I regretted the smart-ass tone they were dressed in, believing for a moment that I might have blown the deal.

Fortunately for me, she took no offense and ended our conversation with a cheerful, "Well, I'm definitely going to recommend you to the agency Hank."

Several weeks later, after a trip to Austin and several extensive interviews, I landed the job.

Similar questions and responses have emerged in my travels over the years—not unlike a recurring dream or better said a persistent nightmare—my responses often causing furrowed brows and looks implying, "Does not compute." Back In the late '60s and '70s, those kinds of exchanges very often taught me that the more I declared my identity, the more I found that many non-Hispanics had difficulty coping with my self-descriptive terms. Some found the label Chicano particularly distasteful. I remember a White guy I met at a party had the audacity to assert, "Oh no Hank, you're not a Chicano. You can't be."

Even after I insisted repeatedly that indeed I considered myself a Chicano, the refutations continued. I found the guy's attitude astounding in light of his being married to a lovely Mexican American woman.

Encounters such as those convinced me that stereotypes of Mexicans were so entrenched in the minds of many that I decided to create a presentation to help shed some light on the subject and perhaps influence a muddled mind or two.

The "Frito Bandito" Strikes Again and Often

In preparing for my presentation, I decided to dig around, do some research, and find out where some of the stereotypes of Mexicans may have originated and how they influenced the low esteem and even hate felt for the group. I knew that most of the information people acquired about Mexicans and other Latinos must come from the mass media. I also surmised that even if Americans learned about Latinos from personal contact, their perceptions could remain colored by the influence of what they had been fed by the media. Being a serious movie buff, I had seen the endless parade of bandidos, loose women, and other one-dimensional portrayals on the silver screen. I already knew that movies contributed to the countless erroneous perceptions held by many. As I conducted my research, I quickly learned that radio, television, magazines, and even textbooks were also active culprits in the act of tainting our image.

In addition, I found out that some of the thinking behind the negative images held by so many Americans could be traced all the way back to the rivalry between England and Spain during the colonial period. Descendants of those with strong anti-Spanish and anti-Catholic feelings would later encounter what they considered the inferior Hispanic character in America's Southwest during the eighteenth and nineteenth centuries.

The derogatory accounts I read from that period not only floored me but also left me wondering if I should catch the first plane out of the country. One such account, written in 1837, referred to Mexicans as "... cowards, cruel, tyrannical, bloodthirsty, but also humble, sycophantic, crouching, deceitful, treacherous, weak, promiscuous and indolent." A nineteenth century California legislator, G.B. Tingley, expressed the general attitude toward Mexican-origin workers: "Vicious, indolent, and dishonest...with habits of life low and degraded; an intellect but one degree above the beast of the fields and not susceptible of elevation; all of these things combined, render such a class of human beings a curse to any enlightened community."

After reading such vitriol, I thought to myself that if just a small percentage of those attitudes prevailed as I was growing up, my not wanting to be Mexican must have stemmed from an astute sense of reality.

Gathering more information for my speech, I discovered that often advertising practitioners chose to employ Mexican stereotypic images in a highly insensitive manner. Not surprisingly, given the influence of movies, the bandido became one of advertising's favorite devices for getting attention and laughs while trying to sell products in the late '60s and early '70s. In fact the industry seemed almost obsessed with the bandoleered, mustachioed, and crude stock caricatures—the most famous of those being the "Frito Bandito," created for an ad campaign to sell the Frito-Lay Corporation's corn chips. The campaign became highly successful but also created an uproar among Chicano activist groups who persistently and vocally complained about the demeaning and slanderous nature of the commercials. After several years of battles between Frito-Lay and those groups, the "Frito Bandito" was retired, banished to the boot hill of old ad campaigns.

Frito-Lay had plenty of company in using the bandido image. Granny Goose (potato chips), Elgin (watches), Bristol-Myers (deodorants) and Liggett & Myers (cigarettes) all created their own variation on the theme right around the same time. Further, as I took photographs for my presentation from magazines, newspapers, restaurant signs, billboards, and even garden figurines, I kept running into the same old images. I found no lack of similar negative examples. In my presentation I would show slides of those narrowly drawn stereotypes and then, by contrast, show pictures of real Latinos and the incredible range of looks they displayed—to make the point as I had said on so many occasions, "We go from black to blond and everything in between."

Armed with this newfound information, I felt ready to go out and change the world. My "dog and pony show" could now be unveiled before business, student, and any other groups that cared to listen. I had gathered some salient facts about stereotypes, had compiled an impressive photo collection of Latinos of all ages and backgrounds, and taken slides of several variations of the primarily three stock caricatures so commonly seen—the bandido, the loose woman, and the cactus-friendly, sleeping Mexican.

Other than presenting some serious, sometimes shocking materials, I occasionally tried to be entertaining. Taking aim at the producers of American Westerns for their blatant use of stereotypes, I dug into my bag of acting techniques to perform a parody of a commonplace scene from a Western. My attempt to use humor as a teaching device sometimes produced some liberating good laughs, other times just uncomfortable squirms. Here is my version of the typical tale.

It begins with a stalwart, tall, rugged, steely blue-eyed lawman standing in front of the saloon. A group of dusty, rough-riding, unshaven, chattering Mexicans ride up and address the lawman. Grinning to show his corroded teeth, conniving, and cowardly nature, the scar-faced leader of the pack displays his envy and admiration for Anglo possessions by leaning over and saying to the lawman in a friendly but condescending tone, "Hey, gringo, that chure is a nice horse jew have there. How mosh you wan for eet?"

The lawman gives his disdainful, unequivocal answer; "It's not for sale, Pancho, at least not for the likes of you."

The bandit laughs hysterically, along with his compadres (sidekicks), but abruptly stops and with a wave of his hand orders the others to do the same. He then squints, sneers, and threatens, "Okay gringo, okay, but wash out that it don get stolen." With that they ride off, like bouncing rag dolls glued to their saddles, howling with laughter and firing their pistolas (pistols) in the air.

Of course, the bandits posed no real threat because everyone knows that the White, bigger-than-life lawman could single-handedly take care of the whole gang of bad guys if he had to. If they happened to steal his horse, our man will surely bring the sneaky thieves back to justice. Surely, the undeniable moral character and stalwart stance of our hero is the reason that Conchita, who works in the cantina on the Mexican side of town, is absolutely crazy about our hero and constantly begging him to take her lustful body. Therefore, when downtrodden Pedro, the noble dirt farmer, who is in love with Conchita, asks her to marry him she takes the rose out of her teeth, shakes her head, and answers by saying. "No, I can marry jew Pedro. I'm in loff with dee chereeff." So poor Pedro simply walks away kicking the dust, back to his comfortable old cactus plant for another afternoon snooze. Such is life on the sleepy Mexican side of town.

My attempt at instructive humor didn't always work, and my presentation didn't exactly burn up the lecture circuit either. I did find enough interested and attentive audiences to make my efforts worthwhile, to feel as if I was making some sort of difference. Sometimes I would walk away displeased, feeling I had not affected anyone. One such audience involved a college class at USC, as I recall a Sociology class. I arrived to find a very enthusiastic professor and an equally unenthusiastic group of students waiting. My presentation fell flat, instigating more yawns than laughs or approving nods. The majority of the students were not even remotely interested.

As I began speaking, I noticed that several young men attending the class were unusually large and muscular and that one of them could quite easily be Mexican American. It soon dawned on me that they must be members of the USC football team and that the very tall, dark one must certainly be the Trojan's All-American lineman, Anthony Muñoz. I had seen enough pictures of him in the *L.A. Times* sports section to finally recognize him. Anthony was truly an extraordinary player. He later proved his prowess beyond question in his professional career by being named all-pro eleven consecutive times and by being inducted into the Pro Football Hall of Fame in 1998.

I walked away disappointed that Anthony acted as disinterested as the others the day I spoke in his class. That he chose not to come up and engage me in further conversation about the subject disappointed me further. Given my history of struggling with the questions of ethnicity as a young man, I certainly understood that peer pressure might have prevented Anthony from doing so. On the other hand, the issues I raised may not have qualified as a pressing reality in his world.

To this day, I can't be sure what Anthony must have thought about the presentation. I do remember feeling a natural kinship with another Mexican American, west coast, college football player, and I wished we could have connected. Although today more Latinos are playing the game in college, still the numbers are few. In the late '70s when I visited the class, their presence in the college football ranks seemed almost non-existent.

I made the presentation for a couple of years with varying reactions and degrees of success. Very often people of all backgrounds would come up to me and thank me for either enlightening them or setting the record straight, but I often found myself wondering why more people didn't see fit to challenge some of my notions or opinions more frequently. Occasionally, someone would dare to say to me things like, "You know, you people have to learn to laugh at yourselves."

My response to the suggestion often carried an extra bite, "Gosh, we don't mind laughing at ourselves. We have a great collective sense of humor. We just don't especially appreciate others laughing at us. And if we are seen only in silly or degrading roles, that ain't too funny." The discussion frequently ended there.

On other occasions, I would get, "Ahh, come on Hank, what's the harm in those pictures, nobody really believes all that stuff anyway."

To that question, I would sometimes come back with, "Unfortunately, they do believe it. The additional harm comes from the lack of balance. No one would mind the occasional negative portrayal or news item if they were balanced with a fair amount of positive ones."

I would argue further that, if along with gang members, prostitutes, and maids, Hispanics were seen as business people, doctors, teachers, and even poor, uneducated people as honorable, hardworking and dignified, I wouldn't be so upset. I often finished my assertions by remarking that the dissemination of negative pictures clearly outweighed the positive ones, an assertion true to this day maybe more than ever. After addressing a group of faculty and students at the Graduate Theological Union, a consortium for advanced theological studies centered in Berkeley, California, I finally decided I would stop making the presentation. My friend Hector Lopez, a staff member of the Center for Urban Black Studies, invited me to speak to the group. He found himself excited about the prospects of some lively exchanges and debate, thinking that students and faculty members at this academic level would not hesitate to challenge my opinions or conclusions. I discovered as I had with so many other groups before, that they were strangely quiet, almost sheepish after hearing the presentation. One polite question out of the whole bunch, then a quick move to the refreshments, caused me to think seriously about this all-too-common pattern. I asked myself what I might be doing to cause the reaction, or lack of it, and took a long, honest look at all aspects of my words and delivery. The realization struck me as if I'd been slammed hard at the line of scrimmage for no gain, and then a voice in me calmly and unwaveringly stated, "Man, you're a fraud."

In the beginning I had convinced myself that I was making the presentation to teach, inform, and help others understand the practice and impact of stereotyping. Certainly, an honest part of me wished to accomplish those lofty goals. Another part of me had an ulterior motive that my brutally candid, inner voice clarified further, "Pretending to enlighten, you are simply working out your anger and frustration on your audiences."

When I asked the inner voice, "What anger?" It replied, "The anger for all the extra bullshit you've lived with all your life as a result of being Mexican. Face it."

I decided immediately the voice was correct. I realized I had been standing up there dressed in my preppy glen plaid suit, with a feigned carefree, objective attitude but with my fists cocked and implying, "Come on, all you White people, I dare you to take me on. And if you do, I'm going to run right over you."

The competitive fervor of my football days had not yet fully ended. The text of my presentation may have included well-turned phrases about the injustice of racism and discrimination, but the running subtext delivered an underlying fierceness that no doubt intimidated many.

Those realizations caused me to stop the speech making, reevaluate, and admit that I still had some important healing to do if I were to reach for a higher level of self-actualization. An equally valuable insight came to me soon after. Because of the preponderance of false, misleading images non-Hispanics took in by the media, I stopped blaming and judging people as harshly for their attitudes towards Mexicans, however damaging. What else should they be expected to believe after years of unrelenting conditioning by the mass media? I truly came to believe that to some degree they too were victims of the same misinformation, of the lies fed them about their Latino neighbors and fellow citizens. Why should they see Hispanics as a good and honorable people if the majority of pictures they took in communicated the opposite?

I realize that today Hispanics must still live with an old collection of stereotypes, the most prevalent being the brand perception as foreigners or recent immigrants. In spite of a Hispanic presence on this continent since before the Pilgrims, the brand image persists. While recognizing that Juan, or several Juans, may have crossed the river from Mexico or Central America just last night, I wish more Americans understood that Juan is not the whole story, however necessary and courageous his reasons for coming here may be. The Spanish settlement of St. Augustine, Florida is the oldest city on the U.S. mainland, founded forty-two years before the English colony at Jamestown, Virginia. The establishment of Santa Fe took place in the late 16th century. Neither qualifies as a recent event.

Due primarily to the proximity of the mother country, Mexicans have flowed across our borders almost daily for many years, influencing many Americans to think of all as recent immigrants among other undesirable perceptions. That major flow from Mexico has now stopped, and immigrants from farther south have replaced them. Still the preponderance of Spanish names identifying states, cities, streets, mountains, rivers, and lakes should partly convince others of a long-standing presence and a broader set of identifying traits. I have always found it perplexing that so many Americans forget that all those Spanish names exist because large parts of the U.S. were once a part of Spain and later Mexico.

Not too long after I decided to stop speaking on the subject of stereotypes, I met a thoughtful Chicano young man who offered me a bit of wisdom that caused me to reassess my stance. As I spoke of racial pride as an effective means of counteracting narrow perceptions, the young man said to me, "You know, I'm not proud of being Mexican. I'm just happy about it." Impressed by the young man's uncluttered insight, I set out to make the statement my reality.

Convinced that everyone suffers on either side of the racial divide from the erroneous, degrading images of Latinos we see in the media, I ventured to express the predicament in verse.

IMPRESSIONS

How can you say you know me,
With your vision of me shrouded,
With the picture of my people
On the screen, obscured and clouded?

Performing as "bandidos,"
Fools or maids, all bowing low,
Clowns and whores to entertain you,
For a price, a bogus show.

One truth we share for certain,
Hollywood has harmed us both
By distorting your perception
By impeding my full growth.

~ 1976

Hank anchoring a high school winning relay

Chapter Sixteen
A Brand New Ballgame

My dad got back from Guam to discover that his temporary absence had created a greater rift between my parents rather than giving them the time to heal their differences. My mother had discovered that living without my dad made her life easier, that she managed better without the habits of their relationship. I'm sure he didn't want to break up, but as usual he didn't know what to say or how to fix the problem. My mom and I moved into an apartment. She decided he could have the house. She didn't care. I think she now just wanted to carry on with her job in the tailor department at Macy's and come home to less tension. She and I had found a mutual comfort zone, an area where we could live together with respect and a newly discovered affection.

I was saddened by the breakup but relieved that as I entered junior college my home base would be free of the old familiar stress our family had endured for so long. As I prepared to make it into Cal, I didn't need any distractions. I was almost glad that Daphne had gone away to college. I would miss her, but I had work to do. I had to pass those college prep classes I blew off taking in high school, get good grades, and think about playing football at Cal.

So there I was at San Jose Junior College. I enrolled in all the normal classes. Fortunately, I didn't have to take bonehead English like some of my buddies. I finally started taking Spanish, and my first day in class failed to turn into the seismic reaction I had anticipated—the entire world learning I could speak the language so well because I was Mexican. I suppose I still worried a little bit about it, given that a couple of my high school pals, Ragone and Dudley, also enrolled in the class. I guess they were thinking they might want to play football at a major four-year school also.

As I suspected, Spanish was a snap. Frank and Denny seemed surprised how easily I breezed through the course or else they were just shocked with how difficult the lessons were for them. Hell, by then they must have known I was Mexican or had just gotten accustomed to going along with my Spanish and French label. Since we never talked about it all those years, I assumed to them I just remained their old friend Hank. I decided not to worry about it.

I was also forced to take a terrifying six-unit math course, a combination of algebra, geometry, and trigonometry, to satisfy Cal's entrance requirement. I felt like I was about to be tossed into the ocean off the Santa Cruz pier without knowing how to swim a stroke. After avoiding math since the eighth grade, I doubted in my ability to count to ten let alone figure out equations, formulas, and logarithms. Fortunately, I had a sympathetic teacher who must have sensed the terror and intimidation I felt about the subject and acted as my willing tutor whenever I needed the extra help. Especially with the damn math course, I was forced to put my nose to the grindstone and study harder than I ever had in my life. I set up a routine, set hours when I would study, and set my mind to doing well.

My social life at JC turned out to be a real drag. I didn't find any of the girls very interesting, and I still missed and thought about Daphne. All of that made studying easier. Strangely enough, I started to enjoy hitting the books.

Fred Silva, my former gym teacher and the guy who talked me into competing in track way back in junior high school, turned out to be the head football coach at JC. What a coincidence. He seemed happy to see me, probably thinking that I could become a pretty good college player. Still I knew I would have to earn my slot on this team. There were several halfbacks getting the nod ahead of me, players Fred knew more about. I was going to have to prove myself.

Prior to the start of the semester, we suffered through two practice sessions a day and soon learned the difference between high school and junior college football—drills, drills, and more drills. Ragone and Dudley were also trying out for the team, and it was good to have someone you knew also suffering beside you. Another ex-Lincoln High player who graduated a year ahead of us, was also on the team, Al Tognetti. At five feet, eight inches tall and weighing in at around two hundred fifty pounds, he was very fast for his weight and one hell of an athlete. We affectionately referred to him as "Tanknetti." We also had a group of older players on the team, guys who had been in the Army and had come back to go to college. Some of them looked like tough, old beat-up pro players that made me think we might field a good team. They seemed to have some trouble moving easily though. We would soon see.

Once the season started, I had to claw my way up to the first-string halfback spot. Ragone had to do the same thing, and he became one of best linemen and linebackers in the league. Early in the season, Dudley tore up his knee and appeared to be finished for the year, probably for life. Some of those old guys didn't pan out so well, and we missed having a winning season by several games. Through it all I kept improving with each game and ended up as the team's leading rusher. I also finished the season with an 8.6 yards-per-carry average, one of the best marks in the nation. While I was at it, I broke all of Johnny Stewart's records from the previous year. Johnny also had attended Lincoln, where he made all-everything, graduated a year ahead of me, and spent a semester at JC before transferring to Cal.

All the great athletes from our high school seemed to be ending up at Berkeley. Doug Weiss had gone up there to play baseball as a pitcher, and Don Bowden, who shattered the national high school 880-yard run record in track his senior year at Lincoln, had also headed up to become a Golden Bear. I almost felt obligated to attend Cal.

Because of my preoccupation with everything else in my life, the question of ethnicity hadn't popped into my head very much. There were a couple of Mexican guys on the football team. Benny Guzman, who played the other halfback on the team, was a good football player and a damned nice guy. I wondered what he had gone through growing up Mexican, but I never asked. We did experience an incident having to do with race that rattled a few of us.

The team took a long, two-day bus ride to play Boise Junior College. On the way up we sang songs, told jokes, almost anything to stop from going stir crazy. I even got to show the ham in me by entertaining the troops with a comedy sketch called, "What Is Was, Was Football," by Andy Griffith. I delivered it, complete with a well-rehearsed southern accent, to loads of laughter from my teammates.

As we headed toward Idaho, we made a stop in Reno, Nevada. Several of us decided to take a walk through one of the glitzy casinos, including our Colored end Eddie Brewer, one of the most well-liked and talented guys on the team. Soon after we walked into the club, some guy came up to a couple of the older ex-Army guys and said, pointing to Eddie, "I'm sorry, but you boys can't come in here with him."

Eddie saw the whole scene, lowered his head, and headed for the door with a hurt look in his eyes. One of the old guys turned right into the nose of the potential bouncer and yelled, "What the hell are you people doing, still fighting the goddamned civil war around here? You can keep your goddamned fleabag joint to yourselves!"

Before the shocked employee could respond with, "We don't want any trouble around here," we left. As we all walked away, a little quieter than when we arrived, we were feeling proud of our teammate for fighting back just a little.

During my JC season, the Cal Athletic Department sent me tickets to see one of the games. They kept in touch with me, especially after reports that I had been tearing up the gridiron. I asked Ginny Peterson, a girl I dated occasionally in high school, to go with me. She was still a senior at Lincoln and a neat gal. We headed up to Berkeley, got stuck in traffic, and arrived late to the game. Parking was impossible so we ended up at a fraternity house where a guy offered to drive us up to the stadium, drop us off, and then take the car back to the house and park it for us. After the game all we had to do was walk to the fraternity and pick up the car. We agreed. How was that for trust?

Except for a few stragglers, everyone was already seated inside the stadium when the frat boy dropped us off. The outside of the place looked almost deserted. As we started walking up the stairs into Memorial Stadium, a strange silence surrounded the structure that made me wonder if anyone was even in there. Just as I was about to mention it to Ginny, the concrete stadium pillars came alive with a thunderous roar from the crowd, one that sounded as if it was emerging from the throat of an unseen prehistoric monster. The roar continued as we walked through the entrance leading to our seats and into the sunlit expanse of the vibrating, cheering oval.

At that unforgettable intersection, the glare of the sun, the dancing colors, the teams battling on the field, the electric excitement of the bands, all combined to send a thrill of anticipation rushing through me—telling me I could be a part of this, turning the play of my senses into an instantly plausible dream. There in the wide-open air of Strawberry Canyon cradling the stadium, I decided to take the feeling of awe and turn it into the engine that would drive my determination in the months to come.

Pushing the Year Along

I finished the intimidating, humbling math course with a solid C grade. When I learned about it I let out a screech heard in the next county. That's all I needed to get me into Cal, along with straight A's in Spanish and the A's and B's I'd earned in my other courses. I was on my way. Now I just wanted the school year to hurry up and end.

In the spring, I competed in track and field for Coach Maury Goldner. He was a Cal alum and had been checking up on me all year, making sure I was getting the grades and staying on course with my studies. I went out for the team but wasn't overly enthused. I liked Coach Goldner, made an effort to please him, and proved to be his top sprinter. He constantly touted Cal to me, telling me what a great experience I was destined to have there. We talked about all sorts of things and about the only thing we disagreed on was music. He didn't like jazz, not even swing. He and his wife loved to dance to something he called "smaltz," square old music played by a guy by the name of, believe it or not, Guy Lombardo. Man, was that crap corny.

During track season, I won the sprints in several meets and my speed kept improving, something that would definitely help my football playing. One weekend Rene and my brother-in-law Nels invited me up to their cabin for some late spring skiing. We had a lot of fun, and at the end of our final day on the slopes I took the last run, the one I was too tired to take. It resulted in a bad fall and a severely sprained knee. I could have kicked myself for taking that last dumb run. When I got back to school, Maury got really pissed off at me for my stupidity. I didn't blame him. The injury pretty much put an end to my freshman year track efforts. Knowing that my major interest was now football, Maury forgave me for my bad judgment and genuinely wished me the best. In spite of not finishing the track season in a blaze of glory, I was voted athlete of the year at San Jose Junior College.

My mom and I maintained the comfortable rhythm of our lives. She was very happy to see that I had settled down and was headed for the university. I knew she was proud of me, but I sensed a little sadness in her. Perhaps she anticipated the day in the near future when I would have to go away and leave her alone. I was glad we had the year together. Unfortunately, I didn't bother to see or talk to my dad.

Summer arrived and Daphne returned from college. We were going out but I felt as if she didn't love me anymore, not like she did in high school. She probably felt she was more sophisticated and advanced than I because she had already been to a four-year college. I didn't know. I tried not to let it bother me and just think about the upcoming fall when I too would be attending someplace very special. When I told her that I didn't think she cared for me like before and that maybe we shouldn't see each other anymore, it shocked her. She seemed to be truly surprised and hurt by what I said. She apologized and started acting sweeter than ever. I wondered what would happen to us when we both went our separate ways at the end of the summer. Until then, I was glad just to be feeling close.

I ran into Al Francis, a high school All-American who went to Bellermine Prep in San Jose. Out of high school he enrolled at Notre Dame, like a good Catholic boy should, but as it turned out he hated it there and transferred to the University of Georgia where he enjoyed playing football much more. He talked Georgia up to me and told me I would love going there. After my great year at JC, a few more schools were now interested in recruiting me, but they probably had never heard of me at Georgia.

Through Al, Wally Butts, the head coach at Georgia, got in touch with me, and after several conversations on the phone I sent my transcripts to him. He then called me back, talked to my mom, and offered me one hell of a football scholarship, one that included, room and board, tuition, books, laundry, four trips home, and two trips per season for my parents to go see football games. I was very impressed and began to have second thoughts about going to Cal, where the scholarship was adequate but considerably more modest. I spent several days debating the choices and ended up very confused, so I decided to talk to my wise, old high school coach and get his advice.

After listening to my dilemma, Lee got right to the point in his usual no-

nonsense manner. He said, "Son, do you plan to make your living in Atlanta?"

I answered, "Probably not."

"Then why in the world would you want to attend a university way the hell over there?"

I answered with a subdued question of my own, "It doesn't make any sense, does it, Lee?"

After being convinced that I'd seen the light, he gave me his wise, old, grey fox grin, a hearty pat on the back and said, "Sure glad I'm going to get to see you play at home, son." His comments also reminded me that I would eventually be forced to decide what to be when I grew up. At this point I didn't have a clue.

Summer settled in, and Ragone and I were working the night shift at Mission Valley cannery. With all the extra overtime, he and I were making some good bucks. He loved my mom's peach pies, so she liked to pack an extra piece for him in my lunch. When he would come over to visit, he would sometimes eat half a pie without even taking a breath. Man, that guy could put it away, and my mom loved seeing him chow down.

We spent a lot of time together that summer, working, getting in shape for next fall, and just goofing off when we got the time. One weekend, after several weeks of hard work, we decided to spend a night on the town, or I should say the city. One of the great things about growing up in San Jose was being close to San Francisco, a city always offering plenty to do. So we checked into this little hotel with a couple of other guys working at the cannery. They too were football players but from Monterey Junior College. The four of us planned the trip to take in a Forty-Niners pro-football game on Sunday.

We enjoyed an exciting game and saw some of the all-time star players like Leo Nomellini, Hugh McElhenny, and Joltin' Joe Perry. The Saturday evening before, we headed for the jazz clubs to catch clarinetist Buddy DeFranco and sax man Vido Musso at The Downbeat. Later I sat just about two feet away from one of my all-time favorite pianists, Earl Garner, at the Black Hawk, an experience that stands out as one of the thrills of my life. We were under-age so we ordered cokes and slipped a little whiskey into our glasses from the bottles we'd hidden in our large overcoats.

It was a big night on the town, and ended up at the "International Settlement," the area of San Francisco where all the strip joints were located. The city's finest burlesque beauties performed for us in shady, sinful places like "The House of Blue Lights" and "The Barbary Coast." My favorite performer that night was "The Cuban Bombshell." Wow! What a body and what a dancer. That was major fun.

The summer wound down, and I got ready for the big move. The time had arrived for goodbyes. I had to report for two-a-days at Cal, two full weeks of practicing twice a day before school started. I had been gradually saying goodbye to my mom for some time now, and I think we were both prepared for the final exit. For some reason, my departure from Daphne became more difficult. We took a long time to say our final goodbyes at my mom's apartment. I think both of us felt like it might be the last time we would see each other feeling the way we did at that moment. At one point I almost weakened and asked her to marry me, but I knew the time had arrived to move on, to allow our futures to flow away from the backyard fence of our youth.

~ FAST FORWARD ~

Flipping Labels and Perceptions

Sometimes athletics can level the playing field to some extent regarding questions related to race. It can make some people more acceptable regardless of their background. Nevertheless, perceptions die hard, and even after someone has gained success or praise in sports, ethnic or race issues can emerge, however innocent. I remember my friend Frank Cardenas telling me about winning a high school batting championship his senior year in Arizona. At the sports banquet honoring his feat, his was the only fried chicken that had been served lathered in a hearty salsa.

Perceptions associated with sports, race, and even nationality, sometimes get tangled up in the strangest ways. In 1994, an exhibition game between the Dallas Cowboys and the Houston Oilers took place in Mexico City's Azteca Stadium. More than one hundred twelve thousand enthusiastic Mexican fans packed the arena, shattering the NFL's previous attendance record of one hundred five thousand eight hundred forty. The American television broadcast commentators seemed surprised, almost shocked, that the fans understood the game so well, given their reactions to various aspects of the contest. I found it curious why they would think otherwise. Did they believe one hundred twelve thousand people showed up and paid good money just out of curiosity? They may have assumed Mexicans were only interested in soccer games and bullfights. My buddy and ex-partner in advertising, Raoul Rodríguez, proudly asserted his life-long, loyal standing as a Dallas Cowboys fan. He equally asserted his disdain for bullfights, in spite of being born and raised in Mexico City.

I naively believed that when I came out of the closet and began declaring my true ethnicity to the world that everyone, including members of my own ethnic group, would accept the labels I chose for myself. I soon learned the task would prove more complicated than expected. Strangely enough, I discovered that the individuals I anticipated would most enthusiastically support my declarations were sometimes the least accepting. My so-called "own people" sometimes rejected me, as dramatically illustrated in the following story.

Mistaken Identity

In my position as SER-Jobs for Progress' Communications Director, I visited projects across the country. My duties involved assisting those projects in the area of outreach, public affairs, and media relations. The assignment had me feeling almost giddy with excitement. I could finally give something valuable back to the community, putting my talents to work as my ex-wife Shirley had often pushed me to do. One of my first visits took me to Dallas, the town where just a few short years before I had so effectively passed for White. Now on a clear path to fully embrace my Mexican roots and the richness of my heritage, I returned with a renewed sense of self and a more accurate self-assigned label, Chicano. It felt a little surreal but right.

The sudden bang from the jet slamming on to the runway of Dallas Love Field instantly shook me out of the short snooze I had fallen into a few minutes before. As my eyes shot open, the plane lurched up for a quick second, slammed down again with a less violent thud, and finally settled into its regular taxi. The tall, lanky Texan sitting next to me complete with Wrangler jeans, massive silver belt buckle, and Stetson in the overhead, grinned and drawled, "Don't worry, son, he's jus' tryin' to shake the water out of it."

I answered with, "Feels like he's trying to adjust my spine with the landing gear." We shared a chuckle over our small-talk exchange. I hadn't said much to my traveling companion through the whole flight, preferring to concentrate on some paper work and a book of Pablo Neruda poetry I picked up in L.A. before starting the trip. I also assumed we couldn't have much in common and weighed the possibility that the guy might qualify, in my limited view, as a racist redneck. Although we hadn't spoken more than a half dozen words, I still felt sorry for him sitting there uncomfortably in the middle seat with his endless legs propped up almost to his chin throughout the whole flight.

As we began to deplane, I hoped I would recognize the guy meeting me at the airport from the Dallas project. Told only that a staff member by the name of David would be picking me up, I felt a little nervous about knowing exactly how to identify my new colleague. Furthermore, I was experiencing some apprehension about appearing overly assimilated to what I anticipated would be a group of grassroots people completely comfortable working in the barrio (neighborhood). It occurred to me as I was getting off the plane that my gray herringbone suit and penny loafers might be totally wrong for my first excursion into unfamiliar territory.

As I approached the usual crowd of people waiting for arriving travelers, I quickly scanned the group looking for some obvious clue to identify my man. It didn't take a Sherlock Holmes to spot my target. There on the outskirts of the crowd stood a scrawny, unshaven young guy with a disinterested, almost vacant look in his eyes, long dark stringy hair, and a medium-brown complexion. As I walked in his direction, the total picture came more clearly into focus. Headband, poncho, beads, old jeans, and huaraches, with the usual recycled tire soles, adorned his body. The young man held the next clue in his left hand, a small wrinkled brown paper bag with the name Enrique scratched on it. He held it loosely just above his waist, as if suffering from its weight and tilted sideways at the same angle as the passive lean of his head.

As I drew nearer a creeping fear welled up inside of me. If wardrobe mattered, I was about to experience the worst cultural clash in North America. Controlling my anxiety, I boldly walked up to the young man and with a pasted smile and cheery tone announced, "Hey, you must be David. I'm Hank."

The slouching figure gave me a disdainful once-over, ignored my extended hand, and snarled, "The name is Dahvéed." After crumpling the paper bag and dropping it on the floor, turning and gesturing with a "follow me" move of the head, he shuffled towards the exit. I assumed it was a signal to follow and quickly caught up like some little kid chasing his dad. I soon realized I might be in for a difficult visit.

He lingered to the side at baggage claim while I picked up my bag. We then drove towards the office in the local program director's borrowed car with barely more than a handful of words spoken between us in spite of my feeble attempts at polite small talk. David did bother to ask, "What kind of name is Hank? Isn't your real name Enrique?"

I told him it was really Henry and generously offered, "But you can call me Enrique if you like."

He shrugged and said, "Hank's okay," his greater interest focused on constantly straightening his headband emblazoned with the words, Chale Con Coors (Down with Coors), the Chicano slogan calling for the boycott of Coors beer for employment discrimination. He temporarily became lucid as we approached the streets bordering the barrio. His speech, filled with lines sounding like excerpts from a political rally, resounded with the current rhetoric on the oppression of Chicanos and delivered in a kind of slangy, slurred barrio accent that somehow didn't ring true. I attempted to concur with nods and an occasional, "Right on, man." Even my ¡Simón! (yeah) and ¡De acuerdo! (right) received little or no acknowledgement. Helplessly stuck listening to my chauffeur's sermon, I endured the one-way conversation.

We reached the local project office, and I was delighted to meet a small but friendly and enthusiastic staff. Most were dressed modestly but neatly, none looking at all like David. A quick meeting with the director included expressions of appreciation for my being there. The amicable director went on to ask that I work closely with David, bragging that his young staff member was a recent University of Texas graduate and quite a good writer. For an instant I thought that maybe David was a little less working class hero and more mainstream than he choose to reveal.

During the remainder of the morning and through much of lunch, I tried to engage David in genuine conversation but without success. Even my attempts to connect by speaking Spanish were met with almost blank stares, and I began to question if David knew any more than the few Spanish or "Spanglish" words with which he punctuated his English soap-box monologues. For hours the bulk of our exchanges involved my making suggestions on this brochure or that flyer, while David categorically shot down the ideas with a flippant, "Our people just don't go for that kind of shit, man. It doesn't appeal to our raza (race), to our culture."

My frustration grew from knowing full well that we weren't there to write the great Mexican American novel, just a few clear announcements about the programs and classes the project offered. Given the task before us, any heavy-handed cultural appeals seemed ludicrous to me. Still I remained polite and respectful of David's comments, wanting to establish my role as a team player interested only in getting the job done. David was at least now talking to me, however combatively.

Through the time we spent together, I noticed David constantly checking me out, seemingly trying to assess what kind of character the national headquarters of the program had sent him. Whichever of his glances I caught, they all seem filled with a kind of disapproving judgmental smirk. Tiring of having to display an accommodating attitude, I felt the limits of my patience edging in on me. I knew the exercise in futility could not go on indefinitely.

At one point in the tedious pattern of suggestions and subsequent rejections, I casually mentioned that I felt Chicanos like anyone else would respond positively to a straightforward message communicating an authentic opportunity for skills training. At that point David apparently hit the wall of his own impatience, and with a sneering, contemptuous tone of voice asked, "Hey, man, are you really a Chicano or are you just faking it?" The feeling that engulfed me at that point took me by surprise. I felt a giant wave of unresolved resentment beginning to roll through me, gaining momentum. It surged toward the surface in a controlled, unswerving way, much like a relentless flow of lava. The emotional backlash of all the ethnic, racial games I had played in the cultural teeter-totter of my young life hit me at that very moment, and David stood directly in the path of a deadly, gathering tempest.

I leaned slowly and deliberately over the table towards David and with a commanding and emphatic tone of voice said, "Who the hell are you, man, chairman of the goddamn membership committee?" Barely taking a breath,

I spoke again with the same determined, measured tone, drawing from some past compartment of my background I had almost forgotten, by saying, "¿Sabes que, vato? Si no te gusta el pinche tipo de Chicano que soy, me vale madre, ese. Si no te gusta, tú escribe las pinche mierdas que tienes allí."

David, with eyes wide as saucers, slowly inched back in his chair as if to calmly escape from the unyielding assault of passion aimed directly at him, as if fearing for his life. He stammered embarrassingly, admitting he really didn't speak Spanish very well, but that it was cool, whatever I said was cool. He ended with an almost tearful, "I really didn't mean to say anything to offend or insult you, man, honestly."

I interrupted his bumbling apology and continued without loosing a beat in my own feigned version of a barrio accent, "Yeah, right on, vato, it's cool. So let me repeat it in a language you can understand and so it's real clear. If you don't like the type of Chicano I am, I couldn't care less, man. If you don't like it, you write that pile of shit you have there. And something else, ese, I've done a dance for the man all my life, and I'll be goddamned if I'm going to do one for you now. So you can tell your boss I'll be getting back on the plane to L.A., and like I said en español (in Spanish) you can write that shit you seem to know so much about." ¿Me entiendes, Mendez? (You get it, Mendez?)

As I quietly and purposefully began to gather my belongings and put them in my briefcase, David got up from his cowering position and began to fidget nervously as he continued to apologize. In just a short two minutes, he experienced an almost mystical transformation in attitude, from smug and uncooperative to amiable and thoroughly obliging. He asked, almost pleaded, that I please stay, that he could use the help and believed that together we could produce some valuable materials for the program. He even lost the barrio accent I had correctly suspected was something of an affectation.

As my inner storm subsided, I felt a measure of embarrassment for having allowed myself to indulge in what I now considered a temper tantrum. At the same time I sensed I had plunged through a personal barrier plaguing me for years. The burden that came from juggling a number of identities or from not knowing which part of my background or personality to reveal began to dissipate. The sudden and unexpected burst of truth had somehow pulled me free from the psychological maze of being too Anglo, too Mexican, not enough of this, or too much of that. A renewed courage to act as I saw myself, regardless of potentially displeasing anyone on either side of the cultural gulf, settled in on me, and I almost felt like embracing David for helping to trigger an overdue epiphany. Without a doubt, I lifted the weight of carefully calculated words and actions from my tired shoulders and felt on my way to solving what I had defined as a behavior crises.

After the skirmish, David and I spent a productive day together. You could almost say that we became friends, discovering how much we really had in common including a college education. David even allowed himself to be impressed that I had played in the Rose Bowl along with another Chicano and revealed his understandable gabacho (White) love of football. Perhaps he even understood further my capacity to take him on with the fury of a linebacker.

At the end of the day, any lingering ill effects from the encounter disappeared over a couple of beers, and we both knowingly chuckled when some common experience emerged that caused us to ask, "Wow! Has that happened to you too?" David and I parted with a warm abrazo (embrace) and a promise to keep working together for the good of the program and the community.

Feeling content with my renewed feelings of self-assertion and with it a newfound tolerance of others, I boarded the plane bound back to L.A. the following day. As I approached my assigned seat, I was surprised to see the tall Texan from my earlier flight seated nearby. Recognizing me and showing his own surprise with a quizzical but broad smile, he quipped warmly, "Hey partner, good to have you back on the bumper cars." He then reached out his hand and said, "My name's Billy Ray Walker, what's yours?"

I extended my hand and replied, "I'm Hank Olguin. Good to know you."

Billy Ray, a little surprised but obviously pleased with the sound of my Spanish surname, responded in perfectly enunciated South Texas Spanish, "Orale, compadre, mucho gusto." (Right on, friend. It's a real pleasure).

Caught off guard but amused by another unexpected twist provided by my eventful trip, I blurted out, "Oh yeah, right. Mucho gusto." I continued down the isle but quickly turned back and awkwardly waved at Billy Ray as we both grinned and shook our heads in mutual, friendly disbelief.

In that instant I reminded myself that one can't always tell from the costumes other people wear or the labels we assign to them what sort of human beings live behind either. In addition, I adopted the clichéd but appropriate axiom I had been longing to live by, one that best expressed my new-found mindset: "What you see is what you get." Later I enjoyed writing about the multiplicity of roles and labels assigned to describe us—sometimes to the level of absurdity.

NAMES

Hi, my name is Henry, Enrique, Quiqui, Quique, Olguin, Garcia,
Cosio, American, Mexican, Mexican American, American Mexican,
American of Mexican Descent, Latino, Latin, Chicano, Spanish,
Hispanic, Indo-Hispanic, Brown.

Mestizo, Manito, Indito, Paisano, Pocho, Guero, Vato,
Mano, Ese, Gringo, Carnal, Californian, Caucasion, Breed.

Student, Frat Rat, Cat, Safety, Running Back, Sprinter, Long Jumper,
Football Player, Brownbelt, College Grad, Actor, Player, Singer, Son.

Sibling, Brother, Father, Cousin, Husband,
Uncle, Ponka, Grandfather, and Friend.

Boyfriend, Baby, Lover, Straight, Sweetheart,
Partner, Companion, Dreamer, Male.

Man, Mister, Sir, Dude, Adult, Citizen, Senior Citizen, Democrat,
Homeowner, Taxpayer, Team Member, Breadwinner, Liberal,
Professional, Alum, Old Fart, and Geezer.

Advertising Exec., V.P., Writer, Copywriter, Creative Director, Lyricist,
Officer, Salesman, Public Speaker, Seminar Facilitator, and Poet.

Greaser, Greaseball, Beaner, Bean, Freehole, Tortilla, Coconut,
Chili,Chilidipper, Chilipepper, Chilibelly, Chilihead, Enchilada, Taco,
Fruitpicker, Foreigner, Vendido, Wetback, Meskin, Mex.

Lazy Mexican, Dumb Mexican, Dirty Mexican, Sneaky, Spick, Frito, Boy.

Pachuco, Cholo, Pancho, Chuke.

Human Being, Homosapien, Member of the Human Race,
Everyman.

Or you can just call me...

Hank.

~ 1996

Chapter Seventeen
Into the Bear's Lair

I arrived at Cal as a scholarship football player in the fall of 1956, excited, grateful, and a little scared. We checked into Bowles Hall, a men's dormitory that looked like a medieval castle and where the football team stayed for two weeks during two-a-day practices. Surrounded by lush trees, the dorm symbolized every fantasy I ever imagined about college life. It resonated with decades of tradition going all the way back to 1928. Nowhere did the past ghosts reside more firmly than in the majestic dining hall, straight out of every British boarding school movie.

Bowles sits on a hill not far from another impressive and massive structure, Memorial Stadium. As I walked down from my temporary home on my way to the practice field, I glanced over and admired the giant arena. For a moment I allowed myself to dream that someday I might run through its north tunnel out to thousands of cheering fans as some of the greats from Cal's football past had done—All-Americans like Brick Muller, Vic Bottari, Rod Franz, Jackie Jensen, and Johnny Olszewski. Between the present reality and that possibility, countless, grinding practice sessions stood in the way, and they began that day.

Putting on football gear in a locker room felt familiar and routine. I had put on shoulder pads and hip pads many times before but never in a setting that felt this alien. My feelings came not from the lack of friendly or welcoming greetings from coaches and even some players but from the unfamiliar locker room blur of teammates I didn't know, from the sounds of old friends laughing and reuniting, from coaches commenting on plays unfamiliar to me, or from equipment managers explaining something I didn't quite understand. Everyone seemed to know exactly what they were doing, while I felt as if I was groping around in the dark, feeling an unintentional exclusion from this strange new mix of people and activities. The only player I knew was my old high school running mate Johnny Stewart. Johnny did his best to teach me some of the ropes, to help me get through this new maze. He acted like a true pal, and I sure was glad he was in my corner.

My apprehension grew when I fully realized the overall size of my new teammates. Everyone seemed gigantic to me. I had always been a little guy wherever I played football but here the contrast seemed even greater. Those guys were huge. As we ran on to the practice field, another halfback I would be competing against, Darrell Roberts, looked me up and down and asked, "How much do you weigh?"

I deepened my voice slightly and, with a little added bravado, told him, "A hundred and sixty-eight."

He looked at me suspiciously, suspecting correctly that I had tacked on at least another five pounds. He came back at me with, "Yeah, sure." A part of me wanted to tell him to shove it, but I decided to save my fights for the field.

After a few inspirational words by our head coach Pappy Waldorf, a true University of California legend, the most difficult practice of my life began. I felt almost overwhelmed by the hard, exhausting regimen. At times I wondered if I'd be able to get through a particular drill let alone the day. I tried to find the extra energy for taking my play to the next level, and I knew it was not going to be easy. It was going to involve learning some serious lessons about striving itself.

The coaches paid particular attention to the new guys during wind sprints, and I was quickly noticed. My speed impressed them, and I felt a surge of new life arriving to help me get through the difficult practice. After several days of running, blocking, and tackling, they moved me up to run plays with the second string. I suddenly began believing I might have a chance to make it, to get some playing time.

Learning the plays for a new system I'd never seen did not come easily, and I made my share of mistakes. Missed assignments or critical tackles are sins that quickly begin to pile up, offenses that after a certain period are unforgivable. I moved down the ladder more gradually than I moved up but inevitably straight down in the direction of the fourth and fifth strings. I felt myself sinking and wondered if I could recover. I had my doubts.

Off the Gridiron

Before moving up to Cal I knew I was going to go through fraternity rushing, the time when you visit the fraternity houses, get checked over by the members, the brothers as they say, to find out whether you're acceptable or not. I couldn't help but think here we go again. Here comes that old persistent push to fit in. I didn't see any Mexican students on campus, at least not anyone who had a typical look I recognized. I didn't give it much thought, but I couldn't help but wonder what my chances would be if the houses were to know about my Mexican background. Something told me some of them would not approve, but with a name like Olguin, pronounced ALL-gwin, I probably would be able to slide by. A Martinez or Gonzales hanging on me would make it more difficult.

I rushed a few houses and ended up liking the guys in Stewart's fraternity the best, Sigma Alpha Epsilon (SAE). I got a warm reception from Johnny and his brothers and was asked to join the house. It felt great. I found a place to live with instant friends, a whole houseful of them all at once.

I was surprised and pleased to discover that one of the upper classmen in the fraternity was a guy by the name of Mike Diaz, confirming that at least one house invited Mexicans to join. I thought to myself who wouldn't want Mike as a brother? Handsome, a good student, and a varsity basketball star, Mike also exuded a warm personality that made everyone like him. I started figuring out that if Mexicans display enough winning traits they can become more acceptable. Mike treated me well, but we didn't talk much about our common heritage. I think it was just quietly understood.

Living in the house would be no sweat with my scholarship paying for expenses. The only crappy thing about it was living there as a pledge. The pledges, what they called new members, did all the dirty work in the house for a whole semester. Our job amounted to taking an inordinate amount of shit from the upperclassmen, bonding with our pledge brothers, studying hard, making our grades, and getting through "hell week" so we could be officially admitted into the house. Next to my initial stumbles in football, I suspected it would be a snap. Making my grades and competing academically at a great university was another matter, and it did cause me some anxiety.

I was starting to get the lay of the land at the giant institution, although registration for classes proved to be a confusing, tiring series of long lines, forms, and IBM cards. The process also caused a good case of writer's cramp. While I was at it, a complete stranger told me off. I was standing in the registration line waiting to pay my tuition with a voucher supplied by the Athletic Department as part of my scholarship. When the student managing the line saw that my tuition had been paid for, he scowled at me and grumbled, "Another free-rider, huh?" He then reluctantly pointed me in the direction of the proper window. I thought to myself, I guess I won't see that guy at any football games. I found some relief in that at least he didn't call me a dirty Mexican.

Pre-enrollment for classes turned out to be even more trying than registration. The university had devised a method of primitive torture, requiring that one rise at the crack of dawn, stand in more endless lines, and creatively juggle choices in order to enroll in the proper classes. I concluded that if I could live through that ordeal the actual classes might not be so bad by comparison. I quickly learned the error of my thinking. I found out that just locating classes in a building called Dwinelle Hall amounted to looking for disappearing doors in a labyrinth. The first day of classes I bumped into untold numbers of students asking the same question repeatedly, like meek, lost sheep, "Can you please tell me where such-and-such room is?" Arriving finally at the proper classroom and taking a seat felt like a major accomplishment. I heard some students joke that freshmen had been known to get lost for days in the bowels of Dwinelle.

It didn't take long for me to start feeling comfortable with college life. It occurred sooner than I expected. I quickly found the groove of courses with five hundred people in them, making early eight o'clock classes, and taking midterms. Winding my way up campus at dusk after football practice and hearing a men's chorus rehearsing in the distance reinforced my "ivy-covered halls" glamorous image of college life. The Campanile, Sather Gate, Bancroft Library, and the Student Union, revered landmarks of one of the country's leading institutions of higher learning, all became fixtures in my daily routine.

My social life revolved mainly around the fraternity house. As pledges we adhered to our nightly duties of enforced study table and our daily work details. The other aspect about fraternity life imposed upon us involved the push to automatically like all of our pledge brothers. The rebel in me struggled considerably with the forced camaraderie. I ended up becoming close friends with really only one of my pledge brothers, an older guy by the name of Gordon

Nixon. He and I thought alike about the artificial brotherhood shit and both definitely leaned toward the hell-raising side of life.

The active members gave us a little static about our attitude, but we simply went on our merry way. One day we pulled a stunt that almost made them forgive us for our lack of adherence to brotherly love. It was All-U Weekend, a time when all the UC campuses came together for festivities and a couple of football games. Fraternity brothers arrived from the other campuses. The house opened up for parties, and students from other fraternities and sororities swung in and out of our living quarters. The following Monday morning we discovered that someone had stolen our SAE chapter flag over the weekend. We also learned through the grapevine that the Fijis, members of the Phi Gamma Delta fraternity house, were the culprits. When our house president called theirs and asked if by some chance they had our flag, they vehemently denied it, pissing off the brothers even more over our embarrassing loss.

Gordon, another pledge John Sutherlin, and I got together and secretly plotted a scheme for getting the flag back. We calculated that we needed to steal something belonging to the Fijis valuable enough for them to make a trade. So we decided on the perfect article, their front door.

At two-thirty in the morning, the three of us drove to the Fiji house, parked about half a block away, and snuck up the street. The large stone staircase leading up to the huge front door, one clearly in sight of the street and any passing campus police, complicated our task. We tiptoed up the stairs and with a hammer and screwdriver began to work on the hardware as stealthily as mice. Fortunately, we only had to tap on the hinges two or three times, but each tap conjured up visions of being heard, getting caught, and either being axed to death or tarred and feathered. After our delicate, silent operation, the door slipped off its hinges. Shocked by the weight of the massive chunk of solid wood, we barely managed to carry it down the stairs, up the street to the car, and awkwardly load it into the trunk.

As quickly as we could, we drove back to our house, unloaded the newly acquired prize, and hid it in the basement. The next day the three of us let our pledge brothers in on the caper, one that sent them into fits of ecstasy.

We suggested that we make a formal presentation to the house and offer the door as a gift from our pledge class. I made the announcement to the unsuspecting brothers as they were all seated in the dining room having lunch by pronouncing, "On behalf of the 1956 SAE fall pledge class, we would like to present to the chapter a token of our brotherly passion for and dedication to the house. More importantly, this valuable gift will allow us to retrieve our honored chapter flag and gain our justified retribution for a most grave and cowardly insult." Just before I uttered the last line like a ringmaster, several pledges hauled the door in and placed it on the dining room floor as I shouted, "THE FIJI FRONT DOOR!"

The brothers went berserk, howling, screeching, and stomping on the door, pointing at it and making mocking comments, and praising the three valiant night raiders who were able to pull off the unlikely theft. Not long after our presentation, the president of the Fiji house called and inquired if we happened to have their front door. We again asked if they happened to have our flag. They admitted their crime, and a formal exchange of stolen property took place. In the meantime, we made sure that we told as many friends as possible in other fraternities, and especially sororities, to please drive by and see the gaping hole in front of the Fiji house compliments of the SAEs. I basked in the special praise and acceptance as one of the boys.

The season began, the starting team had been picked, and I got relegated to nothing more than an afterthought in the minds of our coaches. I remained on the team, maintained my scholarship, but so far down on the roster I was in danger of falling off the list. Sophomore halfbacks Darrell Roberts and Jack Hart would probably see a lot of playing time as well as sophomore quarterback Joe Kapp. Stewart for sure would also be lettering, probably starting. After the great year I had at junior college where I broke all of Johnny's records, I concluded that I had turned out to be a disappointment to those who recruited me. Worse, the hotshot junior college transfer with an 8.6-yard average had now become a major disappointment to himself.

In those days Cal had a junior varsity called the Ramblers, and we were scheduled to play other junior varsities and military teams fielded by bases like Fort Ord and the San Diego Naval Training Station. I was definitely assigned to play the less-than-glamorous schedule. Our coach John Ralston, a smart and enthusiastic mentor, told us that the Rambler program provided us with a real opportunity to improve as players. He thought it would be especially worthwhile for us sophomores, with three full years of eligibility, who could end up playing varsity the following two years—that is if they worked hard.

I didn't pay very close attention to his encouragement. I knew he was probably right, but my attitude had turned me into something of a robot—going through the motions, doing just enough to get by and stay on the team. For sure I didn't want to lose my scholarship. I had never felt so discouraged, inadequate, and sorry for myself. I attempted to rationalize that maybe I hadn't received a fair deal, feebly looking to blame someone else for my situation. Coach Ralston played me but always seemed frustrated by my performance. I learned later that the whole time he believed strongly in my ability to do much better.

After a game around the middle of the season in which I played with a faint-hearted attitude, John came up to me, visibly upset, and in a firm, castigating voice said to me, "Son, you're just going to have to stop backing down." That's all he had to say before walking away. His simple words burned into my mind like a branding iron, and I instantly submerged into feelings of shame and remorse. John had found the fitting words and manner to challenge and shake my sense of manhood and pride.

After that incident, I felt a strong urge to run away, and I went home for a couple of days. My mom was glad to see me, but I really didn't go home to visit her. I returned to think, to be alone. I rode out at night to my high school and slowly walked out to the deserted football field and track stadium where the cheers from past glories still resonated in my ears. As I paced from one end of the dark field to the other, I seriously contemplated what Coach Ralston had forced me to face—that I had been cheating my team, my coach, and, most of all, myself.

I had often fought with the idea that we are forced to play many different roles, variations on ourselves, and of being compelled to decide which role to pull out and when. Losing the sense of time, I found myself sitting in the empty stands, dismayed and angry with the me that had emerged in the last several weeks, contemplating what I must do to change that person.

Finally, as I slowly walked away from the echoes of earlier triumphant days,

I vowed to return to the university and, even if I never played one minute of varsity football, to give it all I had—to make every effort to recover my integrity and courage. I decided the time had come to put off childish things and test the extent of my character.

I played out the season with a renewed spirit of dedication and enthusiasm. I began steadily to improve as a football player, and Coach Ralston happily confirmed my progress. I learned again to take every practice and game as an opportunity to gain something, and I finished the season with an outstanding performance. In our last Rambler game against the San Jose State Junior Varsity, I scored touchdowns on runs of 21, 35 and 13 yards. We easily beat the Spartans, 39-13.

I was allowed to suit up for some of the varsity games and actually got into one game for one play. Late in the fourth quarter, with almost no time left on the clock, I was sent in because of my speed to attempt a last-minute, desperation pass that never even got thrown my way by the quarterback. It served as only a token appearance, but it gave me a fleeting taste of how it must feel to play in our great stadium.

The season ended with Cal winning the Big Game and with our sophomore quarterback Kapp outperforming Stanford and their highly-touted senior, All-American quarterback John Brodie. In spite of the Big Game win, the season proved disappointing and Coach Pappy Waldorf decided to step down. His decision caused a great deal of sadness among loyal players, friends, and fans that held Pappy in the highest esteem and affection. It spelled the end of a notable era of Golden Bear football, filled with great teams and extraordinary players. I felt grateful to have been a small part of it.

I made my grades in the first semester, went through the bullshit of hell week, and became a full-fledged active member of the SAE house. The fall semester rounded out with parties, dates, burgers from Kips or the Smoke House, catching an occasional jazz concert, and looking forward to a great spring. I saw Daphne only twice in Berkeley. She came to Cal for my pledge dance and for one other party at the fraternity. I hadn't been great about writing, and we seemed to be growing apart. Our lives had changed dramatically in a short period of time.

I initially dedicated my spring sports activities to running the sprints on the track team. I performed reasonably well, in spite of finding myself in some blazingly fast company. My teammate Leamon King easily qualified as one of the fastest humans alive. I also competed against Ray Norton, another world-class sprinter, along with some other speedsters in the Pacific Coast Conference. Nevertheless, I ran fast enough to take my share of seconds and thirds, enough to win the honor of my first Big C, my first varsity letter.

The arrival of our new head football coach Pete Elliott created quite a stir. He was a University of Michigan graduate, where he earned an impressive twelve varsity letters in several sports during his college career. That had to be a record. He came to Cal after coaching at Oklahoma with the legendary Bud Wilkinson who had led Oklahoma to impressive winning streaks and national titles. Pete brought with him some of those Sooner players and the split-T offense, a system I was going to like. It seemed to be suited for quick hitting backs like me. Pete decided to keep Rod Franz and Coach Ralston as assistant coaches from Pappy's staff. It made me happy that a man who had taught me a critical lesson would be staying on.

I met some of the assistant coaches for the first time when they came to watch me run in the Cal-Stanford track meet, including our new backfield coach Buck McPhail, an All-American fullback at Oklahoma. I took a close third in the 100 by running a 9.8, a time that Buck told me in his distinctive drawl he thought was "reeeal good." I quickly learned that "reeeal good" served as Buck's favorite phrase, and I looked forward to hearing him say it to me many times in the future.

Spring football, when the team practiced for several weeks to get a jump-start on the following season, amounted to dreary business. It offered no large crowds, glory, or instant rewards for all the hard work. That year in particular, spring ball mainly involved learning an entirely new system and even an entirely new way of practicing. In Coach Elliott's system, every phase and drill, precisely timed and measured, left little or no room for rest. His practice sessions moved at a much faster tempo than Pappy's, and getting and staying in the best possible shape was going to count greatly in making the team. I starting feeling that with hard work I had a good shot at getting some playing time.

It looked as if Darrell Roberts had the inside track on staying as the team's first-string left halfback. He had a whole year of varsity experience under his belt even though it was under Pappy's old system. I knew other backs would also be giving me some competition next fall, but Darrell remained the front-runner. He ranked as a fine, tough, and talented back, and probably didn't worry in the least about me replacing him, rightly so. I had to improve even more, but he had become my target; he was the one I had my sights on.

We ended spring practice with Darrell clearly in the driver's seat for the starting position, but something took place in a scrimmage that gave me added incentive and served notice that I was ready to fight for the slot. In a practice game, I was playing safety on defense against Darrell's squad as they tried a running play with him carrying the ball to the outside. I came up and tackled him hard on the line of scrimmage with a force that caused the suspension unit on my helmet to break and the exposed rivet to dig into my scalp. As I was getting up from the tackle over Darrell, a small spurt of my blood from the cut landed on his face. Lying on the turf for an extra moment, Darrell looked up at me and said, "Nice hit," with a look of surprise and disbelief that I was the one who came up and nailed him that hard.

I helped him up, said, "Thanks," and thought to myself, I'll see you next fall for more of the same.

~ FAST FORWARD ~

An Array of Exceptional Coaches

I have been fortunate to have had several coaches and mentors who helped me to succeed, not only in athletics but in life—beginning with Fred Silva, the gym teacher who inspired me to compete in a little track meet and who jump-started my athletic career way back in junior high. Fred always held a special place in my heart for that role and for serving as my dedicated, tough junior college head football coach.

Fred's sometimes-volatile nature made playing for him an interesting experience. One night, after tying a game that the team should have clearly won, he got so pissed off he called out the whole team. I didn't think even some of the older guys would have taken him on that night.

Overall, he treated me with warm respect and displayed the utmost confidence in my athletic skill. He even tried to talk me into postponing my transfer to Cal and playing for him another year, a request I took as a compliment. Years later I felt proud of Fred, watching him became a top official for the National Football League (NFL). I remember seeing him perform as the head referee in Super Bowl XIV, between Pittsburg and the Rams.

With a name like Silva I assumed Fred's background was probably Portuguese. I had friends in high school with names like Santos, Fernandes, and Pacheco, names that sounded Spanish but like Silva were Portuguese. As usual, I didn't know for certain because I didn't ask. My friends and I continued to skirt the subject.

I often wondered what Fred would have thought about race issues. He certainly always treated his players even-handedly regardless of their backgrounds. By the time he became a leading NFL official, being color-blind must have turned into a major job requirement, given the racial make-up of the NFL.

During the illustrious career as a coach that John Ralston enjoyed, including leading Stanford to Rose Bowl wins in 1971 and 1972 and winning the UPI AFL/AFC Coach of The Year Award while coaching the Denver Broncos, he surely served as an inspirational influence to countless players. Of course, no words of wisdom or inspiration were ever as important to me as the ones he spoke to me in the fall of 1956. Years later I took to heart the axiom that "one small thing can make a great big difference." The few words that Coach Ralston chose that day made an enormous difference in the direction of my athletic career and life.

Other than John's special contribution to my passage into manhood, Coach Pete Elliott and his great staff continued where John left off. Playing under Pete and his assistants provided me with valuable and lasting lessons. Pete's pushing for excellence and integrity in sports, instilling in me the desire to reach for every ounce of effort my mind and body could deliver, and instructing me in the pride necessary to never quit are values that have served me well. Drilled and reinforced by respected and admired assistant coaches like Buck, Gene Stauber, and Bobby Herndon, the benefits of their instruction have stayed with me throughout my life.

As I look back at the many paths I have taken, other people, less famous or celebrated than the group of outstanding men who tutored me in sport, also served as life coaches. During the journey several individuals have appeared, some described on these pages, to offer their friendship, support, advice, inspiration, and even benevolent kicks in the ass. Two especially loom large in my own personal pantheon of teachers.

Ed "Bear" Robles

Ed Robles waltzed into my life while I was working at SER-Jobs for Progress. Having arrived for his first day of work, I saw the two hundred fifty pound plus frame strolling toward me down the hallway with an apparent nimbleness unusual for a man of his size. As we passed in the hallway, Ed flashed an engaging smile at me and casually threw out, "How you doin', man?"

I replied with a quick "Good. How are you?" As I entered my office and sat down at my desk, an overpowering intuitive sense told me that the guy I had just seen for a brief moment was destined to become a close friend. I was right. Shortly after our first encounter, we began developing a deep, enduring, and loving relationship. Ed's wife, "the Feech," a wonderful, playful nickname Ed created for Alice, also formed a lasting part of that friendship. Over the years, we spent uncounted hours sharing the favorite parts of our lives with each other—a joyous unforgettable journey of mutual regard and esteem.

Ed, whose girth caused his friends to lovingly refer to him as "Bear," was an extraordinary man who assaulted life with daring, sensitivity, great compassion, and an infectious sense of humor. He loved the academic life, and he could have easily become a professor of something if other interests hadn't pulled him away. While earning a Masters degree in Anthropology, he conducted the research for his thesis on a Hopi reservation, an experience that spawned fascinating stories I became privileged to hear—magical, mystical tales that matched Bear's own spiritual imagination and expansiveness. In his own words he expressed, "Those were some of the many priceless gifts I received during my time on the res."

Later, Ed earned a second Masters in Education. Under another set of circumstances, he might have continued toward earning a Ph.D. Before all that took place in the more carefree years of his youth, he worked as a radio disc jockey for a time. Folk and Funk with Edward John was the name of his popular show. He also toured with Taj Mahal playing blues guitar, a natural for him since he belonged to a family of great musicians, including his father Lalo Robles who worked for many years as an orchestra leader.

Years later he spent a couple of difficult years, as he said, "Pulling drug addicts out of the gutter on the streets of L.A." He confessed to handling the job pretty well until some guy overdosed in the bathroom of his apartment and subsequently left the planet. It was more than he could take. When I met Bear, he was writing grants and proposals to help economically disadvantaged Latino and Latina youth.

I enjoyed watching Ed's special pride in tuning-up his own car and mine just for the fun of it. He even built his first computer just for the fun of it. He especially loved sports cars and great music. He and I spent countless hours together listening to jazz. In addition he relished in the fact that I played college ball. Once when Joe Kapp was a guest on a local L.A. sports talk radio show, Bear, who could impersonate me with uncanny accuracy, called in and pretended to be Joe's old running mate. He knew enough facts about my playing days to pull it off and make the listeners and Joe believe he was Hank. He then recounted his little charade to me in between outrageous spurts of laughter.

He loved great movies, great food, and great celebrations, all of which he and I shared. He was passionately in love and devoted to his soul mate and wife, "The Feech." He also adored his entire family and extended family. I felt privileged to be called his brother in that context. He was the eldest of ten blood brothers and sisters in one of those Mexican American families whose members went from brown to blond and everything in between. He never cared to pass for White but he could have without any problem. If you saw this guy walking down the street, you would definitely say, "There goes a White guy." When he spoke in his beautifully articulated and colorful speech, no one could possibly question his mainstream credentials.

As much as any coach, he exercised a great influence on my life at a time when we were formulating and fine-tuning our notions of what it meant to be Mexican American. We shared many probing discussions regarding the value of our backgrounds and the mutual trials and tribulations in growing up in a society that didn't always fully accept us. Nevertheless, he loved his country and proved it through his military service. At the same time, he insisted on exercising his freedom to be any stripe of Mexican or American he chose.

His wisdom, including a lack of resentment and the acceptance of the ultimate goodness of all people, helped to provide me with a more generous perspective. He demonstrated a simple but profound joy and love of life. Bright, energetic, and thoughtful, he spent the majority of his time on the planet loving, appreciating, or nurturing everything from little kids to trees, from social justice to books.

He never failed to entertain me when he brought out some interesting bit of knowledge, an event, or episode from his fascinating background. A simple drive to the mountains or beach might cause him to start sharing his fascination and understanding about the migration trails or spiritual rituals of the Chumash Indians. A moment later and just as quickly, he might fall into some silly improvisation, pretending to be driving in a Wells Fargo wagon rather than his big Buick, sparked simply by an especially invigorating passage from an Aaron Copeland piece playing on the cassette deck.

Perhaps the most significant event in his life took place during his tour of duty in Vietnam. In the early days of the war U.S. military personnel acted only as advisors. He was one of them. He recounted that one day while he and a fellow soldier were setting up satellite dishes, they began to see mortar fire walking up on them. Bear remembers asking, "Hey Scott, are they shooting at us?" After a mortar hit a little too close for comfort, he yelled out, "Hey Scott, I think they're shooting at us. Let's get the hell out of here." The last thing Bear recalls is jumping into a ditch and hearing a loud thud before waking up in a hospital with half of his body torn open.

He sustained serious wounds that resulted in the burden of chronic medical complications for the rest of his life, controlling his weight being the most troublesome. He always said he should have died over in Nam. Fortunately for me, he lived long enough to enter and enhance my life with his incomparable dance. The effects of his wounds finally caused him to slip away quietly one evening in 1993.

Rev. Dr. Hector Lopez

Hector entered the University of California in the fall of 1956, a setting miles away in distance and character from the small rural town of Pomona where he grew up. He and I met in the spring of 1958 after I addressed a youth group at an Oakland church. I couldn't help but notice a skinny, enthusiastic little guy sitting in the front row. As I began speaking, this bundle of exuberance sat there grinning up at me. With only a handful of Latinos attending the university, Hector later confessed his delight in meeting another one, especially one playing varsity football. After my presentation, Hector and I spoke—Hector open and friendly, I polite but guarded. I remember thinking that I held no burning desire to connect or create friendships with other Mexican students, however charming and friendly.

Over the next several months my attitude began to gradually change. For some unexplainable reason, I began cautiously, almost secretly, seeking out the company of other Latinos but far away from the center of my social life, the fraternity. Those included an interesting, radical student from Chile and a Mexican American professor teaching Spanish at Cal. Both provided me with some tentative, early steps back to embracing my heritage and using Spanish beyond the classroom. Other than my happy interactions with William Oliver, my Spanish-speaking theater professor, the other relationships remained private, almost hidden.

Running into Hector a year after we first met, I felt more open to sharing casual conversation. Hector's winning personality, first-rate wit and warmth, were hard to resist, and we began to slowly develop a friendship. It grew to the point where I could be brutally honest with him about some of the social choices I had made. Hector learned that in certain social settings I was still not ready to start openly declaring my ethnicity. Hector accepted the deception with a knowing smile and understanding far beyond his years. As our relationship flourished, I learned more about Hector's own personal struggles and challenges. Hector's story still enlightens.

Growing up in Pomona surrounded by miles of orange groves, Hector and his family lived each day with the reality of a small ruling class of White farmers and merchants coexisting with a large underclass population of Mexican workers. Almost absolute power for the Whites alongside servitude and poverty for the majority of Mexicans best describes their relative positions. Most of the labor used to harvest the crops consisted of migrants passing through only during the season. However, some Mexican families had been able to establish their roots in the area and build some sort of stable life. Hector's family qualified as one of those.

Hector excelled academically in school and effectively played the class clown. He also became a starting point guard on the varsity basketball team and was voted the Most Valuable Player his senior year. A Mexican becoming reasonably popular in a high school dominated by the White gentry of the fiefdom might qualify as something of an accomplishment. For Hector it came as no anomaly. He has always managed to plow through the underlying attitudes of racial superiority held by others, perhaps better than anyone I have ever known. Somehow he floated above the discrimination but always challenging it with an irreverent attitude and smile.

The grounding came from his parents, but especially his father who moved through life with an undeniable assurance and dignity in spite of experiencing daily indignities. Perhaps this family found a way to best transcend discrimination in the little Protestant church his parents helped establish. There they could pray and worship in Spanish, find solace, strength, and a caring community away from a callous world.

To be sure discrimination existed in that town. Hector remembers his older brother and sister swimming in the public plunge with the other Mexican kids only on Thursdays. On Fridays they cleaned the pool. Further, the main floor of the local movie theater was off-limits to them. For many years they could only sit in the balcony with the rest of the brown faces. An open seating policy did not take effect until Hector reached the age of twelve. Even after that change, the Mexican kids continued to stay largely to themselves.

Following in his brother Bert's footsteps to attend the University of California, Hector arrived at Cal with no apparent psychological damage from his childhood experiences. He enthusiastically jumped into campus life. He quickly hooked up with his high school friend Artie, who happened to be in a fraternity. During his freshman year, Hector spent an increasing amount of time hanging out with Artie and his fraternity brothers, many considering him an unofficial member of the house. Hector's intelligence, sense of humor, and easy manner endeared him to the brothers. It didn't hurt that he excelled in ping-pong, bridge, and basketball, activities that sometimes counted even more than his academic prowess.

Hector had found a ready-made group of friends in the large and often impersonal setting of the big university. At the end of the spring semester, while he, Artie, and a couple of other guys were playing a game of bridge instead of studying for finals, Artie casually mentioned, "Next fall, when Hector joins the house we'll get even with him for beating us at everything." The others laughed and agreed, leading Hector to believe that he would receive an automatic invitation to join the fraternity in the fall.

When Hector returned to school to begin his sophomore year, he checked into the Shattuck Hotel where he had rented a room temporarily, until rushing was officially over—after which he could move into the fraternity house for good. He had made no plans for permanent housing. He also did not bother to rush any other houses. He barely knew what that entailed, and joining any other fraternity had not even entered his mind. Still he attended a couple of parties at the fraternity house during that period to say hello to his old buddies from the previous year. They all pretended he was like all the other students going through rush to be scrutinized, and many assumed he was one of those shoe-in pledges.

After the week of rushing ended, Hector waited to hear from his friend and make his move. Several days passed and still no word from Artie. Hector finally called him and said, "Man, where have you been? This cracker box is about to drive me stir crazy." Artie seemed to be stalling and avoided the issue until Hector asked more firmly, "What's going on, Artie?"

He answered with a halting whisper, "You got dinged. I don't get it. I'm sorry Hector, but you just got dinged."

"Artie, please, not another one of those crazy frat house terms. What the hell does 'dinged' mean?" Hector asked.

Artie responded with an almost desperate tone of voice, "I know, I know. It's stupid, but it simply means any one member of the house has the right to disqualify someone we're considering for membership. In other words, any brother has the right to vote down, to ding someone they don't like. It was only two guys that didn't want you."

After an awkward pause, Hector joked, "Oh well, I've always wanted to live out of a trash can. I guess that's what it will have to be this semester with no emergency backup housing plan." Hector paused again for a moment as the silence hung on the phone line. He broke it by asking, "Artie, would you mind telling me why? Why didn't those two guys want me?"

Artie answered quietly, "They said...they said, his voice wavered, they, eh, felt you would be a social detriment to the house."

In time, Hector overcame the hurt and rejection of the decision through the support and love of his family. Although painful, he was able to overcome the enormity of the demeaning episode in his young life and become a man with an amazingly positive attitude, one devoid of bitterness and anger. After Hector related the story to me, I often questioned how I would have reacted to such a severe blow.

Following graduation from the University, Hector attended seminary and was eventually ordained as a minister in his denomination. I had never seen anyone begin a career, in this case a serious calling, with such enthusiasm. He represented the epitome of dedication, a man focused on his mission and intent on making a positive difference in the lives of people of all colors, faiths, races, genders, and persuasions—all people.

I believe Hector being different, a member of a minority, a Mexican American, kept the hierarchy of his denomination from allowing him to perform his calling at the highest level of his extraordinary talent and abilities. Over our many years of friendship, I witnessed instances of denied opportunities— times when his gifts as a scholar, administrator, and churchman could have been more fully realized and applied. Throughout it all and in spite of personal disappointments, Hector remained profoundly loyal to his faith and denomination. Although at times I had difficulty understanding the extent of his loyalty, it caused me to respect and admire my dear friend even more.

Several years ago Hector moved from Los Angeles to Portland, Oregon, following his wife Lynne, also a minister, as she assumed the duties of pastor for a Portland congregation. Hector applied for the position of Conference Minister for the northwest region, a position akin to a bishop, and landed it. In my estimation, Hector deserved to be working at this level of service for many previous years. Finally, he had gained a post in which the complete range of his talents could fully shine.

Having learned valuable lessons from the challenges Hector faced, they served as only one small aspect of our relationship. Over the years, we have shared many memorable moments together. We have transcended our personal setbacks and celebrated our triumphs together, along with mutual friends and family. We have shared a special brand of camaraderie while mourning the loss of loved ones, rejoicing in the arrival of others, or while discussing a good book, film, or piece of music together. We have also shared the agony and ecstasy of living and dying with Cal's inconsistent sports teams' performances. Since our college days, we have laughed, cried, argued, protested, and worked together for what seems like several lifetimes. We have remained so consistently connected that he rightly belongs on my A-list of cherished friends and extraordinary mentors.

Here's to all the coaches who have enhanced my life. Here's to all the winners.

ODE TO A BEAR

Once upon a magic time
I met a dancing bear.
A great and gentle bear he was
With a spirit light as air.

The very first time that we spoke
He took me by the hand,
Said, "How'd you like to dance with me?
Come on, strike up the band."

At first I was a bit amused,
For I'd never heard a bear
Address me quite this very way.
It was almost like a dare.

He said, "You gotta learn to dance
To get through life, you know.
And so I challenge you to live
By truly letting go."

Slowly I began to take
A step or two or three
With my new partner in this dance
Designed to set me free.

'Round and 'round for many years
We kicked up both our heels
To vast arrays of rhythmic treats
As he taught me how life feels.

It really was a joy to see
This big bear pirouette
With zest and grace throughout his stay,
A dance I won't forget.

After I had learned the steps,
He stopped me to converse,
And said, "I think I'd like to dance
Across the universe."

For him to take this giant leap
We'd have to say good-bye,
And he would have to shed his fur
To dance away that high.

I didn't want to see him go
But felt it must be right.
For who would want to keep a bear
From reaching his full height?

And as he slipped out of his coat
And drifted off into his trance,
He made me promise on my soul
To never cease the dance.

Each day I miss him very much.
No one can take his place.
Yet every time the music plays,
I see his smiling face.

~ 1993

NORTHWEST WIND CALLING

My brother, friend,
So many years ago,
Heeded his generous spirit
Calling him to serve,
To minister unto the flock,
To understand the rites of life,
To elevate the way we bond.

Through many years,
He honored well the call,
While artificial structures
Often failed to see his worth.
Sought justice more
For others than himself,
And stayed on
Steadfast, faithful and direct.
Until a northwest wind,
Invoking like an ancient psalm,
Sang, come and lead,
We welcome all your gifts.
Come pastor, take your place.
Here finally is your due.

~ 1997

Chapter Eighteen
A Season of Change

Going back to San Jose for the summer proved to be uncomfortable at times, especially when getting together with my old high school and junior college teammates who expected me to shine brighter my first year at Cal. Without talking too much about it, I sensed their let-down as much as I felt my embarrassment for not having played up-to-speed. I figured the summer would give me a chance to do some more serious thinking about how to turn things around.

My mom was glad to have me home, and I was happy to be able to eat my fill of her luscious Mexican cooking. Soon after I returned, she made me a batch of gorditas (little fat tortillas filled with savory goodies), and my sister Lucy brought over some of her superb Mexican rice. I had myself a long-awaited comidota (big fat meal). I still hadn't contacted my dad and didn't expect to very soon—maybe never.

The first couple of weeks of the summer were always a time just to screw off, go the beach, drink beer, and recover from finals. Then the time came for going to work and earning some money to supplement my scholarship for the coming school year. One of the great advantages of living in the Santa Clara Valley was the abundance of good paying summer jobs, especially in the canneries. I landed one of those again.

That summer I ended up working on a boxer in a cannery warehouse. My job entailed loading cans of fruit into cardboard boxes for eight hours a day, sometimes ten, using a boxing machine that helped me package the parade of tedious cans. Man! The job was a big, huge drag. Good thing the money was great. I thought to myself that if I didn't use my mind while on the boxer I was going to go nuts.

I remembered Coach Elliott saying, "In preparing for a game, you should carefully review every single play assignment and imagine in detail what you have to do." A good way to occupy my mind and not die from boredom, I began following Pete's instructions while working all day like an automaton. I decided to create my own mental movie, complete with pictures of the opposing team, the sounds of the crowd, the feel of taking a tackler head on, and even the sweat on my brow. In my imagination, I created game-like scenarios completely under my control and from which I emerged as the star. I discovered a way to play the writer, director, and actor in the great playing field of my mind.

A Winning Mental Movie

I start with a running a play, taking the ball and making a perfect cut off of the block and running it down the field for ten, twenty yards. I do that repeatedly. The next time I go for thirty yards. Forty and fifty on the next play. I make a great head and shoulder fake, get by the safety, and sprint eighty yards for a touchdown on the following play.

I try another run around end, the linebacker misses me, and it turns into a foot race past the defensive back. With my speed they can't catch me, and I streak down the field ninety-five yards for another winning touchdown. The crowd goes crazy. My teammates and coaches pat me on the back and shout, "Way to go, Hank. Way to go, man!"

Buck comes up, grabs me by the shoulder pads and yells, "Reeel good, Hank." Even Darrell reluctantly gives me a quick, "Nice goin'."

I run that particular play over and over again on the screen of my mind. Strangely it looks and feels good. It looks and feels real.

Next I try a beautiful pass route, fake to the inside, cut back out, get in the clear, and catch a perfect pass from Kapp on my way to pay dirt. Again, I run the same pattern. This time I have to stretch out for it, but I still haul it in.

I never drop a pass in my fantasy field, never. I can do whatever I please since I'm writing the script. I even imagine I have glue on my fingers, making it impossible to drop a pass that's thrown near me.

On the next series of downs I'm playing safety on defense. Gene Stauber, our great defensive backfield coach, has taught us how to run backwards or obliquely one way, spin quickly then go in the other direction. I do it better and faster than anyone. I keep my eye on the receiver and quarterback all at the same time, and just as the receiver is about to catch a perfectly thrown pass I come up and collide with him, making the ball fly off his hands and on to the turf. In the next similar sequence, I knock the ball away. In the following one,

I step in front of the receiver and intercept the ball for a touchdown.

Again and again, I see everything in sync, in perfect timing, like one big well-oiled, flowing machine. I even feel the crunch of the grass under my cleats as I cut, run, and pump—breathing hard like a stag racing for the trees. The din of the crowd always fills my ears to pour more voltage into my legs, lungs, and heart as I perform better than I ever have in my entire life. I even see headlines in the newspaper the following day shouting about my accomplishments.

Time on the boxer shot by. I rarely felt bored or tired, even when I stayed up late drinking beer the night before. I had stumbled on to something remarkable: self-made entertainment, a daydream I could control, new and powerful chunks of food for thought. I wondered if my self-produced mental movies would make me a better football player. I started getting in shape a little sooner than usual and with more determination than ever. I couldn't wait for the summer to end and the season to begin.

Endings and Beginnings

During my first spring semester, Daphne and I talked only twice on the phone and I might have written to her just a couple of times. I remember getting a note from her with the first sentence facetiously inquiring, "How are things at Africa State?" I couldn't blame her for feeling as if I had become as remote as that. I hadn't stopped caring for her. I just let our relationship slip away, let it become replaced by the overriding and pressing concerns of my new life. When I learned that someone else had taken my place, I was not terribly surprised. Daphne had met and fallen in love with Ray Horne at Chico State, and they had decided to get married that summer.

When she got home, Daphne and I had a kind and gentle talk about the changes in our lives. She told me about her newfound love. She shared that he played trumpet in a band and that he cared deeply for her. As I learned just a little more about him, I became flooded with contradictions. I couldn't help but think that he was probably a nice guy, and I felt happy for the beautiful girl who had been such an important part of my life for so many years. At the same time, I felt a little jealous and certainly saddened knowing that this was finally and truly the end of our relationship.

I got an invitation to the wedding and attended with Dudley and Rodda. I met Ray, and as I anticipated he came off as nice guy. Still it felt so very strange to be in the company of all the Lewises and no longer close to Daphne. Her parents, sisters, and brother probably wondered why it didn't work between us. I had been an extension of their household for so long. I think they must have known how I felt, that I would always care for Daphne.

The wedding proceeded and during the part when the minister says, "If anyone has cause why this man and this woman should not be joined in holy matrimony, let them speak now or forever hold their peace," Dudley gave me a firm poke in the ribs. I turned and saw him looking down with an impish grin. I poked him back and shot a look at him that said, just shut the hell up, asshole. Rodda joined him in the grinning.

I got through the reception but with some difficulty. A part of me felt like an intruder, an appendage from the past that had outlived its usefulness. I wanted to bolt for the door several times and run all the way back to Berkeley, the place where I was building new comfort zones for myself. No way could I do that, so I just left after saying my good-byes and good luck to Daphne and Ray. Harry and I ended up quietly having a beer, just the two of us, before we headed for home. We couldn't help but fall into a state of nostalgia about our high school days and how this event seemed to clearly mark the end of our youth. Although it was my childhood sweetheart who just got married, we were both equally feeling a little more alone and transformed. As we parted, we softly realized our lives would never be the same again. Forced to accept this ending, shut the door behind me, and move on, I found some comfort in looking forward with optimism to all that waited for me in the following chapters of my life.

Fall, my favorite time of year, finally arrived. With the smell of burning leaves in the air, we returned to Bowles Hall, two-a-days, blocking dummies, taped ankles, giant lemonades after fluid-draining practices, training table, learning plays, honing skills, getting into top shape, old friends and teammates, and a few new ones. This time I didn't feel like a stranger. Stewart didn't have to lead me by the hand anymore. No questions on where to go, what to do, or who to see. Nothing was unexpected. I could focus squarely on the game.

The mental movies I had run during the summer somehow made the two-a-day practices flow more naturally, helped me get through the murderous drills and disciplined steps needed for attaining superb physical conditioning. Coach Elliottt had a process he called "tempo," a hurry-up way of running plays intended to wear down the opposition. It worked fine as long as we were not the ones to first die from fatigue. No alternatives existed for getting in shape. I concluded early on that trying to cruise through practices only postponed the agony. I resolved to suffer in practice rather than in the middle of a game.

The mental movies seemed to have positively affected my play. I knew I had to become a better player, and my early placement on the second team proved it. Unlike last year, this time I stayed there through two-a-days. Darrell would definitely start in our opening game at home against Southern Methodist University, but I'd see my fair share of action too.

I took my first varsity game in stride. I felt fully prepared, but the tension in the locker room and the accelerating atmosphere outside began to make the butterflies start zooming around in the pit of my stomach. The first hit in the game and they disappeared, but the action on the field moved at a faster pace than I anticipated. As an opposing runner came at me, he seemed to jump step, move through a strobe light, miss frames like in an old movie, causing me to miscalculate and miss too many tackles. Everyone shooting around made me light-headed. I wanted to grab them and slow them down. The blur would take some getting used to.

We lost a close evenly fought game 13-6, one we should have won. The coaching staff was naturally displeased with our performance. They were far from delighted with mine, but I retained my second-team spot. We also lost the following game by a small margin and then took on a powerful Michigan State team at Berkeley. By then the blurring images on the playing field had begun to slow down some, and I started feeling more in control. Although we lost 19-0, I had a good day running and pass receiving. After the game, a major newspaper article appeared with the headline reading, "Elliott Hails Arrival of Ex-Rambler Olguin." The text read, "....he came from virtual obscurity as a football player to rip off yardage on rugged Michigan State." In the article, Pete praised my improvement and Coach Stauber proudly commented on how my stinging tackles made receivers drop the ball. While reading the article, I recalled how I once thought of the junior varsity team as beneath me. I also recalled the gift of Coach Ralston forcing me to see its value.

Although we kept losing, I kept improving. It felt like a mixed blessing. Early in the season, during the halftime of a game and before returning to the field, Pete announced, "Hank, in the second half I want you to go in with the first team at left halfback." I was shocked but thrilled. The level of Darrell's play had fallen off and mine had risen. None of the whys concerned me, and I felt more than ready to take over.

Kapp came up to me before we went back on the field, grabbed me and growled, "You know why you moved up don't you?" Before I could answer he growled again, "Because you want it, goddammit! Now let's go!"

As we ran back out through the tunnel, I remembered dreaming of the very moment I was experiencing, a moment that had floated across my mind many times. It occurred while coming down the stairs of Bowles Hall and glancing over at an imposing Memorial Stadium. I also quietly recalled feeding the dream with dancing pictures while standing at a warehouse boxer. I had finally become a University of California first-string varsity football player.

The remainder of my first season as a starter turned out to be a terribly frustrating experience for all of the players, coaches, and fans. We played competitive football, losing our last four games by a grand total of fourteen measly points. One example of special frustration involved the game against Washington in which a pass play from Kapp to me went eighty yards for a touchdown—at the time, the second longest pass play in Cal history. In spite of that effort, we lost another close one, 35-27. Everyone was playing their hearts out, but luck seemed to have deserted us. Hell! It was maddening. We deserved better.

Some developments offered consolation. My sister and her husband Nels went to every home game and finally dragged my mom along with them to see me play the second half of the season. It pleased me, but Rene told me that our mom still covered up her eyes when I got tackled. I anticipated that by the following year she would get used to it. On another satisfying note, Stewart and I had been seeing a lot of playing time together, and we both started against Stanford in the Big Game. Two Lincoln High, San Jose boys on a starting Cal backfield we knew would make Coach Lee Cox beam with pride once again. A final bit of comfort came from knowing I had accomplished what I set out to do and felt motivated to continue improving.

As I was about to leave the locker room feeling down after losing to Stanford in the last and most important game of the year, Kapp in his usual fiery, tight-lipped, never-say-die attitude, yelled at me, "Okay, Hank. Next year, man! We come back and get 'em next year!"

Before I left, I shook his hand and tried to match his determined tone as I said, "Okay, Joe. Next year, damn it! Next year!" As I walked away I felt a little better and started running a new set of mental movies in my head.

Fitting In Further

Life in the fraternity had become routine and comfortable. Having a good year in football earned me some star status among my fraternity brothers and to some degree on campus. Academically speaking I found myself more confused about my major than I was about my social life. I changed from General Curriculum to Industrial Relations and soon realized I'd made a mistake. I was almost certain I'd change majors again but didn't even want to think about it. I just wanted to enjoy myself. I had definitely postponed contemplating what to be when I grew up.

I met a beautiful girl that helped feed my avoidance mechanism. I started dating Margie Thomas, a freshman in the Tri-Delt sorority. At first our relationship was relatively casual. As time passed, we become more serious about each other. Wowed by her gorgeous looks, I soon discovered her challenging intellect and passions impressed me as well. I learned that she felt deeply and compassionately about social issues. At some point without daring to discuss the subject with her, I simply trusted that my ethnicity would never matter to her. Eventually, she met my mom and most certainly recognized her Spanish accent. Happy to see that it apparently didn't matter to her, Margie, my mom, and Rene established a genuine, mutual admiration society.

Margie and I shared parties, dances, and cutting classes to meet for coffee, afternoons at Tilden Park, weekends at Rene's house on the peninsula, driving to the beach in my sis and Nels's classic MG, listening to music, and sweet moments of passion. I made her laugh with my clowning, impressions, and accents and made her sigh when I played the piano and sang for her. Both sounds pleased me.

The International House sat about a half a block up the hill from the SAE house. The I-House, as casually referred to, provided housing for more than five hundred foreign and American students who lived together and shared the world's cultures. A part of me supposed that maybe some of them lived there, especially the foreign students, due to not being wholly appreciated or enthusiastically welcomed in other living situations.

In the mornings, a handful of my fraternity brothers sat having coffee and reading the newspapers next to our large picture window where we could see the parade of students coming down the hill on their way to classes. As some of the foreign students walked by, several wearing the typical garb of their countries, some of the brothers thought it funny to make snide remarks. "Here come the A-rabs," or "Looks like they just let out the zoo" were some of the comments they spouted.

A part of me wanted to tell the jerks to shut up, but I didn't have the courage. Their behavior only reinforced my opinion that prejudice against anyone different existed in our ranks. Margie would really hate hearing those remarks. I knew not everyone felt that way, but I sure wasn't going to start proclaiming I was Mexican anytime soon.

Richard Ball, a real cool Indian student born in Shanghai, talked to Kapp and me, expressing that the foreign students attending the university represented the cream of the crop from their countries. He felt we didn't make enough of an effort to welcome them and make them feel comfortable while they were attending Cal. Since many of those people would return to their homelands and become leaders, the three of us agreed that trying to do something to enhance their attitude about America served as a good idea. Dick came up with the idea to have an assigned athlete meet a designated student at the airport when they first arrived and then act as a kind of buddy throughout their stay.

We didn't work out all the details but ran the idea past a few of our athlete friends. It fell mostly on deaf ears. With little interest in the idea shown, we threw up our arms and dropped the whole scheme. Deeply disappointed,

I realized it was going to take some time before those indifferent attitudes changed.

In the meantime, I was feeling more relaxed about the whole matter of being Mexican but always kept my guard up a little. One night while several of us indulged in some serious beer drinking at the fraternity, Stewart began to tease by laughing and saying, "Hey, did you guys know, that Hank's a Mexican?"

The moment he said it my defensive dukes immediately went up. I shot an instant and irritated, "Screw you, Stewart," at John, along with the appropriate, insulting hand gesture. My reaction made him laugh and tease even more, knowing he had hit a tender spot. While the kidding went on for a couple more minutes, I started seeing that John's attitude was more mischievous than malicious. After all, I recalled that two of his favorite linemen on our high school football team were Mexican. Finally, his light-hearted taunts had little influence on the brothers and did not even come close to disqualifying my membership in the group. After thinking about it, I assumed it was Johnny's way of saying, "Hey, I'm on to you about that Spanish-French shit you've been claiming all these years. Relax. It's no big deal." He laughingly shrugged off my over-reaction, and we all went on to tease and joke about other more pressing matters. Maybe, just maybe, a healthier perspective on the whole damn thing was beginning to take over my thinking.

Spring came back around, filled up with classes, track competition, and spring football practice. Our spirits were high and preparing our bodies and attitude for a winning season next fall took over. There was nothing left to do but perfect plays, pass routes, and assignments to make everything work better. The feeling of anticipation ran through us all, and we were getting ready, ready to win.

On the extra-curricular side of life, three fraternity brothers, Jack, Bob, Ron, and I formed a quartet we called The Four Most. We had another fraternity brother, a transfer from UCLA, who wrote vocal arrangements for us styled after the popular group, The Four Freshman. Before long, we were singing and performing to accolades from our friends and others. During the annual Spring Sing competition at the Greek Theater, the SAE's and the Tri-Delts, Margie's sorority, performed together and won the grand prize. The Four Most competed for the only open entertainment spot. We won the competition and got backed-up by an exceptionally cool, student jazz ensemble. After the win our two houses celebrated like never before. I was on top of the world and believed the next year was going to be even better— as Margie's looks, smile, and walk continued to knock me out.

~ *FAST FORWARD* ~

A Persistent Pattern

When I heard fraternity brothers making derogatory comments about the foreign students attending Cal, I assumed attitudes like those would be rare a full forty years later. I also suspected that athletes might be immune from such biases. I wished that my assumptions in 1958 had been completely right. In 1998, *ESPN The Magazine* published an article on the then number-one tennis player in the world, Marcelo Rios from Santiago, Chile. The article attempted to point out his arrogant, ill-mannered behavior on the court, comparing his rude antics to players such as Jimmy Connors and John McEnroe. Not content with focusing solely on and criticizing Rios's boorish manners as he certainly would have done with a Conners or McEnroe, the writer Curry Kirkpatrick chose to spice up his piece by adding the most flagrantly stereotypic language I had heard in a long time. He referred to Rios as,"...a glowering, nasty-mannered, ponytailed greaser..." and "The Dark Hot Chili Pepper..." One of his other digs that I found particularly disturbing was, "Ask the 22-year-old Rios to stop over and, if his previous chivalry still holds, a drive-by shooting could develop." Later in the tirade he described Rios as, "...a dead ringer for those friendly neighborhood heroin dealers who starred on Miami Vice." He finished by talking about one of Rios's coaches saying, "Luckily, for Stefanki, Rios did not go for his switchblade."

At the time of the article, I was operating my own creative services boutique with my partner, Raoul Rodríguez. Although busy with a group of demanding clients, my shock and outrage over the magazine's audacity compelled me to react. My letter to the editor-in-chief got the magazine's attention.

May 4, 1998

John Papanek
Editor-in-Chief
ESPN The Magazine
19 East 34th Street
New York, N.Y. 10016-4303

Dear Mr. Papanek:

Being a greaser myself, I was delighted to read the wonderful article Curry Kirkpatrick wrote on a fellow-beaner, Marcelo Ríos, in the April 20 issue of your cutting edge magazine. It is truly gratifying to see that a quality publication such as yours so thoroughly understands the nuances and subtleties of spic culture.

As I was eating my tasty, spicy tacos, here in my nice filthy, dirt-floor cottage, I realized further what an ingenious and socially productive piece Mr. Kirkpatrick produced. Not only did he demonstrate truly original thinking, none of the cheap shot writing so prevalent today, but he also provided an invaluable service to the whole Hispanic/Latino culture. He applied, in a marvelously simple and elegant way, an intelligent, broad brush to characterize us as one people.

I'm tired of others trying to distinguish between Chileans, Mexicans, Puerto Ricans, Cubans, Spaniards, Argentineans, Dominicans, Colombians, Venezuelans and others, when we are truly one big, unwashed, Spanish-chattering, happy-go-lucky family. What good is it to play up the differences? It only promotes racism and stereotypes. After all, we really do all look and sound alike.

Judging by his clear, perceptive and pithy writing, I'm sure Mr. Kirkpatrick would agree that we are a clannish, hardworking and passive people, who only get angry when others make disparaging remarks about our pet Chihuahuas, graffiti or the bright colors we all like to wear. Otherwise, we are more than content to stay in our places playing our guitars, drinking our beer and tequila and having a lot of loud sex. Caramba, we really know how to live.

In closing, I simply want to say, muchas gracias to Mr. Kirkpatrick and your breakthrough magazine. This contribution to the image of Hispanics is so inspirational that I am considering encouraging my kids to get into sports writing and out of the gangs, drug dealing and car jacking.

Thank you, once again, for your insight and enlightened sense of social responsibility. I hope Marcelo Ríos and other wetbacks understand and appreciate all you have done for them. Surely, many will run out and pronto cancel their subscriptions to Sports Illustrated and start reading your fine magazine.

Sincerely and Happy Cinco de Mayo,

Henry Olguín
Secretary/The Imperial Chucos

Mr. Papanek responded with a kind letter of apology, complimenting me on my writing ability and assuring me that he and his writer Curry Kirkpatrick got the message. To this day, some twenty years later, I regret having to write such letters and hope I won't be forced to write similar ones any time soon. Nevertheless, I cautiously have decided not to put away my protest pen just yet. I have seen too much evidence to suggest that the battle is far from over, that some of the attitudes I encountered in my youth continue to surface.

Blond, Blue-Eyed Mexicans

When I first met Raoul Rodríguez to begin our eleven-year tenure working for GSD&M Advertising, Raoul had recently moved to the States from Mexico City. He came in to head up the newly formed Hispanic division of the agency. At the time, GSD&M ranked as a mid-sized ad agency, billing around $45 million and definitely on the move up. A third partner David Hepp joined the team as a copywriter.

For the next eleven years, I enjoyed the pleasure of working for a dynamic agency that grew to claim billings at a later date of more than $1 billion and rank as major national player in the advertising industry. Those years proved pleasurable and rewarding for many reasons, but

primarily because of the interesting and talented people I met and worked with within the agency. None proved to be more engaging than my two closet colleagues, David and Raoul.

David Hepp, born in Dallas, Texas, at an early age moved with his missionary parents and family to Puebla, Mexico. David quickly found himself immersed in the language and culture of his new home. Often he stood as the only güero (light-skinned, blond) in his elementary school classes. Those experiences helped shape his successful professional career and form many of his significant interests. It would stand to reason that David might gradually lose his facility for and interest in Spanish after returning to the States. On the contrary, he eagerly maintained his adopted language and culture through a vigorous reading regimen over the years as well as through the habit of constantly seeking out opportunities to converse in Spanish.

His love of the literature of Latin America and Spain, read primarily in Spanish, led David to become an expert in, among other subjects, the history of Mexico and particularly that of the Aztec and Inca empires. David's command of the Spanish language served him well in creating advertising for clients such as Coors or Taco Bell. Whenever he, Raoul, and I were not hard at work coming up with ideas for commercials or delighting in the hilarious comedy routines of Mexican comics such as Héctor Suárez or Polo Polo, I had the pleasure of picking David's brain to learn some historical gem about his own heritage. To this day, I consider David as genuinely Mexican as anyone I know in spite of his obvious northern European bloodlines. My perception was reinforced by his ability to converse in English, Spanish, or Spanglish with equal ease and pleasure.

My other colleague, Raoul Rodríguez Hatfield, was born and raised in Mexico City. Hatfield, his mother's maiden name (the use of which is customary in Mexico), comes from his grandfather who immigrated to Mexico from Liverpool, England. Granddad proved to be one tough Brit by living through and surviving the Mexican revolution in an area of the country where some of the most heated battles took place. That part of Raoul's background partially explains why he may be the most completely bilingual and bicultural person I have ever known. Attending American schools while growing up in Mexico City contributed to Raoul's attractive dual personality and style.

Raoul spoke in glowing terms, equally well in Spanish or English, about several aspects of his beloved country, from the food and customs to the people and the music. He could as easily turn around and boast proudly about his revered St. Louis Cardinals, Dallas Cowboys, his alma mater, Southern Methodist University, or the incomparable steaks at Sullivan's in Austin, Texas. I have enjoyed hearing him chastise Americans for some ignorant comment about Mexico or Mexicans for some stereotypic notion about Americans. I may have grown up straddling two cultures, but Raoul grew up straddling two countries.

By the time I met Raoul in 1983, he had already been a top advertising executive for several international ad agencies, D'Arcy being the most notable. Being new to advertising when we teamed up at GSD&M, I relied on Raoul as both a trusted peer and willing mentor. For the eleven years at GSD&M and the six during which we partnered to run our own creative services boutique, we worked on innumerable advertising projects together. Throughout the process, I learned countless lessons from Raoul, many about advertising but many more about human relations. His consistently kind and respectful attitude and dealings with people at all levels revealed his charitable spirit. His dry wit always stood ready to jump out and lighten up a dark moment. Raoul remains a respected and cherished friend whose association and conversation on any subject never fails to enlighten or entertain.

Throughout the years David, Raoul, and I worked together, we experienced a variety of interesting, humorous, sometimes bizarre, and memorable occurrences. One evening the three of us met at a Mexican restaurant near the agency to celebrate some triumph. As we walked in we noticed two tall, dark young men sitting at a table and looking like they could be descendants of Aztec or Toltec warriors. We tacitly identified the young men as Mexican American, exercising a fairly well honed ability to recognize our own. Dressed like any other Texans proud to sport the typical Texas uniform, they wore cowboy boots, Stetson hats, blue jeans, and massive metal belt buckles. Since they were within earshot, we could hear that they also spoke with thick Texas drawls that would have made even President Lyndon Baines Johnson proud. My compadres (pals) and I sat at the table next to them, ordered our golpes (shots) of Tequilla, and proceeded to converse in a loud and lively fashion—mainly in easy, flowing Spanish.

After a while, we began to notice that the two Tex-Mex boys were glancing at us politely but quizzically. They were probably scratching their heads and wondering what planet these two "gringo-looking" blond, blue-eyed guys talking to a third, light-skinned, gray-headed old boy could have possibly come from. I later guessed that they may have also been thinking to themselves, "Who the hell are these three loud, White guys sitting there talkin' away in the lingo of our grandparents, one we cain't speak a lick of?" After they left, Raoul, David, and I chuckled over the encounter and agreed that we must have presented a picture of contrasts many would have found perplexing.

The first piece of business the Hispanic team pitched and landed at GSD&M happened to be the Coors beer account. Coors was experiencing major market share losses among Hispanics and they needed a major fix. Much of the brewery's problems resulted from a boycott against Coors launched by a national Hispanic veteran's organization, The American G.I. Forum, protesting the brewery's employment practices. The boycott had seriously damaged the Coors image among Hispanics, and GSD&M was hired to help repair it.

When some of my Chicano and Chicana friends found out that I was working on behalf of Coors, they gave me an ample amount of grief, claiming I had sold out. I could not deny the charge completely but pointed out that working for Coors also presented some special opportunities to create positive changes from within. Because of our Hispanic team's influence and counsel on a wide range of issues, we were able to affect the attitudes and awareness of many people working within the company. After several years handling the account, we felt comfortable taking some credit for helping to institute a landmark agreement between Coors and several national Hispanic organizations. In the arrangement, Coors pledged substantial corporate support for a variety of ambitious and worthy Latino community projects.

In the process of creating and launching a Coors' corporate image-building campaign, my colleagues and I also managed to present and disseminate positive, uplifting images of Latinos. For example, the TV spot celebrating the then thirty-seven Hispanic Congressional Medal of Honor recipients struck an emotional chord among many Latinos, especially veterans. Some went so far as to remark that it was about time someone set the record straight about Hispanics fighting and dying for their country. The idea to commemorate a bronze statue of one of the "Tejanos" (Texas Hispanics), Toribio Losoya, who died defending the Alamo also hit a homerun with the Mexican American community. Many other similar campaign ideas helped to promote the Coors brand while simultaneously celebrating the accomplishments, contributions, customs, and holidays important to Latinos.

I felt especially proud that through our collective efforts we were able to halt Coors' slipping market share among Hispanics and affect record sales. The achievement received recognition by Advertising Age, calling it "...one of the most dramatic marketing turnarounds in modern corporate history."

One of my special pleasures while working at GSD&M involved my duties in creating music-driven radio and TV commercials. Writing jingles in Spanish and English allowed me to play with words in a new way, especially when trying to make the Spanish match the English and vice versa. With Spanish being twenty to thirty percent longer than English, the process often seemed akin to tackling the challenge of a Rubik's Cube.

Our team effort generated some welcomed praise from peers in the form of awards for advertising excellence. Many of our commercials, including the two TV spots earning Clios (advertising's highest honor), used music to drive the action and sell the products. Our team would conceptualize and write the spots and then turn to talented individuals who helped make our concepts come to life. Meeting and working with these people personally provided me with hours of special job satisfaction.

For the very first jingles we created in Spanish for Coors Light, we called on the services of an extraordinary composer/arranger/conductor, Carlos Franzetti. Born in Buenos Aires, Carlos moved to New York in 1974 to further develop his musical career. Since the day I first met and worked with Carlos, his career has soared to unbelievable heights, excelling in multiple genres including symphonies, film scores, big band jazz, chamber work, and opera.

As we started producing some of our first radio spots, Carlos recommended a lead singer for one of the jingles, an unknown to us then by the name of Ruben Blades. The guy had a great voice, and I took Franzetti's suggestion and hired him. The spots turned out beautifully, and later Ruben's career as a singer, actor, writer, and even Panamanian presidential candidate, flourished.

I have not spoken to Carlos in many years, but if I should I'm confident this exceptional talent would still be as modest, amicable, and gracious as the first day I met him.

In addition to working with numerous superb studio musicians, I considered myself lucky to have worked with other outstanding Latino artists such as Little Joe, Freddy Fender, Johnny Rodriguez, Luis Conte, Flaco Jimenez, and Tish Hinojosa. Our team also created and produced a set of Coca-Cola spots performed by the one and only Selena. The occasion involved a set of circumstances that forever placed Selena at the highest rung on my ladder of respect.

One afternoon my music producer and good friend Carl Thiel and I drove down to San Antonio from Austin to meet Selena in a studio to record the Coke radio spots. Selena and her husband Chris were driving up from their home in Corpus Christi. When Selena and Chris arrived we discovered that Selena had been in bed for a couple days with a bad case of the flu. The severe cold symptoms fiercely assaulting her throat immediately caused me to suggest that the session be cancelled and rescheduled at a later time when Selena felt much better. Selena would have no part of it. Like a seasoned old pro, she had arrived with lemon tea, medicinal sprays, and lozenges, fully prepared to go on with the show. No amount of my urging, even pleading to postpone the date, could convince Selena to shirk what she considered her professional duty. In spite of her pain and discomfort, we completed the spots, creating a polished final product that equally delighted the client and agency. After the session I praised and thanked Selena profusely. We also worked on a corresponding TV spot, one on which she again showed her consummate cooperation and professionalism.

When I learned of her premature death, my deep sadness stemmed from knowing that a great talent had been lost to the world of entertainment, one unquestionably destined to become a mega star.

Daniel (Dani) Indart

In 1984, I met a special young man who had recently graduated Magna Cum Laude in film scoring from the prestigious Berklee College of Music in Boston. After meeting Dani and his wife Sara, we quickly became friends. Dani had moved to L.A. to make his mark in the music business, and I had started working for GSD&M the previous year.

Dani inherited his passion for music from his mother. A world-renowned dancer and choreographer, she continued performing Flamenco dances through her seventh month of pregnancy. While on tour, she gave birth to Dani in Guayaquil, Ecuador. Raised in Caracas, Venezuela, he simply could not escape from the genes nor from the influence of musicians and dancers he grew up knowing and emulating. In 1977, RCA International signed him to its stable of performers and two songs from his album became number-one hits on the South American charts.

By the time I met him, he was trained and eager to make it big in L.A. As usual, success moved at its own tempo. Meanwhile, I set out to convince Dani to jump into the advertising music game. At first reluctant, he couldn't resist when I offered him an assignment. I asked Dani to create music for a radio Christmas greeting card in the tradition of the Mexican estudiantina (student madrigals) style of music. Dani nailed the assignment and since then has affectionately referred to me as el padrino (the godfather) for getting him started in this career direction.

Dani and I have worked together on many large and small projects and always with a mutual respect, high level of creativity, cooperation, and attitude of fun. Sara, now his ex-wife and trusted business partner, has kept us both on track. More importantly, Dani has helped enhance my knowledge and appreciation for the tremendous Latin musical menu available to him. From Salsa to Samba, Merengue to Latin Rock, Dani continues to experiment with and expand the options offered by his extensive catalog of Latin music. Aside from the compositions and arrangements he creates, selections from his vast Latin Music Specialists library can be heard to this day on national and international television, film, and advertising productions. Dani and I have also developed a Latin music-driven, animated, children's TV series.

Dani is one of the special, extraordinary people who has become a trusting and loving part of my extended family—truly a brother. From friendships and ties shaped in my school days to those created in recording studios, I measure the value of my life by the enduring and affectionate connections I have formed with family, friends, and colleagues. I'm grateful to all those who permanently remain along a tender path that reaches many pleasurable years back.

THE MOMENTS OF FRIENDSHIP

The meaning of genuine friendship
Is elusive as clouds drifting by.
We never know how to define it,
No matter how hard we may try.

For friendship is born in the moments,
Individual, unequaled, and rare.
Then nurtured through loving and sharing,
Expressions of how much we care.

Though our lives may take different directions
As friends go their own separate ways,
We will always cherish the memories
Of the moments and joys or our days.

~ 1996

Chapter Nineteen
Driving Towards the Goal

The spring semester ended. I borrowed my mom's car and drove Margie home to Southern California for the summer. We spent a few leisurely days with her family, enjoyed the beach and each other. Our relationship, although sweet and comfortable, felt as if it was drifting away from me. I cared for and respected Margie, but I couldn't bring myself to say I loved her. My heart seemed to belong somewhere else, but I didn't know where.

I returned home and ran into Pat Cochran, Dudley's steady girlfriend and Daphne's best friend all through high school. I thought of her as a friend also, having seen her almost everyday for three of the most important years of our lives, often double-dating with her and Dudley and being part of the same social circle. I remembered the first time I saw Pat the first week of our sophomore year of high school. She was looking for a classroom and I was looking at her, gawking is more like it. At the time I thought to myself that she had to be one of the most beautiful, cool, classy girls I had ever seen.

She and Dudley broke up just before he went into the Army, and Daphne had become an old married lady. We were the odd-couple out of an old familiar foursome and picked up on what we had in common. At first we just got together for coffee, dinner, drives, or for easy conversation and casual company. An innocent kiss and then another and very soon the emotions took over, and we thought we were falling in love. Were we? It happened so quickly. Yes, we were in love. Mad, fun, exciting, almost dangerous, and all too quickly we said, "Oh, what the hell let's get married."

The most important football season of my life awaited me just a few weeks away. Getting in shape that year felt like a religious experience full of fervor, drive, and purpose. Wherever the other Golden Bears were getting ready, I'm sure every step they took in preparation was designed to redeem themselves, to erase the pain and disappointment of our last season. Winning was the only option. The mental movies I ran as I was working, driving around, or running wind sprints all ended happily.

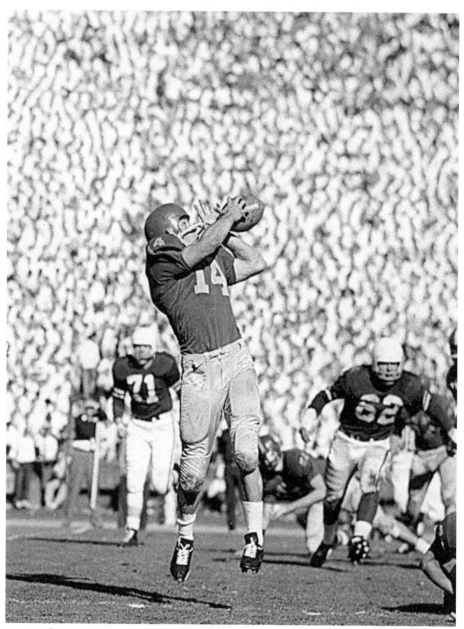

Catching a pass from Kapp in 1957 Cal/Stanford Big Game

Although my dad and mom had been divorced for a couple of years, they started occasionally talking to each other, and according to my mom, in a more civilized way. I thought they might be able to put their many differences aside and just become friends. I didn't know; a lot of hurt had to be set aside.

My dad and I also met that summer and began to mend our fences. As we played catch-up, I told him about the terrible start to my sophomore year and the tough lesson I had to learn. Although my dad was no great jokester, his sense of humor would occasionally emerge. He reacted to my confession by saying, "No es pecado ser pendejo. El pecado es, quedarte pendejo." (It ain't a sin to be a dumbass. The sin is to stay a dumbass.") I agreed.

He then made his own confession that stunned me. He told me he had bought season tickets to the Cal games the previous season and went to see me play in every home game. He related the event in a matter-of-fact way. He then struggled emotionally to tell me further how he admitted to the people sitting around him that I was his son. He and the other season ticket holders had suffered together through a heart-breaking season. After the games his new friends apparently made comments like, "Tell Hank, good game. Tell Hank, to keep his spirits up when you see him."

Of course, he never told me anything, never delivered the messages. Instead he quietly left the stadium and drove home alone.

Before returning to Bowles Hall and the grind of early fall practices, I reluctantly met with Margie back in Berkeley to tell her about Pat. We got together at her friend's apartment and when I saw her I couldn't suppress some of the old feelings of affection and even desire stirring inside of me. The feelings turned into regret after telling her that Pat and I were to be married and seeing how deeply the news had hurt someone for whom I truly cared. I walked away saddened and sorry after my announcement but determined to bury any emotions getting in the way of my driving towards the goal line.

That year the practice field atmosphere had an extra emotional charge.

Moving better, faster, and smoother, we were beginning to perfect our quick-hitting Split-T system even if no one else could see it. The sports pundits had predicted that we would have trouble improving on our dismal 1-9 season of 1957. They wrote that we were too light, with a puny one hundred ninety-two pound line that gave away a full twenty-three pounds per man to our across-the-bay rival, Stanford. Piestrup, one of our finer minuscule linemen, always summed it up best, "We may be small, but we're slow." They dismissed us on paper for our lack of speed and star power, Jack Yerman and I being the only exceptions in the speed department and Kapp and Jack Hart in the star category. We were dying to make them eat their words.

We knew what it would take to overcome the apparent lack of talent. An exceptional amount of physical and "mental toughness," as Cal All-American and former line coach Rod Franz liked to preach, would head up the formula. We planned to be in better shape than anyone we played. We knew we could do that. There wasn't a dog in the bunch, and we knew our coaching staff concurred. It gave us added incentive. So did co-captains Kapp and Hart who drove us hard to excel. We were also feeling sure in the strength of our backfield with probable All-American Kapp, Hart, and me seasoned and sound. That year we were happy to have young promising fullback Bill Patton join us. Billy had a great year on the freshman team in 1956 but sat out the '57 season. At 192 pounds, he qualified as a potent straight-ahead runner, a good blocker, and a rugged defensive player.

The first team looked good in pre-season scrimmages. In one, I returned a punt for ninety-seven yards and a touchdown. In another I got three of the six touchdowns scored. The rest of the Bears were also clicking.

We opened against the College of the Pacific (COP) and scored plenty of points, but their great running back Dick Bass tore up and down the field almost at will. We lost another close one, 24-20. After the game, the frustration ghosts from the previous season returned to haunt our locker room. In spite of all the angry helmets being slammed around, we couldn't scare them off. In preparing for our next game, we knew what we had to do. When we got too tired to run we had to run harder.

The following week we traveled to East Lansing Michigan to take on the powerful Michigan State Spartans. The close COP loss didn't dampen our spirits, and we still felt confident. I especially felt upbeat going into the game, having played well against the Spartans in our last season's 19-0 loss. I didn't dwell much on my individual past performance. My focus stayed on winning the upcoming contest.

I played just okay. I got off a quick kick for fifty yards and returned a punt for thirty-five yards. Other than that, my performance proved to be unspectacular. On one pass play, I beat the defender by five yards. Joe threw one right into my hands, and I watched in disbelief as the ball trickled off my fingertips. It was not like me. I hadn't been dropping passes. When I returned to the huddle, I was surprised Joe didn't punch me in the mouth. I thought he should have, since the catch would have led to a sure touchdown. No matter, we got trounced, 32-12. The fact that Michigan State was being touted to win both the Big Ten Conference and a national championship offered us no consolation. We returned to Berkeley pondering what the hell we had to do to win.

Next we opened our Pacific Coast Conference competition against the Washington State University (WSU) Cougars. They had the greatest passer in Cougar football history, Bobby Newman, as well as a dangerous receiver in Gale Cogdill. In the previous season, Newman had led the nation in total offense. In their opening game, WSU crushed Stanford 40-6 and then lost by only one point to Northwestern. In their first two games, they had already scored a total of sixty-eight points. We were clearly the underdog but didn't bother to read WSU's press clippings. We just got ready to play like never before.

My teammates and I assaulted the week of practice with a driving determination I had never experienced in my life. Moving beyond some ordinary winning attitude, we had entered into a high-purpose zone, one in which we were collectively breathing, running, executing—transcending our deficiencies, disregarding our past losses and adversity. We appeared blinded by the task at hand and silently asserting, "It is impossible to lose this game. We will die on the practice field first. The practice field is where we create the unquestionable outcome. There in that moment is where Saturday's contest takes place, where it is truly decided within each of us."

Even our coaches understood that they might have been managing the practice, but our resolute spirit was propelling it. As we ran our offensive plays for timing and precision, the coaches required that we run each play downfield for ten yards. We followed their instructions for the first few plays. Then Kapp and Hart ran one all out for fifteen yards. Soon after we went for twenty, and before long the entire team was wind-sprinting on every play, twenty-five and thirty yards down the field, shouting and howling like a pack of ravenous, wild dogs closing in on a kill. Washington State had no idea what was about to descend on them.

Before our nationally televised game began, Kapp gathered the starting unit out in the middle of the field. We stacked our hands in the center of the circle, and Joe announced with stern, steely determination, "Anybody who doesn't know we're going to win this game get the hell off the field. Now!" He had no takers—only resolute warriors.

We lined up and quickly and inexorably proceeded to thoroughly dismantle the Cougars. Exhibiting our most complete team effort to date, our line and defense in particular rose like the Phoenix to devastate the opposition. On our first touchdown drive, Joe ran our pitchout play to perfection by lateraling the ball to me at the perfect moment. On one play, I took it for thirty-eight yards. Several plays later, I scored on a thirty-nine yard dash around end. I finished the day with a nearly twelve-yards-per-carry average, but everyone on the team had stepped up big-time just like in my mental movies. We routed favored WSU, 34-12.

The day after the game I asked Coach Elliott if he thought my getting married during the Christmas holidays would interfere with our Rose Bowl team practices. He looked at me with an amused grin and said, "Yeah, I think it would be fine." He probably thought I was being overly optimistic. He didn't know I was already seeing the Rose Bowl game films in my mind's eye.

We were now off and literally running exceptionally well. Our next opponent, Utah and their All-American quarterback Lee Grosscup, didn't stand a chance against us, and we took them out 36-21. With our defensive line pressing Grosscup all the way, he didn't shine until our third unit went in to play most of the second half. The game was never in question. Although I was playing well, our backfield coach Buck grabbed me before our next game and demanded, "Hank, you have to start running over people."

I looked at him, wondered if he'd lost his marbles, and asked, "At a 162 pounds soaking wet how do I do that, coach?"

Through clinched teeth, Buck answered, "With your speed and velocity, you just put your head down and drive into 'em."

I told him, "Okay coach, I'll try."

He smiled and said, "Reeel good, Hank."

The USC Trojans were next. We played them in the Los Angeles Coliseum where the temperature hit over one hundred degrees on the floor of the arena. I actually attempted what Buck suggested. It started feeling "reeel good," and I got a couple of extra yards as a result. In the second quarter, I was involved in a pile up. I felt my ankle twist unnaturally and a sharp sting of pain under the tape. Shit! I limped off the field and the half ended. During halftime, I got the ice pack followed by a shot of Novocain and Cortisone. Come hell or high water I was going back in. Good thing I did.

In the fourth quarter Angie Coia, the Trojan's 9.7 speedster, took a pitchout and sprinted thirty-six yards down the sideline. I ran over from the offside safety and at the last moment managed to barely push him out of bounds. Without the bump he would have scored and USC probably would have won. After hitting Coia, I rolled into the USC bench and one of their coaches with a reputation for his own brand of USC zeal, Marv Goux, grabbed me and said, "Goddamn you, Olguin."

As I walked back on to the playing field, I appreciated his passion but at the same time felt glad I was able to make the play and piss him off. After a hard-fought game we came out on top, 14-12. After the game, one in which I had melted down to a scrawny 157 pounds, Marv came up to me and apologized, "Sorry about that, Hank. You know, in the heat of the moment . . ."

I answered, "Yeah, no kidding coach, heat. No problem. Good game." He appeared inconsolable. On the plane back to Berkeley, I almost passed out from the pain. The ankle did not look good.

Oregon was next. I hobbled all week with the injury, but I was still scheduled to play. One of Buck's favorite sayings came back to me, "Is it pain or injury? You can't play with an injury but have to learn to play with pain."

I had to play. I was off to a great year. I was just behind Kapp in total rushing yardage, sporting an 8.29 yards-per-carry average, and just behind Hart in pass receptions. I was determined to hang in there, but on the second play of the game I took a hit to my other ankle. I couldn't believe it. In a dizzying instant I was out of an incredibly important game. My mental movies didn't include that scene. Fortunately, Wayne Crow took over for me and did a great job. We won, 20-6.

We lost one of our next three games but stayed in the driver's seat for Pasadena. I didn't even suit up for the Oregon State game, the one we lost, and saw only spotty duty in the next two. In the UCLA game, I still couldn't cut very well, so I really took Buck's advice to heart and ran straight into tacklers with a vengeance. I didn't just try and run over them, I tried to lay them out. It helped me work out the anger for my lousy, rotten luck.

Jack, our head trainer, did his best to rehabilitate me, but the healing took its time. Even when our illustrious and gracious university Chancellor Glen Seaborg expressed his concern for my wellbeing, it failed to ease the pain of being sidelined. Nevertheless, I felt honored when Glen would come into the locker room and ask, "Hey, Hank, how are the ankles doing?" Imagine a Nobel Laureate genuinely caring about a little halfback's ailing wheels. He was one fine man. No doubt about it.

By Stanford Big Game time, we were on a direct path to the Rose Bowl and Kapp to All-American honors. Our line play and defenses had jelled. Another one of our good young halfbacks, Grover Garvin, had stepped up to fill the void along with Wayne. Patton had become a short plunge scoring machine and Hart, Domoto, and others had a great year. Getting past Stanford posed no great problem. They'd had a terrible season. We were favored by 10½ points. By comparative scores, we should have beaten them by a whopping margin of one hundred six points. That figure came from a sports writer's numbers game where he compared each team's scores against common opponents—interesting but useless. All I knew was that I was ready and eager to play.

Time and time again, we had heard Old Blues say, "Never take the Big Game for granted." They were absolutely right. This one turned into an emotionally exhausting afternoon not only for the players but also for the 81,490 screaming fans that packed Memorial Stadium. I kept expecting to play, but Pete didn't put me in. My own rationale for easing my disappointment was that he was saving me for the Rose Bowl. I never asked.

The one hundred six point mythical calculation became a 16-15 final score reality, with Stanford attempting a two-point conversion and falling a mere yard short of the goal and a win— one that would have robbed us of the roses. We escaped disaster by a hair's breath. Pete put me in for a token appearance late in the game. Kapp ran a pitchout to me, which I fumbled. Fortunately, I recovered my own screw-up. I wondered what the hell was going on? I hadn't fumbled once all year or last. Maybe I felt the fans needed a little added closing drama. Whoa! Too close.

After the game a wild celebration took place. The president of the university Dr. Clark Kerr, California Governor-Elect Pat Brown, and other notables visited the locker room to congratulate the team. Even my old gym teacher and junior college football coach Fred Silva joined us in the locker room. Honored and thrilled by its successful run to the roses, the team basked in the intense adulation. Pete stood on the balcony of the locker room and addressed the Cal student body saying, "I don't know how good a team we are, but I know this—we have been through a tough season, under pressure in every game, and this bunch of fellows put out at all times." That was all the praise we needed, simply hearing that we gave it our all every step of the way.

The time had come to head for Pasadena. That's the movie I wanted to see. Hey wait a minute. I had to get married and did so on December 20. Pat's father threw an elegant and well-attended affair. The morning of the actual wedding the team held its last practice before traveling to Southern California. During the scrimmage, I got creamed in the eye on one play. Well-meaning coaches pulled me out, and the trainers rushed to apply an ice pack that would prevent an embarrassing black eye from appearing on the groom.

With Kapp, Hart, and my other teammates Domoto and Bob Chiappone all part of the wedding party, we received national press. Heading for the Rose Bowl we were absolutely newsworthy. The entire team and coaching staff attended the wedding with the reception appropriately held at the California Alumni House. Everyone regarded it as a distinctive blue and gold gathering, through and through, and a fitting prelude to Pasadena.

Now that I had grown up, I still hadn't decided what to do the rest of my life. I did contemplate becoming a writer and documenting some of the interesting events I had experienced—like playing in the Rose Bowl. Time would tell.

~ *FAST FORWARD*~

Mental Movies Beyond Sports

The summer I started running mental movies of me making touchdowns and catching passes, while working in a cannery, I had never heard of creative visualization. I had somehow accidentally stumbled on a technique that today is common among elite athletes like Michael Phelps, Carli Lloyd, and Jack Nicklaus. Years later, when I first read *Psycho Cybernetics* by Dr. Maxwell Maltz and other books on the subject, I gained a greater understanding about the power of the technique and subsequently applied it to some of my professional endeavors—namely by successfully helping public speakers to eliminate stage fright and by enhancing the creative process in advertising. Today, they have a lot of names for it: mental imagery, mental rehearsal, or peak performance techniques. Whatever they call it, it works. It's such an effective self-development tool that I began to consider its potential application to a pressing problem: the academic achievement of Latino/a students.

Each day it becomes abundantly clear that Latinos will make up an important segment of our future workforce, especially given their youthful demographic. Six out of ten Latinos are millennials or younger. With large numbers of Americans soon retiring in record numbers, some eighty million millennials will be entering the workplace to take their place, many of them Latinos. Therefore, it is imperative that those students excel academically in preparation to effectively help fill our workforce needs.

Rob Lapsley, president of the California Business Roundtable, weighed in on the issue in a *Sacramento Bee* Op-Ed piece in 2015. He emphatically voiced his concern that the academic success of Latino/a students is tied to the future economic health of the state. Recognizing that a full fifty percent of all children under 18 in California are Latino, Mr. Lapsley stated, "California can't succeed as a world-class economy and state if we leave behind half of the population. Education leaders, legislators and the governor need to work together to address these issues now."

Realizing that the lack of positive role models and stereotyping can hinder the academic performance of Latinos, I developed a program idea utilizing creative visualization—mental movies—to enhance the self-confidence and the feelings of self-worth of Latino/a students. While we wait around for the media to begin depicting us in positive roles or reporting on the full spectrum of our contributions, we must find self-motivating methods to inspire our kids. Creative visualization is one such method. If it helped Hank to make touchdowns and catch passes, it can surely help Latino students make the honor roll. Imagine that.

Old Blues and Old Attitudes

Since 1959, the Cal Rose Bowl team has gathered for several festive reunions. At first some of my teammates, now called Old Blues, were surprised to hear me using the Spanish pronunciation of my name. Others were more surprised to learn of my Mexican background. Fullback Billy Patton liked to think back and declare in a hearty, opinionated tone of voice, "I didn't give a damn if any of you guys were Chicano, Black, or Japanese. All I cared about was whether or not you could block and tackle."

To a great degree, Billy expressed a growing attitude. Often sports have proven to help transcend racial divides. The legendary interracial friendship between Brian Piccolo and Gale Sayers, teammates on the Chicago Bears from 1965 to '69, served as an early inspirational example. When I played football at Cal, the country had barely begun to peek at the serious discrimination faced by minorities. An incident involving the Cal team, which included some Rose Bowl squad members in the fall of 1959, illustrated that reality.

At one of our reunions, Terry Jones, the African American center that played on both the '58 and '59 squads, related a story to me regarding Cal traveling to Austin, Texas for a game against the University of Texas Longhorns. As the team began to check in to the hotel, Terry and Charlie Holston, another African American player, were standing within earshot of Coach Elliott. A young hotel employee walked up to Pete, pointed to Terry and Charlie, and whispered, "Coach I'm sorry but those players are not going to be able to stay in this hotel."

Terry remembered that Pete turned to the young man, red-faced and angry, and asked, "Well, where can they stay?"

The young man answered, "There's a hotel on another side of town they can check into."

Without hesitating Coach Elliott demanded, "Well, you see that this entire team gets checked into that hotel or we're not playing football on Saturday." Terry recalled being proud of Pete for his emphatic stance and disapproval. Charlie confirmed that the team got back on the bus and headed for a hotel on the outskirts of town where they all were allowed to stay.

Many significant societal changes have occurred since that fall day in 1959. If today they held a Rose Bowl team reunion in the hotel that once refused Terry and Charlie lodging, everyone would unquestionably be able to check in. To what extent race relations in general have progressed since that time is difficult to determine exactly. Certainly time will tell, and we can only hope that Sayers' and Piccolo's example has helped move us toward real progress.

As a historical gauge, 1966 marked the year that Jerry LeVias became only the second African American football player in the history of the Southwest Conference. For that privilege he suffered verbal and physical abuse, exclusion, and even death threats while playing for Southern Methodist University (SMU). Full participation by African American athletes would not take place in Texas until many years later.

I was living in Texas in the fall of 1967. I remember casually tuning into a televised game between SMU and Texas A&M, with Jerry LeVias as one of the Mustangs' starting halfbacks. Before long, I found myself totally engaged in an entertaining, back-and-forth battle between underdog SMU and the powerful Aggies. Late in the first half, SMU's starting quarterback suffered a broken leg. He was replaced by a pint-sized, five feet, six inches short Inez Perez. Seeing a Mexican American playing for a major college immediately spiked my attention, but watching a young man enter the game who could barely see over his giant linemen didn't provide me with much hope for a great performance. I was wrong.

Before long, I found myself cheering madly for Jerry and Inez, and they didn't disappoint. With less than a minute to play, the Aggies scored a touchdown and went ahead, 17-13. The picture looked gloomy until Jerry ran the ensuing kickoff back 24 yards. Perez then passed to LeVias for 29 yards, to halfback Mike Richardson for 11, to end Sam Holden for 12, and finally to Jerry for the winning touchdown. (I couldn't possibly recall those details, so I went back to the archives to get the stats.) SMU won the game, 20-17, and Coach Hayden Fry referred to Perez and LeVias as "my two little giants." What made the game memorable for me, almost a decade after my playing days, is that I found myself stomping around my TV set and screaming like crazy in support of two minority players I hadn't even heard of—further evidence of my investment in and concern for the state of affairs involving race and sports in America.

While back in Texas many years later, I tracked down Perez to tell him of my admiration for his performance and to chat about our respective experiences as Chicano college athletes. It was a heartwarming conversation in which we discovered an easy commonality.

The Play

Living in Los Angeles in 1982, I had the pleasure of frequently hanging out with my old friend from Cal, Hector Lopez. When it came to Big Game time, Hector invited me over to watch the game at his Hancock Park home. We both had a special interest in watching the Golden Bears that year since my Rose Bowl teammate Joe Kapp had been named Cal's head football coach. The year before, Joe promised not to drink another drop of tequila, his favorite beverage at the time, until Cal returned to the Rose Bowl. Years later, I kidded him about the folly of his promise and his having to drink rum instead.

Hector and I settled with our beers to watch our alma mater go up against the Stanford Cardinal and their All-American quarterback John Elway. As I recall, we played a pretty good game and were in the lead, 19-17, late in the fourth quarter. Some extraordinary pass completions by Elway very late in the game put Stanford in field goal range, and their place kicker, Marc Harmon, hit a 35 yarder that put Stanford up, 20-19, with only seconds left.

With that, Hector got up in disgust and slammed off the TV set, and I equally disgusted got up, climbed in my car, and headed back home. A minute or two later, as I turned on the radio ready to change it from the station broadcasting the game to some comforting music, I heard the Cal sports announcer Joe Starkey going completely bonkers. I quickly learned that with four seconds left, Cal had taken the kickoff and five laterals later scored the winning touchdown for a 25-20 victory. I almost got in a wreck as I squealed my car back around to Hector's pad, crashed through his door without knocking, and yelled, "Put the damn TV set back on. Cal just pulled it out." His perplexed look didn't stop me from continuing to spurt, "You're not going to believe this, man. You're not going to believe this shit."

We watched the amazing, highly unpredictable play over and over, including the entire Stanford band running on the field before the end of Kevin Moan's final crossing of the goal line and right after he had run over the band's trombone player en route. "The Play" caused endless controversy, with Stanford fans and players claiming foul and Cal fans gloating for decades. To this day, it stands as one of the most memorable moments in college football history.

Hector and I were especially proud that our fellow Chicano classmate had a hand in coaching such an extraordinary event, but continued to lament the fact that Joe hasn't been able to enjoy tequila for many years.

With all of the special sports events I have had the privilege of observing in my lifetime, I still see the relationship of Brian Piccolo and Gale Sayers as highly significant in helping us to alter our attitudes about race. It inspired me to celebrate their contributions.

WHEN GALE AND BRIAN SANG

When Gale and Brian sang
I felt compelled to kneel
Not to revere or pray
But to awake and feel

That some new note did sound
To shout that change take place
And drown out bigotry
In tune with their embrace

When Gale and Brian sang
They broke old chains apart
Played to an unheard score
To music of the heart

~ 1988

Chapter Twenty
Rose Bowl Bound

By the time we made our way to Southern California, Elliott had been named coach of the year and Kapp back of the year, well deserved honors for them and by association our team. We arrived and checked into the Ambassador Hotel. When Pat and I walked into our room, we had to laugh that our single beds were located at opposite ends of the room. The coaches apparently wanted to reinforce our natural disciplined inclinations.

We started a tough practice schedule in preparing for the game. Pat and the other players' and coaches' wives got the red carpet treatment with sightseeing trips and planned excursions.

The players were treated to a couple of special events but mainly were involved in hard-nosed preparation for the game. My job felt particularly tough and worrisome. Two fine backs had filled in for me the second half of the season, and I was going to have to work twice as hard to prove I deserved to get the starting nod. I was sure Pete wouldn't announce his choice until just before the game.

I may have had a slight edge being a senior and, in spite of missing five games, remained fourth in rushing with the highest yards-per-carry average on the team at 6.9. I had also managed to stay in second place in punt returns and gained more kick-off return yards than any of my teammates. I hoped all that would help. I desperately wanted that starting slot in the bowl. I had dreamed about it for a long time. The tension had been high in practice, the competition intense. With game day upon, us I knew I had prepared to the best of my ability. Now, it was time to try and relax.

Tight, Loose

Tight, loose. Tight, loose. A big game day can often come down to more than a fight between two football teams. It can also involve a fight between tight and loose—an individual player's battle between a tense or relaxed mind, between a mental picture of bumbling a pass or dancing to a touchdown, between a clinched fist grinding around in the pit of the belly or muscles feeling as though they can fly. The tight, loose fight can have you floating around in a giant, mental, emotional and kinesthetic quandary before the first bead of sweat breaks out on your forehead.

That day was no exception. There we were in the Rose Bowl locker room getting ready for the game of our lives. Cal hadn't been to the Rose Bowl since 1951, and all of us were feeling privileged, honored, even lucky to be there. But the pressure was on. It had been a long dry spell.

Winning the conference championship was no stroll in the park, particularly for a team devoid of size and skill as the sports writers often put it. We had reached that point more on tenacity, hard work, and a burning will to excel rather than on talent. No matter. We earned our way into that locker room, and to us it felt like sacred ground. A lot of exceptional teams and athletes had been there, and we were now a part of that great legacy. Regardless of the game's outcome, no one could take that away from us. The story of how we got there belonged exclusively to us.

Locker rooms before going out on the field are usually quiet places, at least ours was. Quiet makes it feel tight. Joking and laughter would make it more like loose. The quiet, subdued atmosphere sometimes took on a strange dreamlike state. I always thought we should be screaming with excitement, but we moved around politely, almost gingerly as we put on shoulder pads and other battle gear. The scene always seemed contradictory to me given that a bunch of men were preparing to go out and participate in a head-to-head, violent collision sport. As we were about to hit the field, we got a bit noisier but during most of our preparation the locker room felt like a temple of whispers.

Rip! Rip! Jack the tape ripper and our head trainer stood in front of me pulling tape off a roll and ripping it with nothing but his strong hands and fingers. I sat on a tall padded table with my leg extended stiffly over the end and pointed straight at Jack. He stuck on a tight band of tape from one side of my leg just below the calf muscle, pulled it around the bottom of my heel across my shaved ankle, and stuck it on a matching spot on the other side of my leg—all in one smooth, swift, unequivocal motion. Another tight length of tape went on slightly ahead of the first and then another and another, reinforced by concentric strips from the ankle up the leg to, again, just below the calf muscle. Jack gave the other ankle the exact same treatment.

Like a master craftsman, Jack sculpted armored leggings for me made of sticky, white fabric. The leggings felt tight, secure, and solid enough to hopefully keep my previously sprained ankles from buckling or bending from a hard hit. I thought they had better work. I was tired of banged-up wheels and missed games. I couldn't have the damned gristle and bone fail me during this once-in-a-lifetime dream come true. Although it was still hard to believe we were there at the granddaddy of the bowls, the reality of running on to that field got repeatedly validated in my mind's eye and then raced through my body like an electrical current.

As I slipped off the taping table, my ankles firmly in their cast, an intense, tight-jawed Head Coach Pete Elliott walked up to me and asked his ritualistic, pre-game question, one I had heard many times before. And as usual the question carried a field general's somber tone, "Are you ready, Hank?" Meaning of course are you prepared to sacrifice your body, run, and hit until you are thoroughly spent, play with reckless abandon, and die on the field of battle if necessary. Now that's what I called tight.

My response came from some imbedded place in my psyche needing a little bit of loose at that particular moment. It certainly didn't come from a safe, rational place. Coach Elliott's usual stern demeanor and disciplined style demanded a serious confirmation of commitment to the task at hand not some frivolous smart-ass, dangerous remark. Still I blurted out, with a dopey grin, "You betchum, Red Ryder, heh, heh." (A stock line from Little Beaver, a Native American sidekick character in an old western series.)

During a soundless second that ballooned into an eternity, the words boomed in my inner ear, Pete's face froze in disbelief, and my brain screamed back at me, "What in the world did you just utter? Have you gone absolutely, stark-raving mad?"

I stood there with a tentative, frightened look on my face like a five-year old waiting for his angry parent to decide on the punishment to be applied for using some obscene word. After the never-ending moment passed, Pete's face slowly thawed and broke into a smile that surprised even him. I began to slowly breathe again, and we both quickly realized that our shared moment of levity was a necessary gift from the gods of loose. His smile, nod, and relaxed shoulders told me he clearly understood that Hank was indeed ready to play football the Pete Elliott way.

The team ran out for our preliminary warm-up, went through a series of quick calisthenics and other drills designed to get our sweat and the blood moving, and then returned to the locker room. In spite of the workout, we were all feeling emotionally tighter than ever, as if a giant rubber band was squeezing our intestines and vital organs. We were definitely ready to start hitting to relieve the discomfort.

The pace of the preparation accelerated; a short period back in the locker room just before the game started for final inspirational words from coaches, captains, and teammates; last-minute efforts to rev up or release the built-up binding of tension before returning to the field; and final individual battles with the balance of tight and loose.

Before going back out, Pete announced the starting lineup. When he got to the backfield I held my breath until he said, "Hank, you're in at left halfback." I noticed the disappointed reaction of another back competing for the starting nod and understood. I wouldn't expect less from a teammate who wanted to play as badly as I. Nevertheless, it was time to put that competition behind us and seriously gear up for a team effort. After Pete's last words, the team received tacit permission to explode. As we walked out of the locker room, we finally released our caged-up emotions and discharged all the war cries we had been repressing for the last few hours.

Entering the dark tunnel leading into the bright arena, I heard the deafening wave of sound from ninety-eight thousand people mixed with the blares and drum beats of brassy marching bands beyond. I struggled to focus on play assignments through the unseen gnawing of nervousness, anticipating necessary spurts of speed and imagining the first hit that would put me into automatic drive and help me execute what I'd learned during endless hours of practice.

Now, the self-exhortations spewed out of us unconsciously, echoed and trailed off in the tunnel. "Go Bears! Be tough! A hundred and twenty percent! Yeah!"

The multiple clicks of metal cleats on the hard surface of the shaded tunnel met the soft, cushy feel of the stadium's great green turf as we rushed into the sun. We were out of time to think, contemplate, or worry about the struggle between tight and loose. Now we had only to play, to act, and react in this great pulsing theater.

While we ran on to the stage ready for the fierce storm of competition, a question came to me from a far away region of my consciousness. The question was fleeting but clear, "Of the tens of thousands in the stadium and the millions watching on television, I wonder how many knew that Kapp and I were Mexican?" As quickly as the question evaporated, I wished the answer to be all and none.

As we lined up on the first play from scrimmage to face the number one team in the nation, I looked up and saw Iowa's massive line. I blinked to check if my eyes needed adjusting. They didn't. Their line remained massive. Directly in front of me stood their right tackle Mac Lewis. At six feet, six inches tall, and weighing three hundred five pounds, he indeed stood tall. The only thing between him and me was our right tackle Pat Newell. In the program, Pat was listed as weighing one hundred eighty-five pounds, in the press book one hundred eighty. I believed the press book. In both, his height was reported at a mere six feet, two inches by comparison. From my perspective, the contrast was overwhelming, and it looked like a Willow sapling going up against a towering Oak. I assumed running in that vicinity would be no simple chore in spite of Pat's incredible intelligence and unsurpassed courage to take on a giant outweighing him by one hundred twenty-five pounds.

My assumption proved to be correct. We aspired, we fought, we pounded, but it was not enough to overcome the onslaught of the Hawkeye's superior size and speed. They humbled us to the tune of 38-12, the blinding speed of Bob Jeter and Willie Fleming doing most of the damage. Jeter ended the day by gaining 194 yards on nine carries for a 21-yard average. In the third quarter, he escaped the grasp of all of us and flew down the field for an eighty-one yard touchdown run that broke the Rose Bowl record.

We gained enough yards, 344, to win most games except this one. Iowa gained more, 516 to be exact. Our All-American quarterback actually out-passed their All-American quarterback. Joe hit eight of seventeen passes for 126 yards and one touchdown. I ended up as our leading rusher, with a close to 7-yard average—not enough and no great compensation. Our defense failed to stop the attack. We just didn't find the guns needed to shoot down the enemy. After sixty minutes of the toughest most disappointing football we played all year, Coach Elliott summarized the afternoon by saying, "They were the best team we've played all season. And, if it isn't the greatest team it's awfully close to it."

The experts begin their assaults. Some said Cal didn't belong in the game. Others claimed Iowa was better than the score indicated. Still others were content to say we were simply met by a superior force and outclassed. One backhanded compliment asserted that no other team in our conference would have performed any better against the "gang of bruisers." Thanks.

None of the comments injured us any more than our own profound disappointment. A part of us felt as if we had let everyone down, including our conference, our university, our moms, and ourselves. Kapp, sitting in a daze in the locker room after the game, was asked what happened. He answered by apologizing, "I'm sorry. I thought we could do it. I'm sorry I let you down." On the field of battle or anywhere else, Joe has never let anyone down.

After the losing effort, we tried to live with the frustrating, helpless question, "What do we do now?" I couldn't help but think of what my wise, old high school football coach Lee Cox would have kindly suggested. "Boys, ain't nothin' left to do but to just go lick your wounds." That's all we could do, and after the immediate anguish subsided, we began to assess what we had experienced, what we had lost and gained.

We had definitely lost an important game, perhaps the most important game of our lives. To be sure we had also lost a little of our strut. By no means had we lost our respect for one another. A single game could never erase the durability of something earned in the many previous close games, numerous hours of practice, and the moments of triumph and defeat we had shared. We had become a special kind of family.

Our respect extended beyond coaches, starters, and lettermen, perhaps more to those who had seen little or no playing time. Players like Mike Prado, Henry Guidice, and Emerson "Tex" Byrd had spent week after week in the thankless trenches of preparing us for our opponents. Trampled, bashed, and bloodied during the week so we could shine on Saturdays, they clearly deserved medals of honor. They had unquestionably proven their dedication to the Blue and Gold by giving of themselves as much as anyone—this without receiving few accolades or glory in return. For the rest of our lives, they would remain the unsung heroes of this family.

Because our team could not claim an excess of super stars, we made teamwork and maximum effort our stars. We walked away knowing we had done the best we could with the tools we were given. We walked away with our pride intact. For me the season was summed up best by the greatest compliment I had ever received in all my years of involvement in athletics. A couple of games back a quote by Coach Elliott appeared in the newspaper saying, "I have never seen Hank take a loafing step." Fortunately, he had missed seeing the halting start of my sophomore year season.

Nevertheless that statement meant more to me than the long runs, the cheers of the crowd, or photos on the sports page—and it has stayed with me for all these years.

~ FAST FORWARD~

The Game Isn't Over

Completing the story of my youth, marked by my playing in the Rose Bowl, I feel grateful and privileged for having experienced an association with a group of men, coaches and players, who displayed values I cherish to this day—respect, tolerance, and unity, to name just a few. Unfortunately, those values are still not universally embraced in our society, especially when it comes to minorities. We have made some strides, but we still see, all too often, instances of lack of respect, intolerance, and disunity.

Harmful Speech from the Top

Throughout this book I have laid much of the blame for the negative attitudes about Mexicans and other Latinos at the doorstep of the media. Only the most unengaged would fail to see that the rhetoric of leaders also serves as an additional contributor to those damaging perceptions. The most blatant, disgraceful example comes from the speech of the current President of the United States, Donald Trump.

When he announced his candidacy at Trump Tower in June 2015, Trump referred to Mexican immigrants as criminals and rapists, stating, "When

Mexico sends its people, they're not sending their best. They're sending people that have lots of problems, and they're bringing those problems with us (sic). They're bringing drugs. They're bringing crime. They're rapists..."

Although Mexican migration has dwindled to a trickle, he has doubled down on his position, at the time of this writing, especially since it serves his side of the raging debate over a wall on our southern border. His careless, broad-brush comments stain all of us with his fallacious words. Not only do law-abiding immigrants suffer from the onslaught of such speech, so do native-born, well-established, third- and fourth-generation Mexican Americans. The situation feeds my contention that we are often seen largely as recent and downtrodden immigrants—a picture that must change if we are to eliminate actions that cause untold suffering and impede the full realization of the American dream.

With all the many external forces that have influenced my attitudes and behavior about belonging, identity, or justice, I feel I must still return to the depths of self to transcend those forces and to live without resentment, guilt, or envy. At an early age, I found solace and peace by turning inward.

INNER WORLD

Twelve times and more,
The harlequin I am
Leaps through his own delirious hoop,
Grasping for attainable impossibilities.

My inner world, unlike,
Resolves its own confounding traps,
Beaming on ribboned, harmonic tones
A dance with space.

I grope and search
Through folding fantasies
For the clear and final sounds of thought.
Approaching siren truth,
I see the endless hollows of expanding time,
And then fall
Mute.

~ 1969

Hank running in the Rose Bowl

Olguin Kapp reunion

EPILOGUE

Memories are like breadcrumbs we drop along the trail to help us find our way back. They provide clues for fleshing out our stories. They may also help us to find our way forward or even design the future. As I look ahead, I realize I can't be complacent about the state of race relations or the perception of Latinos in this country. Although I know I can have only a minor effect on the big picture, I continue striving to make a difference.

While I focus grateful attention on all the gifts I enjoy in my old age, a supportive and loving wife, the love of family, many dear friends, and relatively good health, I still exert energy and work on a couple of pet projects, both of which I have mentioned earlier. A partner and I have created an animated, kid's TV show for preschoolers using Latin music to expose them to different cultures while fostering universal values. I have also developed a motivational presentation aimed at enhancing the self-confidence, self-worth, and thus, the academic performance of Latino students through the technique that helped me to become a successful college athlete—creative visualization.

Aside from that, watching old and new movies, reading good books, listening to great music, and rooting for Cal takes up my spare time. I also spend some time meditating for peace and serenity and contemplating where do I go from here. With our lives full of experiences, intricate and varied as a changing sky, I have settled on one simple self-admonition for now—to condemn silence.

Without wasting energy lingering on useless regrets, I look back at the numbing silence that prevented me from knowing my father better, from learning more about his family and the early struggles of the labor movement, from understanding his aspirations as a young boy at the turn of the twentieth century, and from sharing the love of wood or grafting fruit trees into succulent hybrids. I condemn silence.

I look back at the crippling silence that prevented me from asking trusted mentors how to air my unseen pain or apprehension; from setting free the clamps of fear that held me down in dreams and playing fields; from daring to openly celebrate in my youth the value of my heritage and all the gifts it offered. I condemn silence.

As I look at our society today, I condemn the silence that keeps us from having an honest, constructive dialogue about racial matters, courageous exchanges about our views, biases, and experiences to help us build bridges of understanding. I condemn the silence that ignores an innocent child's pain from demeaning playground taunts or slurs, the tearing of a fragile self-esteem striving to excel, the disruption of a path toward self-realization or a desired destination. I condemn the silence that masks our neglect, indifference, and complacency and allows injustice and hatred to thrive.

Martin Luther King said it so eloquently: "The ultimate tragedy is not the oppression and cruelty by the bad people but the silence over that by the good people."

I condemn the silence that comes from ignoring the contributions, true history, dignity, and loyalty of not only Latinos and Latinas but also other groups that have helped to build this nation.

As I look out at the future, I choose to praise all those people of good will, of all backgrounds and races, who shatter silence with their cries for justice and compassion; all those who speak out against alienating and distorted views of our fellow travelers on a globe rapidly becoming a neighborhood; and all those who choose to engage, dialogue, and tie together the threads of our fragile mutual destiny and humanity.

We stand somewhere near the opposition's thirty-five yard line. The team of hatred, fear, injustice, and ignorance presents a resolute and fearsome foe. I know we can make it across the goal line, create a world that accepts and celebrates the gift of both our diversity and commonality, and ultimately win the game. The final victory will require the heart, drive, and determination of the 1959 Rose Bowl Bears.

And when you think you're tired,
Dig down deeper, deep inside.
There you'll find out what you're made of,
Learn the measure of your pride.

Excerpt from *The Scrimmage*
~ 1995

ACKNOWLEDGMENTS

Many of the people who have had a positive influence on my life and to whom I owe a debt of gratitude are acknowledged and even praised in the preceding pages. Nevertheless, some deserve additional thanks. When I began writing my memoir, I attempted to try something different with the format and structure. My childhood friend and mentor, Sandra Lewis Nisbet, provided some needed advice and editing. None of it worked, mainly due to my inability, and I threw the project aside in frustration but remain grateful to Sandie for all her support through the years and in the early stages of writing the book. I also want to extend a special thanks to Secretary Federico Peña, Dean Kevin Johnson, Tom Knoles, Alicia "Feech" Robles, Victor Obeso, Roberta Rey, KJ Sanchez, María Gatling and Emilio Delgado who were all kind enough to read the unpublished manuscript and offer their encouragement and support. A special thanks to Hector Lopez, my old pal who over the years has reviewed, supported, and helped me think through my ideas and projects. Many thanks to Bob Paltrow who designed the cover and prepared the manuscript for publication. In addition, I am extremely grateful to Sarah Arney, whose superb proofreading provided some important fixes. Of course, I can't thank my wife, Patricia, enough for her support, inspiration, and fierce attention to detail.

About the Author

Hank Olguin has enjoyed a long and varied career, most of which has been devoted to the advertising and marketing/communications fields. As a writer and creative director, he has written and produced countless advertising vehicles, including dozens of TV and radio commercials; has won numerous advertising awards, including two Clios; written a book on creativity and songs for *Sesame Street*.

Early in his career, he decided to focus his efforts on projects related to the Latino community and market. For eight years, he served as the Communications Director for a U.S. Department of Labor, national employment and training program, SER-Jobs for Progress, serving the special needs of Latinos. During those years, he became an active member of Nosotros, an organization dedicated to eliminating Hollywood Latino stereotypes.

Hank was then hired as a senior copywriter by a major advertising agency, GSD&M, as part of a bilingual/bicultural team in the pioneering days of Hispanic advertising. He soon became a creative director and VP, working on successful Spanish/English advertising campaigns for several major accounts such as Sea World, Walmart, Coors, and Domino's Pizza.

A strong advocate for changing the negative image and public perception of Latinos, he collaborated on the creation of breakthrough advertising and promotions while at GSD&M. A TV commercial celebrating Hispanic Medal of Honor recipients and the commemoration of a statue of a "Tejano" unsung hero of the Alamo serve as prime examples.

Today, he is available for speaking engagements designed to entertain, enlighten, motivate, and challenge business, community, and educational audiences on Latina/o/x issues. He has developed a program to boost the academic achievement of Latina/o/x students by applying the self-development tool of creative visualization. In addition, he continues to facilitate seminars on creativity, branding, and communications.

He holds a degree in Rhetoric from the University of California at Berkeley where he earned letters in football and track & field and was awarded the Sara Huntsman Sturgess Memorial Prize (for outstanding artistic achievement in dramatic art). He was inducted as a Fellow of the Order of the Golden Bear.

www.americanmexicanstories.com

CPSIA information can be obtained
at www.ICGtesting.com
Printed in the USA
FSHW011255060820
72763FS

9 780979 266126